BROKEN TOYS
BROKEN DREAMS

Understanding and Healing Boundaries
Codependence, Compulsive Behaviors
and Family Relationships

by

Terry Kellogg, M. A.
with Marvel Harrison, Ph. D.

BRAT Publishing

369 Montezuma Street – Suite 203
Santa Fe, NM 87501

■ ■ ■ Books offered by BRAT Publishing:

Broken Toys Broken Dreams *Understanding and Healing Codependency, Compulsive Behaviors and Family* Terry Kellogg

Family Matters *The Principles & Roles of Family* Terry Kellogg

attrACTIVE WOMEN *A Physical Fitness Approach To Emotional & Spiritual Well-Being* Marvel Harrison & Catharine Stewart-Roache

Finding Balance *12 Priorities For Interdependence And Joyful Living* Kellogg Harrison Family & Relationship Series

Pathways to Intimacy *Communicating With Care & Resolving Differences* Kellogg Harrison Family & Relationship Series

The Sacred Trust *The Parenting & Guardianship of Children and Creating Healthy Families* Kellogg Harrison Family & Relationship Series

■ ■ ■ Inspirational & Gift Books offered by BRAT Publishing:

Butterfly Kisses *Little Intimacies For Sharing!* Harrison & Kellogg & Michaels

Hummingbird Words *Self Affirmations & Notes To Nurture By* Harrison & Kellogg & Michaels

Roots & Wings *Words On Growing A Family* Harrison & Kellogg & Michaels

Reflections *Guideposts and Images For The Journey* Harrison & Kellogg & Michaels

■ ■ ■ Also Available from BRAT Publishing:

marvel notes™ Elegant & delightful greeting cards

Educational videos and audios on families and relationships

Kellogg, Terry
Broken Toys Broken Dreams
Copyright 1990 Terry Lee Kellogg

ISBN 1-56073-001-3

2nd Printing 1992 - Revised edition
3rd Printing 1995
4th Printing 1997

Printed in the United States of America

Copy Editor: Arthur Hoffman

BRAT Publishing, 369 Montezuma Street - Suite 203, Santa Fe, NM 87501
1-800-359-BRAT (2728) or 505-662-9200; FAX 505-662-4044;
Email «marvel@trail.com«

this book is dedicated to my children

dan
jessica
dave

and *all* children

the dance of childness
dancing in a moon beam
to chimes of our wind song
sprinkling magic dew drops
as we puddle plod along
charting our chataqua
travel teach and train
dancing in a moon beam
to the rhythms of the rain
snuggling in a sleep dream
soaring in a tree swing
walking with a heart sing
gliding beyond the pain
swirling in the twilight
twirling in the sunlight
dancing in a moon beam
with a child bearing my name

terry kellogg 1990

Acknowledgements

For the past 15 years I have entertained the idea of writing a book. I guess it felt like work, and I was working enough. On my own time I really wanted to play. Recently I realized the time had come. Interest in the issues I've been involved with has become extremely high. My friends and co-workers had already published books, and I was beginning to feel left out. Besides, I had so many people that kept asking, "When are you going to write your book?"

I want to thank everyone for their prodding, support and modeling. Without all of you I'd still be considering it. Anything worth doing is worth doing tomorrow—or as my family would have said—"Anything worth doing should be done by someone else."

In March of 1989 I spent some time on a little island in the Bahamas, where I had been a teacher/lay missionary for the Catholic Church in the early 1960s. In that ten days I wrote and wrote—a stream of consciousness effort since I had no notes, references, library, or anything else to back me up. Just my pen, the sun, the sea and the sand. I thought I would edit, reference and complete the book when I got back, but I didn't. So in August I went back to my island and worked again using the same approach as I did in March. This is an island I had visited many times in the past and on my frequent visits I would read. Instead of bringing a book to read, I brought my paper to write on and a pen to write with. This book is the result.

It is a rather global approach to the concept of codependency, addiction and family. It is the result of 19 years of learning from clients, colleagues, friends and family. There is much more I would like to include, but that can wait for the next book.

The island I mentioned has become a second home to me—Harbour Island, Bahamas. I wish to thank the people there for keeping a watch on Paradise. The island is one-half mile wide and three miles long, a natural harbor on one side and a pink sand beach on the other. When I am there I watch no TV, drive nothing mechanical, use no telephones, and read no newspapers. I spend time with the people I care about and the ocean I love.

I want to thank many of the people who have supported and befriended me for the past three decades, the people of the island: Eva Sawyer, the Dencil and Pat Higgs family, including surrogate son Gregory. Nevel Major, Tony Robinson, Gregory Higgs, Glen Roy, the Cleare family, Sybil, Edie, Suzanne, my God children, Gus, Rachel, Harry, Kathy, Jean and others. The Sawyers, the Saunders, Johnsons, Sweetings, Roberts, Barrys, Millers, Currys, especially Archie, Alan, and Barret, Paddy, James, the Alburys, the Malcoms, Kif Brown, the Beans, the Browns, the Percenties, Sharon King, Fr. Jim, Larry, Edgel, Father John H. McGoey, the storekeepers, resort owners, dive instructors, and all the other families and important people who struggle in, and cling to, their Caribbean jewel. This is my chance to acknowledge the gift you have given me. This book belongs to the people of Harbour Island, Bahamas.

There are many others I like to mention: my family, Dan, Jessica and Dave for their encouragement, teasing, and playfulness; my parents, who persevere; my sister Pat and brother Jim, who allow me to lie about them; Kirby our dog, who trampled and chewed my manuscript almost as much as my editor, Marvel; Rokelle Lerner, Carla Brandon, Barbara Cherry, Michael Cox and Bob Subby for their friendship; my mentors Alan Anderson, Renee Fredrickson and Ken Fletcher; the people at the Gillette Corporation, who worked to change a manufacturing plant, Mary Cameron, Ron Peterson, Bob Wood and the Hope team; the children of St. John The Baptist Catholic Grade School of Excelsior for the cover design.

I would like to acknowledge Dan Barmettler of the Institute for Integral Development, for his personal caring and in recognition for his 15 years of offering professional training throughout the country; the PIA Hospital Group; Susan Smith of Baywood Hospital; the Listen to Learn group in San Diego; the U.S.

Journal; Tim Devilbis and staff at Custom Cassette; Chris Stevens for holding down the fort.

A special note of thanks to Marvel Harrison for her continual caring, helping me see my mistakes, letting me keep a few *dangling participles* and finding light at the end of this!

And in memory of Bedford Wynn, who suffered a fatal heart attack at an AA meeting at the end of 1989—a dear friend, a father figure to me and hundreds of others.

Finally, to all Adult Children and codependents who have been, are, and will be discovering recovery.

About The Author

For the past several years Terry and I have been on the same speaking circuit, bumping into each other at airports, meeting at conferences, chatting during speaker's luncheons and becoming acquainted. It wasn't until after I began editing *Broken Toys Broken Dreams* that I got to know Terry. While editing his book I learned much about his perception of himself as he shares his family history, his struggles, personal and professional thoughts, feelings and yes, plenty of opinions! What he didn't say much about is who he is from day to day. Personally, I enjoy knowing a little about the *person* who is also the author so, taking editorial liberties I would like to share a few tidbits I have learned about Terry.

Professionaly, Terry hails from in depth experience in family systems, is an expert in the areas of violence, compulsive behaviors and Post Traumatic Stress Disorders and has utilized this expertise in the treatment of addictions and family dysfunction. Terry is a teacher. He delivers his message with compassion, knowledge, sensitivity and has a terrific sense of humor to boot. Above all else Terry is a man of integrity, dedicated to his professional and personal growth, unafraid to challenge "the system" or others, open to challenge himself, willing to make changes *and* mistakes and most importantly, from an editor's standpoint is *educable!* Terry is a teacher to many, a pioneer in the field of family treatment, a leader in child advocacy and absolutely detests being referred to as a *guru!*

Terry is simply crazy about his children. His eyes light up with excitement as he describes playing hockey with Dan and Dave and the warmth in his voice glows as he brags about Jessica. He could talk incessantly with joy about his family and their many talents and virtues, the roller blading escapades, soccer games and adventures in the Bahamas. My congratulations to the Kellogg kids for an excellent job in planned parenthood!

Terry is a joy to work with, whether it is writing, speaking or brainstorming. His affirming nature, creativity, cheerfulness, easy and contented style, experience, willingness to share, and brilliance shine through. Yes, he gets grumpy and sometimes thrives on complaining and organized chaos and he can go for endless hours without eating but, what the heck! He hates details, cheese, returning telephone calls and airplanes. He relishes sleeping late (don't call too early), is a bit of a daredevil, enjoys making up new words and writing with dangling participles (you'll be reading them), tells terrific stories and can be simply outrageous! Terry lives and breathes playfulness. Frankly, he has an inner brat that just won't quit! In addition, Terry is a spirited man with a life full of meaning and purpose. He is most at peace when in the wilderness. He is deeply concerned about our broken planet, the blatant destruction in the name of progress. Terry's life and message is advocating for the vulnerable peoples of the world and protecting our precious creation.

One of Terry's greatest strengths lies in his ability to be vulnerable, to feel, experience pain, hurt and joy in his life and he is getting pretty good at sharing his vulnerabilities with others. He has a gentle and generous spirit. Our world needs more people like Terry.

Marvel Harrison

A Note From BRAT Publishing

*"It is a BRAT Publishing policy to print
books on recycled paper whenever possible. There has been a shortage of recycled paper, so please, for the sake of
our broken planet, recycle your paper
products. If each one of us in Canada
and the USA recycled a mere 10% of the
paper we use, we could save up to 25
million trees every year!"*

We have decided to donate the standard author's royalty of
Broken Toys Broken Dreams to four special projects. One part will go
toward a fund that provides education and promotes treatment
and recovery for Native Americans, another will go to a fund for
wilderness programs for troubled young people and individuals
with special problems or handicaps, a part will be donated to the
organization "Teachers For Social Responsibility" and another
part will be used to fund the writing and publishing of material to
promote balance, peace and a sense of guardianship for Earth
and her residents. Already we are looking forward to the sequel of
Broken Toys Broken Dreams, which is *Broken Silence* which will focus
more on issues for adults who grew up in dysfunctional families.
In it we will continue to explore the impact of violence in our lives
and culture, the violation of self, feelings, rights, needs, wants, our
bodies, our sexuality, our spirituality and how we have responded
to the violence which happens to us and around us. We will go
further into the family systems with chapters on family roles,
family secrets, family violence and the responses to violence. The
process of recovery will be discussed — the insight processes with a
focus on realizing, linking and debriefing; the emotional proc-

esses, grieving, feeling and healing; the social processes, networking, socializing, parenting; the spiritual processes, forgiving, twelve step work, establishing meaningfulness and values; the self processes of developing identity and integrity—integrity being the integration of sometimes seemingly separate aspects of self, integration of childness and adulthood, sexuality and spirituality, fear and courage, strength and vulnerability, prayer and humor.

BRAT Publishing came about during the writing and editing of *Broken Toys Broken Dreams*. We received calls from numerous publishers but both of us were interested in developing the project ourselves. BRAT stands for **Belonging Recovery And Trust.** Some people have suggested the company is appropriately named because we are both Brats. The truth is Marvel is a Brat and Terry says he is too old to be a Brat, he is simply cantankerous, eccentric and idiosyncratic! We hope Brat pleases you as much as it pleases us! For more information please call: 1 800 359-BRAT (2728). We look forward to hearing from you.

Marvel Harrison
Terry Kellogg

Contents

Foreword

We met Terry Kellogg four years ago when we attended a Lifeworks Workshop near Dallas, Texas. Even though we attended separate workshops we both made a strong connection with Terry. When Terry asked us to write the foreword to "Broken Toys Broken Dreams," we were honored to have an opportunity to express our gratitude for the difference his work has made in our lives. The Family Workshop was the real beginning of our family being on the road to recovery.

In reading through the manuscript we were reminded that recovery is created anew each and every day. The information in this book is a powerful tool for anyone in recovery. Terry Kellogg is one of the most respected sources of information on the interrelation between codependency, addiction and dysfunctional family systems. Terry traces the thread of codependency from self to the outer most reaches of our society.

Gloria and I both came from dysfunctional families. We struggled for years to overcome the reprecussion of dysfunction in every aspect of our lives. After trying all sorts of private therapy that never really seemed to get at the source of the problem, we heard about the workshop that Terry developed. Busy schedules have prevented us from spending as much personal time together with Terry as we would like, but our respect has grown over the years as we have been able to keep in touch through his work. We feel that this book is an example of his finest work. The information on these pages can break the chains of denial and aid you in your recovery effort.

BJ Thomas
Gloria Thomas

Introduction

*"Environmental abuse stems from child
abuse."*

*"Grieving fuels the forward movement
of our lives."*   TLK

We have had a drug problem in this nation since its inception.
Recently, it has received much press, mostly due to the escalating
crime rate and the huge amounts of illegal money involved,
especially with cocaine. Cocaine, the object of most concern, is not
our most serious drug problem. Drug abuse is symtomatic of
other cultural, family and personal issues. The problem is real,
but it stems from poverty, shame, isolation, family violence, power
and greed. It is a spiritual bankruptcy that eats away at a culture
and destroys the core of meaningfulness in people's lives. Chemical dependency is real, it destroys lives. Chemically dependent
people require enabling. They require other people and institutions who support, allow, ignore, encourage, create—actively or
passively—the chemical dependency. Many people who enable are
in relationships with chemically dependent people. We've given
these people the name "codependent," the enabling spouse of an
addict.

We all enable "addicts." We ignore, support and allow addiction.
We do not know how to deal with the repetitive, self-destructive
behaviors in others, in our culture, and in ourselves. Some of us
actively enable while others do so passively, some of us through
ignorance and others through maliciousness. Some of our enabling comes from the depths of our own addiction or addictiveness and some from misplaced beliefs and intent to help.

We are a group of people who enable addiction—a group of people who become addicted. Our addictions, our repetitive patterns of self-destructive, mood altering behavior show up in our personal lives, our political systems, our corporations, our spending, our need for power, our search for a high and a fix for our pain.

Codependency is not just a term to describe people in relationships with addicts. *It applies to a culture that enables addiction.* Even our war on drugs is an enabling posture. It misses the real issues. It ignores the primary drug problems. It is a system of shame and punishment. It is an attempt to change what we cannot change.

In *Broken Toys Broken Dreams* I outline the beginnings of the term codependency, how it has been viewed and defined, how each of us participates, how it can be a set-up for lives of loneliness, relationship problems, and a lack of healthy balance. Since codependence and addiction are inseparable, I will attempt to explore the roots of addiction and certain common addictive problems. This is both a personal and global approach to dependence and its traveling companion, addiction.

Broken Toys Broken Dreams is for anyone who is concerned about themselves, their family, our culture and our planet. In our addictive lifestyles, we tend to ignore the long term impact of meeting short term wants. This affects our survival, our life balance. Even more importantly, it has an impact on the planet where we live.

When children live with people who are not dependable, the child never learns to depend on others or self in healthy ways; they depend on fixes, externals and inappropriate people. They allow people to depend on them, or they isolate and *appear* independent. Dependency on externals becomes addiction. Codependence is a byproduct of abuse and the loss of identity. It is usually defined through its symptoms and is often treated by non-recovering helping professionals.

The key conflicts are control versus self-empowerment, denial versus reality awareness, lack of identity versus self-esteem and boundaries. We get stuck in several developmental stages, especially autonomy versus identity diffusion, a pre-school developmental issue. We generally have problems with trust, initiative, industry, and intimacy. Our resilience to the impact of our family history is primarily based on our ability to have people in our lives to share with and trust. No book, information, workshop or therapist can be a substitute for finding friends and confidants in our lives.

The recovery process is interdependence, a recognition and acceptance of mutual dependency. As codependents we are reactors who polarize our responses and operate in extremes. This polarization can follow us through our recovery as an overreactiveness to information, suggestions and overidentifying with the problem and the labels—including the label codependence. Those of us who lack identity often overidentify with our labels and pathology.

In the Beginning Was The Word
History and Concepts of Codependency

"Codependency is that empty space in our soul."

"Codependency is a byproduct of cultural misogyny, the fear and hatred of vulnerability."

We hide our pain, We hide us from us.
Being denied our basic child dependency needs,
We dwell in shame plagued with dependency problems.
Normal needs and urges become attempts to fill the empty self.
The need for fun and excitement become addictions to intensity.
The need for attention becomes acting out.
The need for self esteem becomes arrogance.
The need for nourishment becomes our eating disorders.
The need for understanding becomes compulsive demanding.
The need for security becomes obsessive worrying and misering.
The need for self care becomes isolated narcissism.
The need for relationship becomes desperation.
The need for intimacy becomes enmeshment.
Our sexual needs become shame, compulsion, fear, confusion and
    jealousy.
The need for identity becomes an overidentification with the
    responses to our childhood hurts.
We overidentify with the labels of pathology.
These are merely windows to lost childhood.

Addiction is a window to the hurting child.
Self destructiveness is a window to Broken Toys.
Hopelessness is a window to Broken Dreams.

During a panel discussion in 1987 in Brazosport, Texas, I was asked to define codependency in ten words or less. I'm not sure if anyone had ever done this. My answer was, "It is the child's reaction to a low functioning family." I did cheat when I repeated the answer and added "short of chronic mental illness," although I had ambivalence about adding this part.

Dependency

In a low functioning family people are not very dependable so children's basic dependency needs are not met. The child may appear to depend on one parent or someone else in the family, but the opposite is usually true. The parent is depending on the child to meet the parent's needs. Developmentally we first depend on others and then ourselves, thereby being able to do both, which is called interdependence.

When we cannot depend on other people or ourselves we also learn not to depend on our feelings as guides in life. Compensation for this is done by becoming very dependable and having people depend on us, or becoming excessively dependent on inappropriate people and externals to fill the emptiness of self—work, food, drugs, sex, gambling, spending, and so on. Codependence is the basis for addiction. It is the inability to depend, in appropriate ways, on self and others which sets up the excess reliance on things that become destructive in our lives, our addictions. Addictiveness moves through the spectrum of society including family, community, business, church and government. All have become addictive systems.

Confusion Reigns

Mental health has never been an exact science. Controversy about what is normal, diagnostic criteria, labels, causes, treatment approaches has been the norm. Little has stirred up professional controversy and has involved the public as much as the concepts of codependence. The problem seems as nebulous as the name itself and perhaps as the people who carry the label, a nebulous name for nebulous people. My mother was married to my father, an alcoholic, so she was obviously codependent. But I took care of her, so I guess I was co-codependent!

2

This is possibly the only emotional disorder that doesn't even have its own name, which is appropriate for the condition that it purports to describe. In the following pages I will touch on the origins and history of the term, what it means and describes, treatment approaches and problems, where it comes from, who gets it, and how it affects our lives. I will also outline a process of recovery. In this effort, of course, I hope to do a very good job, take care of everybody and everything, make no mistakes and admit to none if I do, make everybody like me and all that I write, fix as much as I can, but not so much that you would not need me to write another book, which, if you accept, I will know that I am a valuable person. If in this statement you have discovered that I am codependent you may go to the next paragraph.

A "co" is a prefix meaning "with, an ally, assistant, helper." A "dependent" is someone who relies on or *needs*, it is a person with a problem such as addiction, someone who is unable to function separately. A codependent is one who allies with someone who is dependent, a dependent dependent. This view was held in the early recognition of the issues. The term itself came out of the field of alcoholism. Alcohol dependency came to be accepted as a disease, and our view of alcoholism moved from the concepts of moral ineptitude, weakness of character, lack of will, "possession," or biological flaw to the recognition of an emotional, physical, psychological and spiritual illness with a profound impact on the addict and others. It became a common practice, in treatment, to bring in the family of alcoholics. The family members were also suffering from the problems and pain that result from the disease of alcoholism.

Cold-dependency

Minnesota, the state to which I moved from California when I reached my fifth birthday (already bucking the major social trends), has for a period of time been a leader in the treatment of alcoholism. This came about, not because we already suffered from cold dependency, but it's close. Minnesota was the third state to have AA groups, a spiritual healing process for alcoholics that was founded in New York and Ohio in the early 1930s and made its way to Minnesota, evidently after an Ohio State/Minnesota football game, so the story goes. During a blizzard some of the Ohio fans who were snowed in decided to have a meeting and invited some of their Minnesota friends. I'm not sure who won the game, but upon inviting these Minnesota friends, the AA program was established in Minnesota. Climate also affected the growth of the movement in Minnesota in that homeless alcoholics don't do well in the winter. They were frequently taken to state hospitals as an alternative to their freezing to death. Some might question this as an alternative. The Minnesota AA members decided to bring this new program into these hospitals to help the suffering souls and hence we have the birth of treatment in Minnesota, a new Minnesota industry is born. Some have said that this industry is even more important than mining or logging because the supply never dries up—no pun intended—well, at least no harm intended.

A later development came from the West Coast in the 1950s. It seems a group of hybrid therapists had discovered the family, that sanctified basic unit of society as portrayed in "Father Knows Best," (a concept I've been trying to sell my family on without success for two decades), or "My Little Margie" and "Ozzie and Harriet." The family is a system, with all parts connected and impacting each other at different levels in various ways. It is a system with rules, roles, boundaries, components, and principles, a system that seems to maintain itself intergenerationally. This intergenerationality (longest word in the book, so don't get scared!) seems to be fueled primarily by denial, a non-fossil fuel found in abundance throughout the industrialized semi-civilized world.

These radicals from the West believed that what happens to one member of a family affects the entire family and this is true for issues that are overt, obvious, easily seen, as well as the covert, hidden and denied. They also believed that one or more family members become the identified patients or symptom-bearers of the family dysfunction, which may be addiction, relationship problems, or some other secret issue. This is the one who frequently ends up with the diagnosis: depression, schizophrenia, anti-social, borderline, dependent, manic, bipolar, neurotic or whatever is in vogue at the time.

Meanwhile, back in the East, not to be outdone, a group of recovering addicts (not alcoholics, mind you, but real hard core stuff, the stuff that doesn't get advertised on billboards and in newspapers) were getting together and developing a recovery process that had a real "down home" ("home" being the street drug scene) quality to it, very confronting. Almost mean, one might say shaming, very intensely emotional and shared in a language one only hears in current movies.

4

Sound travels through water, but information does better over land and so the East's Synanon confrontive emotional treatment model headed west, while the California systems theory moved east. During a layover in their travels, they met in Minnesota where, lo and behold, they were not only introduced to each other, but also to the principles of AA. Thus the basis for a very powerful treatment modality was born, and the soil was fertilized for codependency theory. Treatment became more confrontive and affective (emotional) and given the elements of family systems theory and the obvious impact, even trauma, experienced by the families of alcoholics, the concept of alcoholism as a family disease became accepted. This family disease concept grew rapidly but, unfortunately, is primarily given only lip service in terms of real treatment. I will discuss more on that later.

Co-Alcoholism

In the course of dealing with the family it was noticed that the spouse of the alcoholic exhibited many of the symptoms of the disease—denial, delusion, distortion, defensiveness, dishonesty, despair, minimizing, projection, etc. The spouse suffered physical symptoms and exhibited fears and anxieties, often to the point of phobias. They were compulsive in several areas, especially food and nicotine. Many were chemically dependent, often on prescription drugs. It eventually became clear that the spouse was suffering from an illness that in the 1960s and early '70s went by various names, including spouse disease, co-alcoholism or co-addiction. In the 1970s the term chemical dependency became widespread as a way of recognizing that drug addiction was the same regardless of what drugs were used, with some exceptions, most notably nicotine and caffeine (so we're told).

There was an attempt to *wed* the concept of alcoholism and drug addiction. Alcohol obviously is a drug, although in our culture and even in the field of addiction we still tend to separate the two. We call people drug and alcohol counselors, which is a redundancy—or we refer to drug and alcohol treatment programs, another redundancy. This is possibly because alcoholics don't want to be drug addicts or maybe so we can *pretend* to have a war on drugs but ignore alcohol. The marriage between drugs and alcohol never took and for the most part the war on drugs, mostly a war of words, doesn't seem to apply much to alcohol. Regardless, who wins in a war, anyway? The war on drugs is a strategic military error in the waging of a forgotten war on poverty and child abuse.

The term "chemical dependency" as a way of referring to the addiction to these drugs eventually grew into the concept of codependency for the spouse of the chemically dependent person. The coaddict or coalcoholic became the codependent. Thus, the birth of a new mental health issue that has spent over a decade trying to find recognition, identity, and a treatment modality, which seems fitting since that is essentially what codependents seek as well: identity, recognition, and possibly, treatment.

The spouse in an alcoholic marriage becomes addicted to the addict just as the addict becomes addicted to the alcohol. Codependence is the process by which the life of the co-addict revolves around the addict just as the life of the addict revolves around the drug. The addict is the drug. The kind of day one has depends on the kind of day the addict has. The addict's preoccupation with their drug is similar to the preoccupation with the addict. Whether or not one shops, acts pleasant, has a migraine headache, screams at the kids or helps them with their homework depends on the status of the relationship to the addict. It seemed as if a person became sick by being in the dysfunctional relationship with a dependent. If you married an alcoholic you became a codependent.

A relationship with an addict is a wonderful place for the problem to thrive, but we now know that the alcoholic relationship, with its roller coaster rides and lifestyle, neediness, enabling postures and control issues is where we *act out* but the problem doesn't begin there. A person doesn't *become* a codependent while married to an alcoholic; they marry an alcoholic *because* they are codependent.

Alcoholics may seem out of control, but they are extremely controlling. They *try* to control reality and the people around them. They *try* to control their feelings and their use of alcohol. One of the earmarks of alcoholism is the attempt to control what cannot be controlled. As codependents, in our attempt to *not* be controlled, we attempt to control the alcoholic, our feelings, and environment—we try to control the uncontrollable. This makes us feel more out of control, necessitating even greater attempts at control. Like the addict, we believe, "All I need to do is get a little more in control." We need to face that we are out of control, to accept our powerlessness. We too are addicts.

6

These issues were discovered in alcoholic families because the issues are so overt and alcoholic families were the only families that were ever seen in a therapeutic setting for long enough and in enough numbers for this discovery. Other families contain and breed codependency but we haven't studied other families as much.

Enabling

Our enabling helps others continue their self-destructiveness, acting out or helplessness. Examples include lying for a person, minimizing behaviors and feelings, not confronting or noticing inappropriateness, covering up irresponsibility or neglect, empty threats, whining, complaining, *but not changing*. Enabling is a pattern of disrespect since the enabler tends to remove the consequences from inappropriate behavior, thus the behavior continues without the consequences. Lying to a boss about a spouse's hang-over-caused absence may protect the job but it also protects the alcoholism.

Alcoholics find relationships because the alcoholic requires an enabling system and many of us require someone to enable. The addict seeks someone with little ego strength or identity, someone who feels at fault and experiences guilt when things go wrong. Alcoholics tend to find relationships with people in pain, who feel empty, but don't want to face the pain or emptiness. In turn, the alcoholic relationship is a distraction from the emptiness of self. Married to an alcoholic, one can focus on the alcoholic and forget self. Now our pain is not about us but about the relationship. It appears as if the problem is about the relationship with dependents, but it really is about the *absence of relationship with self.*

As enablers, we tend to say things like, "He or she is not really like that." "They really have a good heart, but just lose a little control." "Their job makes them drink too much." "He/She is just smarter than other people and the same rules don't apply." "They see more and know more." We make excuses for the addict; we distort who they are, creating a mythical relationship and then *cling to the myth.* We often come from families in which at least one parent was an addict, missing, or abusive. Subsequent relationships are a reenactment of the childhood experience and a recycling of unresolved childhood feelings and conflicts. As enablers we usually blame ourselves when things go wrong. We have learned to feel overly responsible and small mistakes get blown up out of proportion.

Feelings

A child whose parents are unavailable because of addiction, abusiveness, or emotional or physical absence feels scared and worthless while knowing it isn't safe to express this. The feelings get repressed. Feelings that get repressed get acted out. Feelings that are not expressed, talked out, worked out or affirmed become a basis for acting out self-destructive behaviors. When we repress feelings we often reenact settings that help us feel the repressed pain or fear. These new situations enable us to attach the repressed feelings to something active in our lives, thereby avoiding the original source of our pain, fear and shame. The alcoholic relationship becomes the place to act out the pain of childhood; our worthlessness and the emptiness we felt while living in families with neglect or abuse is renewed.

We seek perfection and focus on details, missing the larger picture, not acknowledging the larger mistakes while focusing on little things. We cannot see the forest for the trees. We are overreactive to the addict's behaviors, feelings, words, confusion, or illness. We lose inner direction and become outer-directed and overreactive. Externals are what count, getting by, the status quo. We focus on looking good, not feeling good. Arrogance, saintliness and martyrdom are worn like prayer cloaks. Empty threats, complaining, minimizing, lashing out and medicating feelings become our norm.

Intervention

In the field of chemical dependency, intervening with the progression of the disease of alcoholism is less and less directly involved with the alcoholic. Real intervention is with the enabling system. When the family gets help, the alcoholic reacts. The disease cannot maintain itself without the enabling system. The best interventions are with the enablers, not the addicts. When an alcoholic is intervened on and is treated their significant relationships often fall apart, especially if the spouse (or other family members) do not attend a recovery program. When the enablers are left untreated, the system breaks up. Frequently the addict returns to using and family members find other addiction-based relationships.

Alcoholism, even though a primary disease, is also symptomatic. The alcoholic may have sexual issues, spiritual bankruptcy, depression, fear, rage, lack of socialization skills, and be developmentally stuck. Take away the alcohol and the other symptoms remain; the absence of identity and the rage are still present. Scratch an addict you'll find a codependent. Addicts lack identity. When the enabler doesn't get help and the addict does, the relationship no longer fits for either person. The addict in recovery no longer requires the enabling the partner needs to do to avoid their emptiness. Recovery of the addict after treatment often does not last due to the pressure of the enabling system to return to the illness. If recovery is good the relationship doesn't serve the enabler's or the addict's purpose anymore. The recovery in the system is a threat to what they do, their role, their reason for living. The alcoholic's recovery may necessitate the other family members to look at themselves. The family's willingness to do this forces open their inability to maintain intimacy. This combined with the alcoholic's absence of dealing with their own codependency issues leaves too much untreated, too many issues are opened up but not resolved. New relationships need to be based on recovery from addiction by the addict and recovery from codependence by the entire family.

Codependents do not restrict their relationships to alcoholics; any addict will do. We choose relationships with people addicted to drugs, gambling, sex, food, rage, power, intensity, money, religion or whatever. We may find a mentally ill person, an abusive person, a physically ill person, a self-destructive person, an offender oriented person. It may be to an institution or a cause that we turn our life over to, over-focus on and over-react to. One can starve themselves fighting for world hunger, be obsessed to the point of illness over an issue, volunteer to the point of collapse and be the constant counseling companion to a host of friends. We find an obsession that becomes the focus of our lives, an escape and distraction from self and the wounds of our childhood.

Independence
Some of us become isolated and reclusive. We call a person who doesn't act out their emptiness in relationships with others an "independent." Independents are codependents that avoid relationships. Independents are led to believe they were always on their own; a hard baby to hold, always squiggling, did things their own way, played alone, etc. The independent buys the myth of their separateness and differentness without realizing they became independent, not because of who or what they are, but because there was no one around for them to depend on. If they do get into a relationship, they worry intensely about losing too much

of themselves, that they cannot take care of themselves, maintain their boundaries or a sense of self. They stay isolated. There are two extremes—*enmeshment* and *isolation*. Some of us bounce back and forth between the two positions; some constantly stay enmeshed, while others remain isolated. *180 degrees from sick is still sick.* Isolation is the opposite of enmeshment, but ultimately it is the same thing. Counter-dependence is a third posture. Some of us become defiant and rebellious. We sabotage and become aggressive and hostile.

Enmeshment

Enmeshment occurs when we can't tell where we stop and others begin. We over-identify and become obsessed with another. We overreact to how they feel, what they are doing and define ourselves through who they are. Enmeshment is defining ourselves through others, suffering for and because of others. *When someone commits a crime, the codependent pays the fine or does the time.* Enmeshment comes from arrested individuation in childhood. It creates anxiety and major control issues. We attempt to over control or change the other person so we can feel better and freer. Enmeshment can continue long after a relationship has seemingly ended, through the lingering anger and suffering. Enmeshment feels close and warm, but eventually the warmth becomes sticky and rigid; the closeness begins to smother and imprison; the codependent relationship struggles begin. The more we struggle, the greater the enmeshment and the more it looks like the other person's problem. (See more on enmeshment in chapter five.)

The very struggle with and focus on the other person is the manifestation of the escalating loss of self. One can be enmeshed by anger and rage or fear and suffering or by romantic love. Eventually whatever the other person wears, does, believes, how they parent, behave in public, handle money and speak, all reflect not on the person but on the codependent. We invented the Boys' Town slogan, "He ain't heavy, Father, he's my brother . . . and the other one's my sister and the big ones are my parents. I'm also carrying three wives, eleven friends and seventeen various committees and causes, as well as a business that employs 40 people and the long-time livelihood of friends and people that I've met. But I can handle it. Well, at least until I drop dead. Just as long as I don't have to carry me, care for one, be responsible for and get to know me or touch my own fears and pain."

Enmeshment could be illustrated by grasping two hands with interlocking fingers and feeling the closeness and warmth, but not knowing which finger belongs to which hand or where we stop and other people begin. Maintaining that grasp feels like the absence of freedom. We can't gesture, we can't use our hands, we can't take care of self or be free to do what we need to do. We begin to pull away, as if our interlocking hands are straining against each other, pulling in opposite directions. It is like the Chinese finger puzzle placing two fingers into a small tube and as we pull out the tube tightens and holds the fingers together. When we push in we are stuck together and when we pull out we are stuck together—that describes our relationships. As we cling to a relationship it is enmeshment, but the enmeshment is also present as we pull away or struggle with the relationships. The harder we pull the more stuck we become. We are as enmeshed in our anger, fighting, frustration and disillusionment as we were in our love, fantasy and obsessions. The one way out of that Chinese finger puzzle is to *let go*, give up, relax, to "Let Go Let God."

Isolation

Isolation is the alternative position. The struggle with the relationship may end. We break away, find separateness and relief because we don't have to worry or care about anyone but us. Now we can focus on our self and do what we please. We can eat what we want, when we want, go to movies, smoke, drink, sleep, work and play as our impulses dictate. Unfortunately, the pleasure is short-lived and soon we are sick of movies and we're working, smoking, eating and drinking too much. The pain returns, the emptiness is experienced and the feeling of not having a place or not being needed sets in. Soon we are back into an enmeshed relationship, obsessing or struggling with the old relationship or finding a new one.

Some of us remain on the enmeshed side, others on the isolation side, many swing back and forth. We need to learn two new aspects of relationships. The two postures of this new line, instead of enmeshment and isolation, could be called intimacy and detachment. On this line, when there is closeness there is still a sense of separateness, boundary, a sense of self. When we are separated, we can still feel close and intimate. On the new line, in this new relationship style, we can have both intimacy and detachment. Detachment means we still care and feel but are no longer controlled.

Recovery

Before we can have this new line, we must develop a sense of self, our limitations and boundaries. Henry Nouen said "The first step in establishing spirituality is to establish a relationship with oneself." The same can be said for codependency recovery which is spiritual recovery.

Recovery is the spiritual journey of knowing self. This is the healing of enmeshment. Intimacy is difficult because we expect it and want it right away. We seek *instant intimacy*. Sex can be the "instant gratification" for intimacy-seeking. Sex, courtship and infatuation all contain elements of feeling intimate, but they are not intimacy. Too much, too soon, too fast, too hard can damage the possibilities of intimacy. Intimacy is the result of sharing, caring friendship built between people. It is the feeling in a relationship that promotes closeness, bondedness and connectedness without enmeshment. For someone who has spent their life struggling in enmeshed relationships it is difficult to recognize. Intimacy is not focusing on each other, having sex or fighting; rather it is growing side by side facing the same direction, sharing the world within and outside of ourselves, building a history of experience and awareness. There is instant sex, instant relationship, instant hot chocolate, but rarely instant intimacy. Intimacy comes easier when we are healthy—when we have a clear identity, live balance, are open to trust, and experience our own pain and fears and ultimately when we know, love and accept self. Experiencing congruency with our own feelings and self acceptance affords us the joy of intimacy with another.

Crystal Clear Concepts
Dependency Problems As Reactions To Dysfunctional Systems

"When we have our feelings, they don't have us."

Codependence has been described as everything from an iceberg to an onion, toxic shame to the white male system, immaturity to kindness. Our institutions suffer from it as do our friends, children, parents and planet. It is generally described through metaphor, simile and analogy with the focus on symptoms. There are attempts to link it to brain chemistry, sexism and religion. The problem is the result of various and often conflicting forces and concepts including cultural, gender, religious, ethnic, philosophical and socio-economic (people in poverty can't afford it yet). It is primarily about low functioning families and child abuse though much of what we call codependence is the human condition in this present stage of our evolving. The basis is the absence of developmental formation and the resulting emptiness of self—our vacant souls. It manifests in cultural pathology, defensiveness, overconsumption, dishonesty, exploitation, monetary spirituality, tokenism and empty slogans. It is also a result of a misunderstanding of men's and women's developmental process, especially around the relational orientations and needs of women.

It is the sibling of Post Traumatic Stress Disorder, the fragmented self that follows a trauma. It can look like caretaking, narcissism, victim posture, offending behaviors, gregarious or isolation postures. It is a byproduct of cultural misogyny, a fear and hatred of vulnerability. The bottom line is the fear of our need for intimacy and a fear of abandonment.

Most of us struggle between a desire for intimacy and the fear of intimacy. Those of us hurt by the people closest to us in childhood have come to need and desperately seek intimacy. Intimacy that will give us the freedom and sense of aliveness that comes with a family, a support system and the affirmation of others. The family socialization process makes us real. When people in our families (the very people we were supposed to be intimate with in the years of our formation) were not available—when they hurt, neglected and treated us abusively—when that intimacy was not available but turned against us, we learned to fear intimacy as well as abandonment. When people get close we become vulnerable and wait for the shoe to drop. We wait for abuse or abandonment; as we seek intimacy, we live in fear of it. Our relationships become cycles of getting close, getting scared, and distancing. In our distance we feel isolated and alone, so we get close again. The closeness may be clinging enmeshment and we get stifled so we isolate. The cycle continues. We attempt to maintain closeness and control and still deny our vulnerability. We keep reenacting all of what happened in childhood by getting enmeshed and controlling. We feel abandoned, hurt and used all the time. We create a myth about a "pretend intimacy" in our relationships. Fear of abandonment comes from having been abandoned. Fear of intimacy comes from being hurt by people close to us. In our relationships we reenact the very core of our relationship fears.

Symptoms

We tend to identify and treat symptoms. The symptoms look as if they are the problem. In the addiction field we have a tendency to focus on these symptoms, even treating the symptoms selectively. We border on paranoia about looking for the causes of these symptoms anywhere but in brain chemistry. We fear addicts will use whatever it is to justify their using. Treating only symptoms has led to the breakup of many relationships and the early demise of many addicts. It has caused much pain for families. Focusing on symptoms affects the ability of people to find recovery. *The most common recovery for addiction in our culture is addiction.* We jump around from one to another, preferably finding an addiction that

14

won't piss people off so much, but will still maintain our denial, delusions and distract us from feelings.

Treating symptoms instead of the problem creates switching from one addiction to another and increased recidivism. (It also keeps many therapists in business!) There is much talk in the field about relapse: relapse occurs because of the absence of *real* recovery, identity development and healing past hurts. Alcoholics often leave treatment with an increased dependence on nicotine, caffeine, food and disordered eating. They leave treatment with the core issues intact. Treatment with a focus on relationships does not touch the *real* needs.

The Kellogg Prism

Codependence is like a prism, a crystal with six sides. The six sides of the prism represent *denial, delusion, distortion, defensiveness, dishonesty and despair.* No one side of the prism refracts light independently, but rather as an accumulation of all sides. There is no specific pattern or process of one side building on another, but rather an endless array of combinations of how the sides are interrelated. The light is only reflected from the outside. There is no internal light.

Denial

Through denial we maintain our pathology, whether it is denial of the problem, the feelings regarding the problem or the depth of the problem's impact on our lives. In our culture are many problems but only one dysfunction. Addiction, incest, abuse, neglect, depression are all *problems* often found in families. The denial is what creates the dysfunction. The denial eliminates the opportunity to resolve problems or deal with feelings about the problems. It also eliminates the alternatives and chances to find recovery for the problem. The problem controls us.

Denial sets up problems to be passed on intergenerationally. What we don't pass back we will pass on. "The sins of the parents shall be passed onto the children for three to four generations." Much of therapy is a process of dissolving denial. The therapeutic process is to take the covert and make it explicit. The covert involves the buried issues that control our life. Once we make the covert explicit we have choices. Freedom requires the ability to choose. As long as denial exists, there is no freedom — no freedom to be us. Addiction is a process of decreasing choice, the decreasing ability to be oneself, the loss of freedom. *Denial is the sustaining force of our self-destructiveness.*

Kellogg Codependency Prism

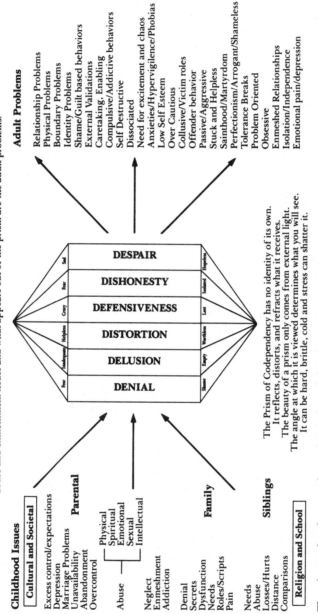

Understanding the Nebulous Concepts of Codependency
and how it comes from a variety of childhood issues and deflects into a range of adult problems.

Codependency is the child's reaction to a dysfunctional family. It will reflect a different pathology depending on the angle from which it is viewed. The child becomes a prism without an identity of its own. The prism deflects the childhood developmental, abandonment, neglect, abuse and enmeshment issues and what appears out of the prism are the adult problems.

Adult Problems

Relationship Problems
Physical Problems
Boundary Problems
Identity Problems
Shame/Guilt based behaviors
External Validations
Caretaking, Enabling
Compulsive/Addictive behaviors
Self Destructive
Dissociated
Need for excitement and chaos
Anxieties/Hypervigilence/Phobias
Low Self Esteem
Over Cautious
Collusive/Victim roles
Offender behavior
Passive/Aggressive
Stuck and Helpless
Sainthood/Martyrdom
Perfectionism/Arrogant/Shameless
Tolerance Breaks
Problem Oriented
Obsessive
Enmeshed Relationships
Isolation/Independence
Emotional pain/depression

© 1988 Terry Kellogg/LifeWorks

DESPAIR
DISHONESTY
DEFENSIVENESS
DISTORTION
DELUSION
DENIAL

Sad — Hopeless
Fear — Isolated
Crazy — Lost
Helpless — Worthless
Inadequate — Empty
Fear — Shame

The Prism of Codependency has no identity of its own.
It reflects, distorts, and refracts what it receives.
The beauty of a prism only comes from external light.
The angle at which it is viewed determines what you will see.
It can be hard, brittle, cold and stress can shatter it.

Childhood Issues

Cultural and Societal

Excess control/expectations
Depression   **Parental**
Marriage Problems
Unavailability
Abandonment
Overcontrol

Abuse — Physical
        Spiritual
        Emotional
        Sexual
        Intellectual

Neglect
Enmeshment   **Family**
Addiction

Denial
Secrets
Dysfunction
Needs
Roles/Scripts
Pain

Needs   **Siblings**
Abuse
Losses/Hurts
Distance
Comparisons

Religion and School

The prism can have beauty and attractiveness, but only from external light. In recovery the light becomes internal and self-produced. Recovery is the process of kindling an internal light source. The beauty and the magic of the child that we are refracting health and spiritual light to the world. The light of guardianship of ourselves, others and our planet that is the winnowing flame of healthy anger, the appropriate responsibility of our shame, the empathy and healing of our sadness and wisdom of our fear and the grateful sparkle of our joy.

16

Delusion

Delusion is "sincere denial," denial we really believe in. Our delusion is a form of a self-deception that allows us to survive with the problem intact. Delusion varies from "It will get better if I try harder," to "There is no problem." Delusion is harder to deal with in recovery because it is sincere and provides a payoff. The ability to believe our life is wonderful in the face of repetitive disaster is quite appealing. The delusion that one is in charge is certainly less scary than the reality of being out of control. Delusion becomes a "crazy maker" for the people around us. Delusion can help us deal with illness and hang together during crisis, but it also makes change very difficult. *Delusion is the survival tool of self deception.*

Distortion

Another facet of the crystal is the distortion of reality as a way to maintain the delusion and denial. We do not see the same reality as others. As the person with anorexia looks in a mirror and sees fat where there is no fat and the alcoholic can distort the consequences of their behavior; many of us distort the reality of relationships, the impact of behaviors, violence, neglect or manipulation in our lives. We distort the world, what we value, and what is said and done. Intervention is done by injecting a sense of reality and awareness of behavior and consequences. *Distortion is the alteration of reality.*

Defensiveness

Before we can see reality, the fourth face of the prism—defensiveness—needs to be addressed. Defensiveness is the 'protection racket'—the focusing on others, their roles, responsibilities and behaviors, while not letting anyone get too close or see too much of us. Guilt is our veneer, fear is the power plant, shame is the fuel. All these distract from the underlying hurt and pain of isolation. It takes a strongly integrated defense system to protect the isolation and to prevent pain and hurt. The following is a list of common defenses that we use:

Manipulation—covertly controlling and altering circumstances and consequences;
Projection—seeing in others what is going on with us;
Blaming—assigning to others responsibilities for what goes wrong in our lives;

Intellectualizing—using words, insights and talk that goes beyond the issue in order to avoid the feelings, bury everything with extraneous data and disconnected issues;

Shifting—switching the issues and the direction of where things are going;

Agreeing—always following the path of least resistance;

Disagreeing—taking the devil's advocate stance;

Levity and humor—minimizing through lightness and joking;

Grandiosity—making things so big *they can't possibly be dealt with;*

Minimizing—making things so small *they don't have to be dealt with;*

Raging—scaring people with the power of our anger;

Passive aggressive—not getting angry, but shutting down, avoiding, withdrawing, being quiet, "getting even but not angry";

Ignoring—pretending not to notice so we don't have to deal with it;

Seducing—being seductive, charming, sexualizing things in order to avoid and control;

Lying—saying what isn't true *and* leaving things out or being dishonest about our feelings;

Reversing—answering questions with questions, placing it back on otherpeople or back where it doesn't belong;

Arrogance—the haughty attitude that distances by putting us above it all;

Bullying and Threatening—scaring people, badgering them, pushing them away from the real issues;

Leaving—going away, running away, distancing, shutting down;

Helplessness—a learned sense of "not being able" that makes everybody want or need to take care of us;

Pitiful—behaving so people end up feeling sorry for us and pitying us, as our way of avoiding responsibility;

Unpredictability—creating an atmosphere that induces fear because people never know what we're going to do or how we're going to respond;

Argumentative—making everything into a fight, a disagreement, a difference of attitudes.

Once I was confronted about being overly defensive, and I, of course, replied, "I am not." Much of our defensiveness comes from a core belief that "I am bad." If someone tells us we made a mistake, we hear it through internalized shame and are convinced they are really saying *we are a mistake*. This personalized interpretation of feedback and criticism necessitates defensiveness. Intervention must deal with the defenses, but not by heavy confrontation or battering at the defenses. The very battering gives them strength. This includes our self-battering, being hard on self. The most effective way of dealing with defensiveness is simply to notice the defense at the time it is being used. This tends to diffuse it so it no longer works. If every time I ask someone a question and they make a joke of it or ask me a question back, or every time I talk about what's going on in the family and they switch the subject, or whenever I say I'm hurt and they get angry, and so on—these are the defenses. What needs to be said is, "You just answered my question with a question," or "You switched the subject while I was talking about what's going on in the family," or "You got angry when I shared my pain." This diffuses the defense. It does not mean there will automatically be recovery or the relationship will be healed, but the noticing eliminates the power that defenses have over us. When we confront and attack defenses with our own defenses and begin hassling with others, there develops a collusion of defenses which prevents any intimacy or recovery from occurring. *Defensiveness is protection and hiding our vulnerability.*

Dishonesty

Dishonesty and distorting the truth occur as the process of our pathology escalates. We lie to cover our tracks or to protect others. We become dishonest about our feelings. When we hate something we say it's OK. When we feel awful we say, "I'm fine." We smile through our pain and deny our anger, becoming dishonest about behavior, addictions and time. Some of us who would never acknowledge dishonesty leave big pieces of information out altogether. The dishonesty creates a disharmony, an electric tension within that can only be quieted with addictive or obsessive behavior. It isn't quieted at all. We just distance ourselves from it. We distance ourselves from ourselves.

We model dishonesty for our children. The basic dishonesty in our culture begins with the dishonesty of families. It is a way or surviving among people who are cruel and crazy making. If it is truth that sets us free, many of us have never known freedom. Our dishonesty becomes delusion and self-deception. There is no chance for recovery with dishonesty. We must seek and strive for rigorous honesty. "Perfect" honesty may be too abusive, rigid or brutal; many people become self righteous and use *excess* honesty to beat up other people. We need to learn privacy but give up dishonesty. The dishonesty we teach our children is the dishonesty we learned in childhood, especially the dishonesty with our feelings. *Dishonesty is the fuel for self-hate.*

Despair

Despair is the hopelessness that things won't and can't change. Despair is the felt sense that we are not in control and are unwilling to let go of control we don't even have. Isolation is the result of the despair experienced in our relationships. Despair mingles with fear, shame and pain, manifesting itself into our last ditch efforts of self-destructiveness—suicide ideation and self-destructive addictiveness. Despair is the absence of hope, truth and light. As codependence is the emptiness of the soul, despair is the death of the soul. It is that hollowness of self, the feeling of emptiness that so many of us carry. Our alienation feels complete; we are cut off from God, self, our family and friends. *Despair is the strangling of our spirit.*

The prism model clarifies the absence of identity. A prism has beauty; so can codependents have beauty. The beauty of a prism comes only from external light, light it collects from outside of itself, which it reflects and refracts in different directions and angles. We have a feeling of emptiness so we collect light from others and reflect this light out to give us a sense of importance, meaningfulness, warmth or beauty. A prism in the dark is cold and hard, possibly brittle and jagged. Only externals can give us beauty and meaning. We can be hard, cold and jagged, brittle to the point that a hit in the right place will cause a shatter. We can tolerate the intolerable, but this is usually marked by tolerance breaks. These may be anything from a temper tantrum to a pre-psychotic breakdown. Stress cracks codependents. These cracks can be called nervous breakdowns or anxiety attacks. In previous generations they have been called spells, or the vapors. If you know about the vapors, you are either a social historian or old enough to be everybody's mom or dad!

A prism only reflects out what enters. We reflect out, in adulthood symptoms, what enters in childhood experiences. Our cultural obsession with treating symptoms applies to treating codependents. We focus on the adult symptoms and ignore the childhood issues. The adult symptoms include:

Relationship problems—problems that stem from the absence of self—relationship, inability to have intimacy, being enmeshed, choosing inappropriate, abusive, clinging relationships;

Physical ailments—illness, somatizing our feelings into arthritis, cancer, allergies, upper respiratory infections, being over-stressed;

Boundary issues—we can't set limits, we do for others what we won't do for ourselves;

Identity problems—absence of self-awareness, strength, directions and goals;

Shame and guilt behaviors—we become controlled by our shame, a belief in our own worthlessness and our guilt, a denial of our uniqueness;

Seeking external validations—others define us;

Caretaking, enabling—we remove harmful consequences from the behavior of others;

Compulsive addictive behaviors—we become addicts;

Dissociation—absence, and split off from self;

Intensity issues—needing excitement, often surrounding ourselves with crisis and creating chaos, only feeling alive when things are falling apart around us;

Anxiety problems—fears, anxieties, hyper vigilance, phobias which control our lives;

Low self-esteem—we feel less than, flawed;

Hyper cautious—timid approach to life, restricting experiences, refusing to take risks;

Collusive role—enabling victim and offender behaviors, enabling violence;

Victim role—behaving and feeling as if we don't have any impact or choice, believing people are doing it to us;

Offender behavior—taking hurts and anger from within and projecting on others, doing things to hurt others, violating their boundaries;

Passive aggressive—not dealing with our anger in straight ways, anger is repressed and covertly expressed. We withdraw, get quiet, become cynical and sarcastic, leave emotionally and physically;

Being stuck—acting helpless so other people have to take care of us;

Sainthood/martyrdom—being perfectionistic, arrogant and shameless;

Tolerance breaks—Tantrums, falling apart;

Problem orientation—Life is a problem to be solved;

Obsessiveness—ruminating, rolling things over and over in our heads;

Pseudo maturity—feigning independence and experience;
Emotional pain—sometimes depression; constant hurting.

These are some of the *symptoms, they are not the problem.* They flow directly from childhood. The input into the prism, the light that goes in, is reflected out as these symptoms. The childhood issues become the cause of the adult pain. We have a childhood developmental disorder that primarily gets acted out beginning in adolescence or earlier and very seldom treated until adulthood, if at all.

A child is pulled off the path of becoming oneself. The spiritual journey of becoming the person we were meant to be by our creator is thwarted. Things that prevent us becoming us are the causes. Violence nourishes codependency. Violence is the violation of self, freedom, needs, rights, feelings, ideas, sexuality or our bodies. It is a violation of boundary, a set-up for loss of identity. It requires the overreaction to the external. The violator, the offender, has the power. The victim loses their power. We try to change who we are so that we won't be noticed, beaten, hurt or neglected. The power is outside of myself. I'll react and change who I am and I'll try to be what they want me to be. I discover that it's hopeless, but I continue to attempt to be someone other than me. I may defy, react or rebel but I am still being controlled by whatever or whoever it is that is hurting me.

Codependence is a child's reaction to families that are messed up. It comes from:
- divorce
- marital problems
- affairs
- addictions
- battering
- abuse of all kinds
- unpredictability
- enmeshment
- abandonment
- emotional denial
- threats
- neglect
- incest
- parents being unhappy about themselves, their relationships and lives

- parents not dealing with problems, expecting the kids to make it OK
- lack of affirmation of self
- parental unavailability which produces self-doubt
- shame
- excess pressure to fill the family needs
- perfectionistic expectations
- covert stress and control issues
- martyrdom of parents
- children's overinvolvement with parents' problems.

It is the *crushing* of our trust, identity, autonomy, safety, reality, self-image, industry, pleasure and creativity.

We learn to react to the needs, problems and dysfunctions of those around us, rather than to our feelings, our reality, our needs and wants. It comes from a child's insecurity of living with parents in a dysfunctional marriage—a family that produces fears, anxieties, worries, phobias, hyper vigilance, and control issues.

As children we tried to make everything better and were unable to. We believed survival depended on fixing the family. We became over-responsible, helpless and hopeless or naïve. The premises, myths, modeled behavior, rules, scripting and repetition all contributed.

We reenact dysfunction. We pass it on as a legacy of dysfunction and denial to our children. Children exist for their parents. Families set up role reversals where parents are taken care of by their children. This happens to many of us in families that are dishonest, bankrupt, hopeless, dysfunctional, empty and undependable.

As crises and problems occur in our present lives, it is back to our families of origin that we must go for our healing. Nothing changes until it become real. We have learned to protect, deny, obey and "live with." We have created a national *parent protection racket*. We try to believe that parents always do their best or at least try their best. In protecting our families and our parents we lose the real source of codependency and stay focused on symptoms. We protect family and stay sick.

Like a conduit, the child receives abuse and delivers dysfunctional lifestyle. We are unaware of the connection between our painful lifestyle and our childhood issues. Hiding what underlies our dysfunction makes change difficult, even impossible as long as denial remains. The behaviors, such as over-responsibility, enabling, excess tolerance of the inappropriate behavior in others, our mood swings or disordered eating, are truly compulsive. We do not choose. They may seem voluntary but we can only choose when we have awareness, not just of the behavior but the driving forces beneath the behavior, feeling and internal conflict. We subconsciously repeat the dilemmas, fears and pain of childhood—or we avoid repeating them to the point of going in the opposite extreme. 180 degrees from sick is still sick.

Many of us maintain our shame so our parents don't have to feel guilt. Our parents often came from families where their parents were emotionally unavailable and dishonest. Children are set up to give meaning to parents' lives and get enmeshed in parents' problems. The issues become intergenerational. What doesn't get passed back gets passed forward. Our problems become our children's problems. Our children's problems become our cultural problems.

Family violence, social messages, school, church, culture and peers all play a part in creating codependents. We live with an educational system that often:
- stifles our ability to become us
- squelches our curiosity, creativity and interest
- smothers awareness of the awesomeness of creation
- breaks down creation into meaningless components
- forces us to stay in the lines with our crayons
- coerces us to memorize and repeat without understanding or interest
- compels us to compete and learn so little in such a long period of time
- denies our ability to question or think critically
- impels us to discover ourselves either as a failure or a success.

Survival in the system depends on one's ability to adapt to whatever school style or teacher style we happen to be in at the time and to be the recipient of the frustration of the teaching profession. This is codependency reinforced in our educational system.

Religion contributes with:
- undercurrents of sexual shame, frequently resting on rafters of woman-hate
- concept of God as a judgmental, powerful, punishing father figure who selects those to favor and those to punish capriciously
- focus on a god of miracles, of power, who alters the course of creation, who is jealous and petty, and vindictive

24

- over-ritualized liturgy
- religion based on intolerance
- institutions operating with addictive greed
- a focus on punishment, shame and threats
- religiosity rather than spirituality
- religious arrogance
- religious extortion and exploitation
- sick spiritual leaders.

A God of Power

We are offered a codependent caricature of a deity, who, rather than creating man in his image and likeness, was created by man in man's image and likeness. It is humankind that worships the power to alter nature. It is humans who look for the technological miracles with no view of the expanded impact or future consequences. It is humans who are jealous, angry and worship the power that would enable us to smite our enemies and grant favors to friends. The sin of Genesis is we have created god in our image and likeness rather than being created in the image of likeness of God. We lost a creator of process, balance and harmony, of the unfolding universe. Our emptiness reaches right down into the roots of our religious beliefs, is a god of control, a god of power, a god of miracles. Our image of god is a projection of us.

In Genesis, with our knowledge of good and evil, we were given the guardianship of the garden. With a worship of power and greed, the guardianship seems to have become the destruction of the garden. We have lost the sense of healthy shame. We have lost a sense of the fragility and balance of the world. We have lost the sense of consequences that we need to be true guardians.

To be created in the image and likeness of this God of life, this God of creation, we must be sensitive to our actions and their impact. We must learn to see and embrace vulnerability. We must have the courage to continue the journey of becoming all that we were meant to be, a journey we lost in childhood. We have lost the ability for prayer, for noticing the awesomeness of creation, for respecting the world. *We don't notice because we haven't been noticed.* We have to be looked at and accepted as the miracles of life that we are. We have to be touched and felt with preciousness and looked at with holiness before we can see that around us. We have to see it within ourselves first and feel it there. We look inward and see blankness. We look at the anger, fears, loneliness and isolation, and we project these out in our relationships with others and our relationship with creation.

We live in a culture that reflects and contributes to low functioning lives. Socially, a person is incomplete unless they are a couple. An abusive relationship is seen as better than being alone. Our culture makes it difficult to meet people but, when we don't or can't, we feel shameful and inadequate. Our culture is ambivalent about work, food, sex and relationships. It's even ambivalent about beatings, abuse and violence. We are taught excess consumption as an economic theology. We practice addictive consumptiveness and disposable everything, from nuclear waste to cigarette lighters.

Codependence is a by-product of
• cultural violence
• crime on our streets and in our cities
• violence on our highways
• dishonesty in our politics, governments, business and religion
• religious exploitation, extortion, exhortation and seduction
• a lack of cultural boundaries
• the worship of wealth and power
• an obsession with defensiveness
• sex role rigidity
• poor treatment of vulnerable people
• little protection of environment

These are all by-products of family violence. The cultural dysfunction is learned in family dysfunctions. Children from sick families grow up and create sick culture which in turn supports a continuing family disintegration.

Sex Role Rigidity

Cultural problems are sustained through sex role rigidity. Most cultures have rigid sex roles, but in this culture these sex roles become the basis for the style of relationship and life choices by men and women. What are women taught in our culture about being women? To have children, nurture, maintain, take care of and do the emotional healing? Women are the fairer sex, the weaker sex and child bearers with limitations. They are sex symbols and beauty objects. Women in our culture start out depersonalized. We have not had a woman president or even a serious contender. Why? Because women menstruate and everybody knows you can't have a president that menstruates; possibly owning a penis is a constitutional presidential requirement—the hidden amendment!

Women are taught that the *right* relationship will ensure their survival, they will be taken care of. Women are taught the meaningfulness of their lives comes through other people, their children and their spouse. Women are taught that love is romance and affection. Women are given fairy tales to use as guides in their lives—Wait for Prince Charming; Kiss the toad and he will become a prince (of course you may have to kiss a lot of toads before you find your prince!); Be Sleeping Beauty or Cinderella and when you wake up you'll find yourself riding off into the sunset with the white knight . . . probably to live with his mother.

Men are taught very different things about *man-ness*. The John Wayne syndrome; Rambo and GI Joe are alive and well. Men are protectors, providers, machines that take a licking and keep on ticking, until the batteries wear down or the machinery breaks and the ticking stops. About 6-8 years before our time, our ticking stops. Men's codependency is different than women's. Men are taught to be power objects and economic symbols. Men are expendable warriors and protectors—not nurturers—non-emotional, competitive, logical heroes who can easily impart the wisdom and strength to handle an insane world.

Men and Women

Men's codependency is the inverse of women's. Women are taught power through powerlessness. Women are taught to portray powerless roles, portray powerlessness, but always retain as much control and power within those roles as they can. Men are taught powerlessness through power. We are given those things to do that look like they have power such as run and own corporations and fight in wars. Those are really the sources of our powerlessness because men don't run and own corporations. Corporations run and own men. Men don't fight in wars, men get maimed and lose their legs and friends in wars.

Men are taught that intimacy is sex. Men are taught that you work hard and intimacy, in the form of sex, will find you. Men become work addicts. Men become money addicts. Men become sex addicts. Women more often become love addicts, romance addicts. Women often become addicted to men who are addicted to other things.

Even when we rebel, when we don't do what we're told or what's expected of us we are controlled by the expectation or the rules.

Once again, the extreme opposite of everything is also true. If we break the sex role stereotypes we are punished, isolated and criticized.

Cultural Misogyny

Sex role rigidity is a cultural dysfunction that helps maintain codependency. The cultural messages about men and women contribute to our isolation, but these messages are perhaps one facet of a much larger cultural issue. This issue is the *fear and hatred of vulnerability*. In a discussion about this concern with Barbara Cherry some time ago, she suggested the word "misogyny" as a term that might apply to this cultural fear and hatred of vulnerability. Currently, misogyny is a term used to describe men who hate women or hate *and* fear women. The hatred and fear of women is really just one part of cultural misogyny. The word misogyny applies better to the underlying sense or the underlying concept that keeps us from achieving a respect for humanity, for women, children and life itself. We have a society that reflects this fear and disdain for vulnerability, a culture that worships power. This is a basis for the codependency that we see in our daily lives.

For the purpose of this book, misogyny will be a term that reflects a fear and hatred of vulnerability, a worship of power, the reason that we hide our inner feelings, the reason we don't respect children, the reason we can't find intimacy.

Offenders

Our cultural system is offender protective. Offenders have power. One of the requirements for offending behavior is the presence of a power differential. The largest offending group in our culture are parents, and they are the most protected group in our culture. Parents are protected, children are not. Victims are often ignored, untreated, uncompensated, and sometimes continually victimized in the process of seeking help, justice, fairness, repair. Victims who ally themselves with power can seemingly beat the system by becoming offenders. Offenders who are punished for being offenders are usually non-parents and in the process of going through judicial penal institutions, still have the offender system protected. They are seldom rehabilitated or treated; in fact, they are frequently taught by peers how to be better or more severe offenders, or they are placed in a victim role, usually a familiar role from their past. They are put in the custody of offenders with a legal back up for their abusiveness.

An offender is a person who has been in the victim role, usually in childhood and has bonded and identified with the aggressors in their life. They often protect the aggressor. Offenders have great denial about where they were victimized, although they often feel like victims in the presence of family, courts, therapists, judges, the system, institutions. They feel a sense of powerlessness, but the feelings about their initial and primary victim role tend to overwhelm them; they take those feelings out on other people. Their fear of vulnerability, which stems from being victimized, becomes an unwillingness to reflect vulnerability—and a hatred of the vulnerability of others. The feelings they have about how they have been victimized get projected out as a way of hurting others. They hurt others with their emotional reality. The pain, rage, shame, fear and disgust of their childhood is projected onto people around them.

If the offender goes through the penal system the system more clearly delineates the victim/offender roles and often continues the fear and hatred of vulnerability. To survive the power structures within the penal system, one must either become offender-oriented or ally themselves with the abusive powers that exist in the institution. The alternative is to get more victimized which gets expressed again as offending behavior upon release.

In the past there has been very little support for victims of child abuse, domestic violence, street crime, robbery and rape. There is little, if any compensation built into our society for victims. Most of the criminals in our culture begin their criminal activity in early adolescence. Most offenders are developmentally *stuck* in adolescence. One of the realities of male adolescence is a fear and hatred of vulnerability resulting in an over-expression of machismo. Offenders are addicts, often to drugs, more often to crime itself. Our culture is the codependent to the crime addict.

It is no coincidence that our crime problem and our relationship problems are primarily adolescent issues. The two key developmental processes of adolescence are identity and intimacy. They are also the key issues for most of us. In developmental theory we need to achieve the first to move on to the next. Many of us go backwards and try to find identity by seeking intimacy. In reality the intimacy follows identity. It is ironic that many of our major cultural issues, crime, drugs and sexual acting out are primarily adolescent issues. We cannot progress as a culture past adolescence until we give children what they need to have healthy identity. We can't help them till we get through it ourselves. We all need identity.

Children who are brutally victimized by their parents and in turn assault their parents are dealt with very severely under the law. Prior to the late 1970s women who were being battered by their spouses who in turn killed the spouse who battered them were given an average of fifteen years imprisonment, while men who killed their spouses by battering them were given an average of five to seven years imprisonment. The "rule of thumb" came from the law that the rod you use to beat your wife can be no thicker than the width of your thumb.

The extent to which the rights of offenders are protected in our culture isn't matched by efforts to rehabilitate, provide insights and recovery for offenders. It isn't matched by efforts to heal, to help mend the wrongs done to victims. We should not regress into older methods of dealing with offenders, but rather progress into better methods of rehabilitation. They need help to find their vulnerability and deal with how they've been victimized and learn better expressions of their feelings. A required twelve step meeting for all offenders would be a great start. We also need to progress in the treatment and healing of the victims. Victims don't have power. Anyone who lacks power in our culture does not tend to fare very well. *We worship power and fear and hate vulnerability.*

Our deity is the miracle-maker, the all powerful god. The wealthy are blessed and frequently, if not beyond the law, only mildly inconvenienced by it. Our government supports power centers — military, corporate, industrial or political. We have a history of supporting abusive, offender-oriented governments in other parts of the world. We have supported and colluded with drug syndicates, especially tobacco and alcohol. We have an obsession and worship of power that goes beyond reason, empathy or care. It seems that the god that we worship is a codependent, meddlesome and power-obsessed deity. We've lost the god of balance and harmony, the unfolding of creation. We have lost the sense of vulnerability of creation. We don't look at the consequences of our behavior in relationships and we miss the long-term effects of our behavior on the earth. We don't accept the true fragility and vulnerability of our planet.

Vulnerability

The problem is beyond families and beyond cultures. The issue is of our survival on this earth. The real proof of cultural codependency lies in our view and guardianship of the vulnerable in our culture, be it the planet itself; animals, plants, air, water or people. Anything that is fragile or vulnerable does not fare well. Survival of the fittest isn't just an evolutionary process but a philosophy of life. Fragile ecosystems are shattered with species of life being lost forever. Clean air and clean water are becoming more scarce. Even the atmosphere itself is showing evidence of the abuse. Vulnerable companies in business and industry are taken over and often dismantled with little regard for the employees, suppliers or customers. The farmers who are the most vulnerable—small, subsistence level farms—seem to reap the least from the government support and aid offered.

Immigrants are seldom really assisted in the integration process of our society, but they are expected to integrate. They have little assistance in maintaining the elements of their own culture so they can have a sense of pride of who they are, a sense of history and a sense of identity. They are sometimes given financial support but seldom given acceptance. The melting pot which our culture was built on is really many kettles boiling over with rage, discontent, neglect, poverty, fear, paranoia and hatred. The gang phenomena is part of this spilling over of these kettles. The dominating culture, ignoring the vulnerability of minorities and ethnic groups, creates discontent. These groups learn to act out power in a culture that worships power or be victimized for their vulnerability.

Native Americans
Native Americans really do not fare much better than they did in the eighteenth and nineteenth centuries. They are still dying of the diseases that were introduced to them (often as an attempt to eliminate them), especially alcoholism. The reservations that we enclosed them into are often places of hopelessness and despair, of alcoholism and death. What percent has entered our middle class lifestyles? What percent of Native Americans is participating in the American Dream? (Or is the dream too abusive to want to participate?) How much land and resources have been stolen? How much pride and dignity shattered? What is our society's view of the Native American person? Our policy toward Native Americans has been extermination, isolation, buy-offs, relocation, arrogant charitable assistance and basically ignoring needs. Ethnic groups tend to fare well only when they empower themselves, through gangs, money, business, property and crime.

Homeless

The homeless, the poor, also do not fare well in their vulnerability. The hundreds of thousands of homeless in our society are virtually ignored. We walk by them in our cities on a daily basis. The people in poverty are being abused by a system that supposedly maintains a freedom and dignity for all people within the system. But where is the dignity in poverty? Where is the dignity in not having a place to sleep? Do we really believe that they enjoy camping out? So many suffer from mental illness, alcoholism, emotional disorders, severe handicaps—not laziness. Are we obsessed with lifestyles of the rich and·famous? Getaways of the rich and famous? Homes of the rich and famous? Do we ignore the lifestyles of the homeless, the get-aways for the down and out and impoverished? One-third of the homeless are Vietnam vets suffering from PTSD.

Sexual Abuse

Women are also a vulnerable group. About forty percent of women in our culture have been sexually abused. About one-third of married women have been battered. Rape is an acceptable practice in our culture and is repeated about every two minutes. Supposedly, the most common kind of rape reported is date rape, friend rape or acquaintance rape. Even though three-fourths of all rape is in this category, it is probably the least reported kind of rape in terms of how often it occurs and very few offenders of acquaintance rape are prosecuted. Perhaps, though, marital rape is the most common kind of rape and probably the most ignored. Even with the recent publicity about rape we don't hear about marital rape. Is it possible that with almost half of all women in our culture having been abused sexually that this would have an impact on a culture, on trust, intimacy, vulnerability and health care? Sexual abuse is the freeway to despair, with major rest stops being in chemical dependency and other addiction. A sexual abuse victim is much more likely to be chemically dependent or practice disordered eating but substance abuse or eating disorders do not necessarily mean one has been sexually abused.

Sexual abuse and how it is dealt with are by-products of cultural misogyny. A person who is raped is very often raped three to four times before they finish going through the legal system. What percentage of rapists, who are prosecuted, punished and rehabilitated, end up with true remorse for what they have done? How many really learn to understand the impact of the crime they've committed? What percentage of rapists ever get reported and of those how many are prosecuted? Of the few that do, the average sentence is six months—in a culture and setting that condones rape. How many people have raped or been raped that don't recognize or accept it, a "no" not heard or listened to, using someone who is vulnerable, drunk, using a position of power or role for sexual gratification: we are taught rape, we believe in rape and many of us have experienced rape.

Our culture has a focus on addictive consumption, power and wealth and ignores the real needs of most of its members. In the United States, approximately 95% of the wealth lies in 5% of the hands. While those hands protect their interest, they give lip service to the needs of the 95%. This lip service is often in the form of arrogant handouts. If our culture is ripping apart from the inside and we do little mending, little repairing or discussing of this tearing of our fabric, it is because the five percent has found that fearing a threat from the outside makes for better business and maintains the balance of the power structure, status quo. Let's fear the Communist hordes, Black gangs, drug pushers, Japanese business, Arab terrorist leaders—not us. Rather than seeking the spirituality of loving, caring, giving, and sharing a social, political, and ecological guardianship—which is spirituality—we enable, collude with, are hurt by, obsess about and feel helpless regarding the social structure as it is. The newest conspiracy we are taught to fear are the drug dealers, but *only* certain drugs and *some* dealers. They are the cause of crime, poverty, and family breakdown.

Our emptiness is reflected in the insatiability of our consumption. Our economics is called consumer economics. It is built on a belief that for our economy to be strong and to grow, we must consume more and more. This isn't economics. This is an addictive codependent process. This is a breakdown of culture rather than the building of culture. Planned obsolescence, excess spending, replace everything, never enough is viewed as strength rather than addictive illness.

Are We A Tad Defensive?

Our military industrial complex reflects the emptiness and fear of our vulnerability. It is wrought with insatiable need, insatiable spending, distortion of reality, fear and paranoia of attack, conspiracy, outside forces. The military is bloated with its own excesses. To have actually spent three trillion dollars in the last seven years on defense is a tad defensive. The need for this excess is built on a semi-religious concept of puritanism. We believe we are good and pure, the elect, but we notice problems in the world, those problems must come from outside of us. If there are problems in our country, the problems must be some form of interference from outside forces. To protect ourselves from the outside, we must be able to destroy the world (great solution). Our focus on freedom in our culture is on one hand a definite value system, a true source of opportunity. On the other hand, it can be a manipulation, a mythology to help us miss the absence of freedom for so many people in our culture. It can help us miss a truth that there is no freedom outside of spiritual values, respect and vulnerability. There is no strength until we can embrace our own vulnerability and the vulnerability of those around us, to cherish that vulnerability. Addiction eliminates choice, so an addictive culture doesn't have choice or real freedom. Many other countries have been abusive, secretive, manipulative, aggressive and oppressive. A world organization is important to deal with these. What is our track record on all of the above, including dishonesty, insatiable greed, human rights, pollution and true spiritual assistance to other countries and the vulnerable people of our culture? Do we support abusive governments because of political compatibility or do we support the spiritual growth of other countries?

Child Abuse

The real test of a society lies in how it treats its children. Children are the most vulnerable group of any culture. In a codependent system children can be focused on and indulged but at the same time used, abused, molested and neglected. In our society we worship youth or at least the look and agility of youth. Many families even revolve around the needs, moods and wants of children. Children become the objects of our needs, efforts, affection, rage, hopes, meanings and frustrations. At the same time we seem to fear, hate, abuse and neglect our children. The U.S. is purported to be the most dangerous place on earth for children. One writer has called it a pedaphobic society, a society that fears and hates its children.

Watch how children are treated when parents feel anonymous in supermarkets, airports and other public places. See how adolescents hanging around MacDonald's are looked at with fear and hatred. The consensus theory of parenting in our country is, "Spare the rod, spoil the child." The rod is a concept, not a device to beat kids with. The concept is about the rod of discipline—that kids need limits, not beatings. Ninety-five percent of Americans were physically punished as children. About 15% of that punishment was punishment, the rest was abuse. Richard Gellis, in his research for a study on violence in America, found that 72% of parents acknowledged violent acts toward their children. Abuse a child and create a codependent.

I believe about 80% of us were physically abused—four out of five Americans. Less than 1% of us are aware of it, dealt with it or talked about it. What impact does it have on a culture if four out of five members of that culture have experienced some physical violence, physical abuse, and almost all are in denial about it? Would it create an altered tolerance level for violence? A collusion for violence? Street crime? City violence? The atrocities of war? It is our denial of the violence in our own background and families, our childhood that is the cause of the violence in our culture. It is collusion. We have a violent culture, not because of offending or victim roles. Not all of us are hurting others physically or being physically hurt. The violence continues because we enable it, feel powerless and refuse to notice reality. We have become immune because of our background. Violence is a symptom of our learned fear of our vulnerability and the growing worship of power.

Physical violence and abuse are on a continuum. Getting hit once inappropriately out of a parent's rage and frustration about their day, is a great deal different than being physically tortured on a regular basis. The denial of any abuse prevents the healing and it alters our baseline tolerance level for violence—what we will stand up to, be appalled by, what we will face, notice, deal with or accept.

When we consider neglect, excess *guilting,* excess pressure to succeed, cruelty, emotional abuse, mind games, I think very few people get through childhood with intact identity, self-esteem, ego development and healthy dependency. Very few of us go through the developmental needs of our childhood to become healthy adults. This absence of our own developmental needs creates codependency. The absence of identity, boundaries and dependency is a result of neglect, abandonment and abuse.

Children are seen as a way for parents to have immortality and meaning in their lives. Children are seen as property. The responsibility of parents is to control and discipline. There is ongoing discussion about permissiveness or authoritarianism in parenting. That is not the issue. The problem lies in our basic view of the child and childness and our fear and hatred of children's vulnerability which causes the resurfacing of shame from our unmet childhood needs.

Our children are not of us or about us. They are not owned by us or there to give our lives meaning. They are not there to be the objects of our affection, rage or frustrations. Our children are, as Gibran said, the miracles of the gift of life itself.

The real measure of a healthy culture is in how children are viewed and treated. The amount of money spent on health, education and welfare for children compared with the defense budget reflects priorities. One group represents vulnerability and the other power. Twenty percent of children live in poverty, a greater number and higher percentage than twenty years ago. The two top executives at Disney Productions, the children's corporations, made several million dollars last year.

The most vulnerable group, even among children, are infants. Our society has one of the highest infant mortality rates of industrialized countries. A child born in Afghanistan has a better chance of living than a child born in Detroit. Neglect of our children is reflected in:

- literacy rates;
- teen pregnancy, 40% of girls become pregnant during their teens;
- child and adolescent suicide, a leading cause of death of this age group;
- accidents, the leading cause of death among adolescents;
- teen prostitution, 80% have been sexually abused in their own homes;
- runaways, usually from abuse;
- adolescent depression;
- adolescent rage, which is the most common adolescent learning disability in our culture;
- crime rate, 90% of offenders commit their first felony in adolescence, usually by fifteen years of age and remain developmentally stuck.

Our children are not protected under the law. Children's rights, child protection laws are frequently unenforced, unenforceable or absent. Major movements in our culture, Moral Majority and pro-family are often misnomers for anti-women and anti-children movements. Children are abandoned, terrorized, hurt, ignored and taught to be obedient and passive. Children act out the feelings of what is happening to them through crime, sex, drugs, depression and failure. A child being abused or neglected sees power as external. Abused children attempt to be or do whatever is expected of them or rebels against the abuse or neglect by doing the unexpected. They often try to be perfect, knowing they are never going to be good enough. Later, they form relationships with people who set them up the same way the family did. Some children will give up, act out or rebel against the dysfunctional system while others will try to do all they can to live within it. Either posture is destructive. One child may be self-involved with low self esteem, another over achieving but no self worth, yet another may become self or other-destructive. Any of these are paths to codependency because the child is denied the ability to become who they were meant to be. They continue the dysfunction or react to it in their adult lives. The power is outside of me and I am worth less than other people and their needs. I need to try harder to make things work. I feel bad about myself for getting in trouble or not learning well. I can never do enough. There must be something wrong with me and I should be what my parents or family wants me to be, be like they are, be like my siblings, be and do what's expected. If I could make my parent happy, my mom less angry, my dad not leave or get drunk, I'll be okay.

Professionals

A final example of misogyny can be seen in our cultural view of professionals. The lowest paid and least respected professionals in our culture are people who deal with vulnerable groups: day care workers, social workers, child protection, teachers. People who work with handicapped, mentally ill, AIDS, homeless, chemically dependent, abused women, Native Americans, immigrants and the poor are often living in poverty themselves. The work is no less demanding, training no less rigorous than other professions, but the disparity in the pay scale illustrates our societal view of the people who do this work. The people working with vulnerable populations in our culture are generally treated with disdain themselves, not only in terms of compensation, but also social position. Many child protection workers feel helpless, are overwhelmed and ignore situations that may be dangerous. They get little feedback or ongoing training. They are operating on trimmed budgets and many times were abused themselves. Our culture has much rhetoric about education, educational concepts, administration, but in the classroom there has been very little change. Teachers are still viewed as servants who don't work enough—they get their summers off and they rebel and whine. Teachers have little control over policy, curriculum and text. Teaching isn't seen as a lifetime prestigious occupation. Teachers are seen as baby-sitters. The teaching profession is not difficult to get into, but there are not enough benefits to keep good teachers in the system. They become disillusioned and overworked. They often project their frustrations on the children in their classrooms. Many teachers get picky and do the same shaming the children are experiencing at home. Kids themselves get type cast as "failures," "difficult" and "acting-out." Teachers are expected to teach children who are too hurt to learn.

Family Problems

Other systems within our culture—religious, educational, political, community, work—reflect and reinforce codependency. They are an outgrowth of the family dysfunction and denial that we lived with. Virginia Satir was once quoted as having said that 96% of the families in the United States were dysfunctional. Not that 96% have problems, all families have problems. The dysfunction comes from denial, pretending there isn't a problem and keeping the secrets and the no-talk rules. When I first started in this field, I used to work with adolescents. Even though I enjoyed working with adolescents, I soon realized the adolescents were reflecting a family issue, a family problem, something they couldn't deal with or sort out. Children's behavior is based on feelings and the feelings are often based on what is going on around them. If I could not affirm the behavior, I could still affirm the feelings. When the things around them didn't change, their feelings didn't change and they continued much of the acting out behavior. I now know this was a family problem. So I began working with families. I learned about family systems and the dynamics of families. I felt like this was having a greater impact. The families would seem to talk to each other differently and do things together more. I noticed families didn't maintain the changes, the same behaviors continued as with the adolescents. I thought this isn't a family problem, it's a marriage problem. I started working with couples. I learned the dynamics of marriage, relationships, intimacy and communications. In working with couples I knew there would be changes because the marriage is the foundation of the family. It's the base on which the system rests. If the marriage is secure, if the marriage is being dealt with, becoming open, sharing and honest, the family will be healthy and secure, the children won't have to act out. Working with couples I found some things changed but the change didn't take hold, it didn't last. In working with couples I was spinning my wheels again because the problem wasn't a problem in their relationship, it was a problem with the individual marriage partners, their relationship with themselves, not each other. They weren't capable of being parents or spouses. One can't be effective in a relationship or a family until they are effective with themselves. I started working with the individuals. In working with individuals I discovered they had to work on what they learned about themselves, what happened to them, where they came from, what they needed and didn't get, as well as myths, rules, premises, beliefs, what they learned about their feelings, identity, and self image. Once individuals within a relationship build a relationship with themselves, they can have a relationship with each other and a relationship with their children. The family then becomes a family.

Family Denial

None of this can happen until the denial is identified. Pathology thrives on denial. There is only *one dysfunction* in our culture, our families and our lives. There are *many problems*—alcoholism, consumptive economics, the military budget, our fiscal irresponsibility, poverty, child abuse and violence, to name a few. *The only real dysfunction is denial.* As long as there is denial there is no opportunity to resolve the problems. Therefore the problem could *seem* to be alcoholism or any other addiction, whether it's food, gambling or shopping. It could *seem* to be mental illness, physical illness, depression, dishonesty, legal trouble or sexual issues. It could *seem* to be any one of these or more, but it is denial that needs to be dealt with before we can effect change.

Children are aware of what is going on. Children may participate in the denial at one level, but there are no secrets in a family. Children are aware enough to act it out. When they are told something different than what they feel or what they sense to be true, they lose confidence in their own judgment and feel crazy, unsure or insecure. They no longer trust themselves and get set up to reenact the problem. Reenactment can help them not feel crazy. The child's life is often controlled by forces outside of themselves which they can't sort out nor understand. This creates stress, control issues, self-doubt, manipulation, insecurity, dishonesty and even severe naivete and self-obsession.

The denial can make one feel crazy enough to recreate some aspects of the system in other settings of our life so the feelings can continue. We may create the same system in a more overt way. If the threat of violence in a family were a covert issue, one might find a system with overt violence in adulthood. The fears of violence would have a realistic basis and won't feel so crazy. The feelings of a dysfunctional system remain long after we leave the system. The fears or shame within the child are still present into adulthood. These feelings need to attach themselves to something to make sense or feel less disconnected. Feelings demand expressions. Much of adulthood becomes the creation of experiences so our feelings make sense or the recreation of the experiences in an attempt to resolve the unresolved dilemmas of childhood. Examples: *How can I function and feel safe around violence? How can I find a sense of balance in my life with all the excess expectations placed on me that I cannot live up to?* We desperately try to fulfill these impossible dilemmas and thereby stay stuck in old childhood patterns. We continue to hang around violence or we become violent. We place excess expectations on ourselves, set up others to do so or stay with people who expect too much. This can be a gift we give ourselves because the recreation of these settings and issues enables us to trace back and see the real problems of our past. Our lives reflect the early issues in our families. They are a way we keep remembering so the conflict can be dealt with.

A child in an alcoholic or dysfunctional family learns to take care of the needs of the system. Survival depends on it. Any basic need that isn't being met by adults will usually be met by the children. The child may provide a sense of pride through achievement in order for the family to exist in the community. A child may nurture or parent the younger children, or be the spouse to an adult who is lonely and isolated. A child may distract the adults from their pain, or become the leader in the family and give it a direction or provide humor in the family or try to give the parents a way to have meaningfulness in their life.

These role reversals occur when the parent functions as a child and the children act responsibly and grown-up like adults. This often makes children look very mature, but it is a *pseudo* maturity. To become an adult, one must first be a child and move through the child developmental stages. When one acts like an adult too early it eliminates the possibility of becoming an adult. We get stuck somewhere in between adulthood or childhood which could be why so many of us call ourselves "adult children." Many of us can't be either much less both.

Children learn roles which help them survive and help the family continue functioning. What we learned is not to be ourselves. We learn to become what other people need or want us to be. We learn to adapt, change, repress and hide. Codependency is the *emptiness in the soul of our being*. We are not really present.

In many families children are used, abused, molested or scapegoated. Children are sexually abused, beaten, traumatized and neglected. They are guilted, shamed, scared and ignored. They are set up to reenact dysfunctional relationships and family secrets. They are lost souls who become lost adults and lost parents losing more souls.

Childhood neglect may show up as adult depression, incest as an eating disorder, abandonment as clinging relationships or excess guilt as stress-related illness. Our adult pathologies have their roots in our childhood. Our dysfunctional lives are learned in dysfunctional systems.

The relationship problem in our culture is our relationship with ourselves, our childhood, our childness. The result of broken self-intimacy in childhood becomes intimacy problems, physical, emotional and addictive problems in adulthood. Those of us who grew up in low functioning families finally have a label, though an inadequate, controversial and nebulous one; at least it's a label, something is real. The label codependence, in its nebulousness, is appropriate to describe those of us who lack identity, just as the label itself lacks identity.

"Who we are is what we see." When one views a prism, the angle it is viewed from determines what is seen. The light reflected out varies depending on the viewing angle. Similarly, the angle codependency is viewed from determines what is seen. From one angle it may look like a bonding disorder, a lack of balance in one's life and distorted relationships. Other angles show spiritual absence and an inability to parent. Another view might show depression or suicidality. It begins to appear that the symptoms themselves are the codependency. Our tendency in treatment has always been to focus on symptoms. This view keeps us from looking inside and through the prism, through the absence of identity, the painful patterns of living, the dependency problems and into the childhood realities. The symptoms vary and so do the theories on what constitutes the problem. The angle from which the prism is viewed is determined by the background and attitude of the

viewer as well as what is sought, which symptoms are predetermined to be codependency, and which symptoms someone is determined to treat.

A medical doctor working with a patient would probably first notice the stress-related illness, particularly a physician who is aware that 60% to 80% of illness is stress-related. The stress is really an inability to deal with one's feelings, set limits or find life balance. Feelings are somatized and become physical symptoms. The physician would begin to focus on the stress and physical health and might well decide codependency is a stressful pattern of living that creates illness. This doctor might write a book emphasizing that aspect of it.

A marriage counselor may view a dependent partner or a person in an enmeshed relationship as codependent, a person who focuses on and obsesses problems in a relationship. Their book would focus on relationships and enmeshment.

A minister or spiritual counselor might recognize the spiritual bankruptcy, the absence of meaningfulness in life, religious confusion, religiosity or spiritual rigidity and decide that is codependence is the absence of healthy spirituality. Another focus, another book.

Developmental psychologists might see the absence of identity, trust, autonomy and decide that it's a developmental issue from childhood. Family counselors working with a dysfunctional family might see over-protectiveness, over-responsible parenting or absence of parenting as codependence. An alcoholism counselor will probably see it as the reactive enabling of alcoholic spouses.

All of the above may be codependence or as least aspects of this broken relationship with self. When we are not on the path of becoming us, we can wander into dark and destructive places. In the absence of nurturing and affirming, we become emotional hostages of our own demons; feelings and thoughts that create pain and fear. The problem has many faces, wears many masks but the real issue is the not knowing what is behind the mask, what is the real face—who am I?

We lead the life of an addict, believing we are making choices, but we aren't. The internal mechanism for choice isn't present. Freedom is the ability to choose, to have choice. The codependent operates by hidden messages, roles, rules and hurts, and is indeed a "prisoner of childhood." Much of our adult experience is the reenactment or reaction to these childhood experiences. Just like a prism, merely reflecting and refracting light from external sources, we also rely on the external sources for light, guidance and validation, buffeted by external criticisms, expectations and needs, unaware or only vaguely aware of one's own reality.

The variance of themes and theories and ideas comes from the viewing of the prism from the angle of our own training, biases and background. So much is frozen and submerged, hidden in shame, guilt, rage, fear, self-hate, pain and isolation. Hidden are the painful self-doubts and mean conversations with self. Hidden is the pettiness, jealousy and meanness. Hidden is the preciousness of our childlike nature with its needs, trust, instincts and awe. In recovery, the prism begins to shed its own light. We build an internal light source. What reflects out from our recovery is the truth of the inside, a warmth and healing, the *power of the crystal,* love, awareness and the giving and growing of self-knowing.

Broken Toys

Many children have lost trust, safety, creativity, spontaneity, awareness and noticing the pleasure and wonder of being. We are Broken Toys, living out lives of Broken Dreams.

Reactors Not Actors

We learn to react and be controlled by the needs around us, by other people's feelings and problems. We learn to ignore our our own needs, feelings and wants. A child coming home from school to an alcoholic family immediately switches on the radar. Approaching the house we check the vibes, the rays emanating. Is the car home? How is it parked—possibly halfway into the garage with the garage door still closed? Entering the house, is Mom depressed? Is she needy? Lonely? Sad? Can I cheer her up? Can I talk to her? Tell her about my day? Let her cry? Avoid her? Get angry at her? Distract her from her pain? Tell her it's OK. Is she suicidal? Talk her out of it? Is Dad here? Is he tense? Or is he drunk? Walk on eggshells. Be careful with him. Try to joke. Or tell him how good you did in phys. ed. today. Or stay away. Keep clear. Are they fighting? Should I try to mediate it? Shall I try to distract them from it? Will they be harder on us or each other if we don't get involved? Should I leave? Can I bring a friend home? Will they behave if we do? If they don't, will I go through the public humiliation if they act out in front of my friend? Should I not come home?

All the decisions of a child coming home from school in a dysfunctional, alcoholic or unpredictable family are not based on what the child needs, sees or feels. They are a reaction to what others need, what others want, what others feel and what others do. We become reactors, and often controllers and manipulators. It is our survival.

Woven into our childhood insecurities from living with a dysfunctional parental marriage are fears, anxieties, worries, phobias and control issues. A lack of affirmation and parental unavailability produce self-doubt, self-centeredness, shame and lack of ego strength. The excess expectations and trying to fill family needs and parental emptiness produce perfectionism, stress, martyrdom, sainthood, over-achieving, rebellion and self-destructiveness. A child reacting to a faltering marriage is set up for isolation, enmeshment, triangulation, inappropriate bonding and emotional incest. We try too hard to make everything better. We become over-responsible, helpless, hopeless and defensive from the secrets, denial, self-deception and reality confusion of sick family systems.

The infrastructure of our system includes false premises about life: It's a dog-eat-dog world. Never trust anyone. The family myths: We're a close family. Modeled behavior: dishonesty, meanness. Scripting: being told what I am, what I will become. Family rules: don't talk, don't rock the boat. Role reversals: children exist to meet the needs of parents.

Many of us have lost our spiritual base and have become broken toys creating a broken society. Some of us offend, wreak havoc on others and the world, hurt others with how we've been hurt. Some of us remain victims, continuing to be hurt, manipulated and violated. All of us are collusive, enabling the continued violence of our families, our culture and society. We have an altered baseline tolerance level for violence, abuse and neglect. We are no longer shocked. We are helpless to change. We do not notice. We are home with a violent culture. This is the ongoing trauma of family violence and addiction. Our helplessness is a post trauma effect. We develop a pretend and surface immunity to trauma and violence.

Codependence does not mean other diagnoses are not present. We may be manic depressive, suffer from anxiety reaction or be depressed. The concepts came out of the literature of alcoholism and the alcoholic spouse. The codependent is frequently viewed as the victim, a victim of the alcoholic's control, abusiveness and unavailability. Because of this view we don't see the offender role or even the addictiveness. We too often ignore the offending role

44

of the codependent by focusing on the doormat posture and spouse disease rhetoric.

Offending

Offenders were victims. They lack identity, boundaries, self-concept and awareness. Some victims bond and identify with aggressors in their lives and become offenders. We often ignore the offender behavior of a person who is in a primary victim role. We don't confront how they abuse, intrude and hurt others with how they were hurt. There is not always a clear cut distinction between a victim role or an offending role. Mothers who are being battered in a marriage are highly likely to abuse their own children. Everyone in a violent family could be labeled codependent—lacking boundaries, identity, healthy relationship and the absence of spirituality—they are victims, offenders and enablers.

The offending behavior is itself born through abuse, inappropriate bonding, unmet dependency needs and developmental processes being stifled. Offending behavior is an extension of victimization. It too is codependence.

We may not maintain a primary offending role but, out of the stress of our painful relationships, an inability to express and deal with feelings in a healthy way. We slide into offending behavior. Tolerance breaks become a lashing out at the people around us. This is difficult to embrace. It holds the most shame. The offending behavior involves trying to get rid of these feelings at other people by projecting and dumping. It is the absence of impulse control over one's feelings. Our undefined boundaries make it difficult to recognize and respect the boundaries of others. We become intrusive and abusive because of our own poor boundary sense. We often project our self-hate, shame and blame on others.

When we tolerate abnormal behavior eventually we lose our ability to tolerate even normal behavior. We build anger and resentment which leads to offending. In recovery, the offender issues are not dealt with, discussed, or shared. They remain hidden where they are steeped in the shame they bring about. They are protected and create secrets, isolation, and further dysfunction. We need opportunities and support to talk about and feel how we have hurt others. This offender debriefing must be built into recovery groups and treatment. We fit the victim, offender and collusive roles.

3

Nebulous Cumulus Clouds
Thoughts, Feelings And Definitions

> *"Much of our adulthood is a reenactment or a reaction to unresolved childhood experiences."*

Codependency has a multitude of definitions and descriptions, each one depicts an aspect of the syndrome. Below is a list of sixty common terms or descriptions of codependency; occasionally, similar issues are described by different terms. Some of these descriptions are:

- enabling
- addiction to destructive relationships
- repetitive pattern of inappropriate relationships
- bonding disorder
- pairing up with improbable partners
- substitution of enmeshment for intimacy
- feelings of isolation often posing as independence
- system of defining oneself through others
- process of external validation
- high tolerance for intolerable behavior marked by tolerance breaks
- overreacting to externals, appearance and form while avoiding substance and the internal
- over responsibility and under responsibility swings
- denial of limitations
- disorder of will
- belief in self-neglect as the ideal state

- focus on spectating rather than doing
- lack of self-awareness
- absence of self-intimacy
- process of self-judging through shame and guilt
- a lifestyle which causes pain
- felt sense of emptiness
- absence of boundaries
- lack of identity formation
- identity diffusion
- arrested individuation
- undifferentiated identity
- pattern of adaptive behaviors
- survival skills for dysfunctional systems
- view of life as a problem to be solved
- learned helplessness
- heroic helpfulness
- stress-related illness
- self-destructive behaviors
- low self-esteem
- hyper vigilance
- feelings of anxiety
- phobias
- obsessiveness
- dependency problems
- posture of defensiveness
- perfectionism
- martyrdom
- victim/offender/collusive roles
- compulsion and addiction
- process of spiritual and sexual bankruptcy
- distortion of reality
- distortion of relationship
- distortion of responsibility
- rigidity
- denial
- emotional inappropriateness
- attempts to control the uncontrollable
- disrespect of others by removing the harmful consequences from other people's inappropriate behavior
- dysfunctional family syndrome
- post trauma stress disorder
- a *learned* behavior

- primary addiction
- relational issue
- cultural phenomena
- loving too much
- When you're drowning and someone else's life flashes before your eyes!

Relationships

The relational aspects receive the most attention. When things go wrong in our lives we often suffer through. When it affects our relationships we tend to react. Our relationship with others is built from our relationship with self. In a low functioning family, we see very little intimacy modeled. There is seldom anyone real enough to get close to. We feel empty and leave home expecting someone to take care of our emptiness and make us happy. We are taught that the right relationship will give us the fullness and happiness that we missed. Our ability to define a healthy relationship is hampered by the "seeming" scarcity of healthy available people and by our own background which frequently sets us up to find someone dysfunctional. If we find someone dysfunctional we can reenact our childhood experience and feelings.

In our families, we didn't learn about working through relationships problems. We often enter relationships with a "Pollyanna" approach that the relationship is going to take care of everything. Love will conquer all, but it doesn't.

Due to our lack of boundaries and ego strength, we become enmeshed. We cannot tell where we stop and others begin. The enmeshment seems like a valid substitute for intimacy. We derive pleasure, warmth and meaning from the other person, often being inseparable. The enmeshment eventually creates intimacy struggles. What was close and warm becomes sticky and restrictive. The struggle creates tension and dissension. The more we struggle, the more enmeshed we become.

Fighting, complaining, threatening, raging and criticizing do not release us from our enmeshed relationships. It intensifies them. Sometimes there is a legal or geographic separation but the attachment is still active. The emotional enmeshment is still present. Persons who are divorced may remain stuck and attached for years to the partner they seldom or never see.

We may leave a relationship. It's over and we are formally and finally alone, we are independent, with no one to take care of but ourselves. We can do, go, be, say whatever we want. It's great, until we go crazy and become self-destructive. We can't stand the isolation so we return to the enmeshment — with the same person or someone else. The entire cycle begins again.

We move from enmeshment to isolation. Some of us stay enmeshed; others stay isolated. Some go back and forth. Those of us who stay isolated are *independents* and if we stay enmeshed we are *relationship-addicted*. Both are codependent postures.

What we want and seek is intimacy. Intimacy grows *first* out of intimacy with self, then with two people side by side, sharing themselves through the world, *inside* and *out,* over time. Before we can have this side by side relationship without getting enmeshed, you must first find our identity. Identity is intimacy with self. In the absence of identity, one achieves enmeshment and isolation. Self-friendship, self-awareness and boundaries create the possibility of intimacy with others. In intimacy we have *detachment,* which means we keep our sense of self even when we are close to the other person. When we are separate from the other, we still have the sense of relationship. Many people cannot travel separately or be physically distant and still maintain intimacy. Many, when close, cannot maintain a sense of self, separateness or detachment. A traveler leaves home and immediately feels isolated, depressed, compulsive and acts out with food, alcohol, sex or gambling. They often become more fearful, phobic, feel unwanted and not cared about. The person comes back into the relationship and again feels smothered, overprotective or over reactive. They become hypervigilent or overly involved in the other person's life, feelings and issues. The ability to travel back and forth within a relationship, the ability to be close and keep a sense of self, the ability to be separate and keep a sense of intimacy is dependent on the ability to maintain a healthy relationship with oneself.

Codependency is not about our relationship with others, it is the absence of relationship with self. When the relationship with self becomes dysfunctional, relationships with others break down. This breakdown is only symptomatic of the broken self. Again, to maintain a loving, ongoing, spirited, warm and friendly intimacy with another, we must first be able to maintain that with ourselves. When we lack it, we can have it with others for a short time, but it cannot last. Our relationships may develop a pattern or be random, but to focus on these relationships does little for our recovery. *Real recovery* from codependency is the building of our ego, identity, boundaries and the learning of self-love, not as infantile narcissism but spirituality. True recovery is internal rather than external. Many of us get in trouble by seeking intimacy before identity. In Erikson's developmental stages, identity is the early adolescent developmental stage and intimacy comes later. These two adolescent struggles are common struggles for people in our culture. Many of us are stuck in our adolescence—no wonder our adolescents are struggling. We work on ourselves in an attempt to find what we missed developmentally but we go backwards. We try to find identity *through* our intimacy. It goes the other way—intimacy is built on identity.

We bond with inappropriate people and over bond with our kids. A healthy bond comes out of our own integrity, the integration and bonded aspects of self. The enmeshed bond may feel like intimacy, a feeling of warmth and closeness, a sense of meaningfulness, but it is a poor substitute for intimacy. The warmth is false, the meaning is based on externals, the closeness doesn't last. We become more deluded. Our relationships take on more and more fantasy and mythical aspects as we struggle to maintain them in the face of their inappropriateness, in the face of the distance that grows. Our focus is still on the relationship rather than on ourselves.

We pair up with improbable partners, selecting an alcoholic, sex addict, abusive person, somebody with a flat effect that cannot share feelings, someone who intellectualizes all the time or puts us down. There is an increased sense of isolation and often a series of painful relationships.

Externals

In the recovery process, the focus must shift from outward to inward, from external to internal. In the dysfunctional family we learn to focus on forces outside of ourselves. In the shallowness of our families we seek externals to make us happy—appearances, approval, addictions. The mood swings and erratic availability of others determines our well-being. Insecurity is the result of not being safe in our environment, not sharing a sense of survival.

How things appear becomes paramount. If they look OK, they must be OK, even if they are not OK, I can work harder, earn more, buy and own more, eat more, have more sex, power, love, mood-altering experiences. It doesn't matter if it's not OK because nothing's ever been OK. Our inappropriate dependency may become addiction. Our inappropriate dependency on people drives them away.

There is less substance in our lives and more form. Our life becomes ritualized. We go through the motions, but we feel the emptiness and over responsibility for others. There is a sense of not being able to take responsibility for ourselves. Speaking of shallow, a client recently told me his family mottos were "better dead than bald," and "money isn't everything but it can buy everything."

Personal Beliefs And Lifestyle

One might call our problem the chameleon disease . . . we change us to fit the environment. It is our best defense, our real survival. We take on the coloring of our surroundings. We adapt to dishonesty, neglect, abuse, relocations, deprivations and twisted messages. We can survive an insane system. We are drawn to these 'insane' systems in work, family and friends. We don't notice the insanity and frequently help to create it. The deep feelings of helplessness, from our childhood, become a charade of adult helplessness. Children may feel and own all the responsibility, while really ignoring what is truly their responsibility. As adults we do the same. We become like the non-abusing parent of abused children who moves from feeling like it's all my fault to saying, "I had nothing to do with this. Nothing is my fault."

In the face of daily tasks, we swing from superpower to infantile ineffectiveness. We can be confused, forgetful, stuck, blind or disabled as is convenient or necessary for survival. Our view of life becomes more problem-oriented and burdensome which increases the sense of helplessness. Barely able to cope, we list our problems for each day. We learn to give up those things we enjoy or what is needed of us because we have burdened ourselves excessively with every possible complication we could conjure up. We can frighten ourselves out of taking risks, out of enjoying basic things. For example, camping is too difficult, equipment isn't exactly right, someone may get hurt and no help would be available. Getting all the food and gear ready is too much of a hassle. We may get attacked by a bear or trapped in a forest fire. The car will break down getting there. Skiing is too much trouble; it's too far away, too many people, too cold and the equipment needs to be checked. Music lessons are offered at the wrong time. We can't go to the movies because the theater is too hot and stuffy. It's all too hard. When we are problem oriented, we procrastinate: "Anything worth doing, is worth doing later." Actually, I think I'll write more about procrastination . . . later. The 'hanging on' and obsessing the problems wears us out, drains the energy so we become too tired to do it . . . in fact, thinking about this section makes me too tired to finish it so . . .

After A Rest!
Simple things can be made difficult with a problem orientation. Difficult things become impossible. We avoid challenges and the challenge of facing each day becomes greater. We create problems faster than anyone can solve them for us. The tension and anxiety that doesn't get acted out gets somatized. Progressively physical symptoms may develop—migraine headaches, upper respiratory infections, allergies, rashes, arthritis, heart disease, cancer, food allergies, or less resistance to infections. We get physically run down, listless, lessened defense and immune systems. The immune system is only one of many boundaries, others are physical, spiritual, sexual, emotional and intellectual. These boundaries are woven together into the fabric of ourselves. When we are repeatedly violated, when there has been violence and we are unable to set boundaries in one area, the fabric is torn and boundaries in other areas become frayed, threadbare and suffer. Incest victims have a higher susceptibility to physical illness. Battered children are more spiritually vulnerable, and more vulnerable to cults.

Most illness is stress-related. Other illnesses that aren't stress-related are exacerbated by stress. We lead a lifestyle of stress. Some of the stress is living in a complex culture, but most of it is manufactured by our obsessiveness, worries, phobias and problem orientation. The feelings and problems that produce the tension and stress-related illnesses can be chronic and terminal. The body keeps score of our lack of balance and integrity, of our inability to take care of ourselves.

Emotional stress usually comes from years of not being cared for appropriately, from unresolved, unexpressed feelings or misidentified and inappropriate expression of feelings. The common fears of childhood escalate to become the anxieties, worries and phobias of adulthood. Living with a parent's marriage of emptiness, anger and dishonesty, family violence or neglect produce fears that escalate and control us. The basic fears are, will my parents hurt each other, will they leave each other, will they hurt me or leave me? The fears produce the hypervigilance, wariness, and need to control. When childhood fears are not affirmed and remain unexpressed, they are repressed and internalized into our lives, resulting in an absence of safety. Without feeling safe, we cannot truly be ourselves or make healthy choices.

We felt so out of control in childhood we can no longer stand to be out of control in adulthood. We try to control others, control us, control the addicts in our life, or control our children. Sometimes the fear of being out of control escalates, especially in the acute stages of our pathology, to become free-floating anxieties and phobias. We can't drive, travel on freeways, fly on planes, ride on ski lifts, be in crowds, be anyplace where we might feel out of control. Anyplace might trigger an anxiety attack and we won't be able to deal with it. We have a fear of panic. We have a fear of the absence of control. We have unknown fears, invented fears which control our lives and families.

Our fears are the 'set up' to over-organize and become compulsive. Our fear is no longer a guide, a source of wisdom, a pause that enables us to make judicious evaluation—it is the controlling element of our life. We are controlled by a fear of abandonment, intimacy, vulnerability; fear of being hurt, out of control, in a panic; fear that people will see us for what we believe we are, of being exposed; fear of finding out about our family, incest, hurt, neglect and abuse. This fear controls us and we in turn try to control it. Control is possibly the most addictive process of all and it comes from the sense of feeling out of control. Our spirituality is lost. There is no sense of being held safely in the hands of a force of love in the universe. We can't hold on to that concept, we feel buffeted by the winds of chance.

Anger
Another difficult emotional response is anger. It often emerges as impatience or passivity. It eventually becomes open or barely repressed rage, sullenness and withdrawal. Our temper flares more frequently, the anger begins to go sideways or backwards, any direction except in the direction where it comes from. Broken expectations set us off. We frighten people away and wonder why no one stays close to us. The anger eventually turns inward. Our violent thoughts become directed toward ourselves. Feelings of self-destructiveness, disappearing and suicide plague us. We get down on ourselves for our imperfections, our isolation, even getting down on ourselves for getting down on ourselves! We hurt ourselves and wonder if it was intentional. We hurt others and are partly sure it's intentional and then we get even harder on ourselves. Our esteem sinks, the image of ourselves becomes dis-

torted, increasing self-consciousness. We hide who we are, developing a belief that no one would love us or even tolerate us if they *really* knew us. We become more and more manipulative, phony or defended. Our rage fuels self righteousness.

The anger eventually becomes apathy toward people, events and eventually the world. The true loss of our spirituality is in achieving apathy. We are no longer impressed and no longer notice. This is a loss of a sense of awe of creation. We no longer participate in creation and we back away from life. The opposite of love is not hate, anger or rage, it is apathy. Apathy often comes when the anger has festered and killed the caring. We become apathetic toward those things that used to mean the most to us. We become apathetic to ourselves. We may no longer even attempt to take care of ourselves.

Guilt

Guilt becomes our veneer, it is the denial of uniqueness. We become more and more controlled by it. Guilt is often delivered as messages disguised as love or through our religious experiences. I think it is possible to become codependent without being Catholic or Jewish, but I consider my own Catholicism a prep school for codependency. I was raised Catholic on my parents' side—guilt and all you could eat. Generally, being Catholic means you haven't been to church for eight years. I did my eight years without church, but I like to think I was shopping for a new religion, mostly in airports where all the great ones are represented. I'm still Catholic and love the church, but I also know that Catholicism is terminal. The guilt kills you, but you die of the shame.

Guilt controls thoughts and behaviors. We second-guess ourselves at every turn. We attempt to guess what people expect of us and do our best to deliver, trying to be what people need us to be so they will notice, accept and approve of us. We must be the problem, it's our fault. There must be something we can do to change what is happening so we try and try and try to give people enough, be enough, do enough.

Our own guilt causes us to be resentful. It comes from a sense of inadequacy and sets us up to attempt perfection. Perfectionism is a set up for failure, it guarantees failure. Our guilt requires us to attempt to take care of everyone else. Guilt makes us feel that we are responsible *for*, not *to*, people. Eventually, responsibility becomes defensiveness and irresponsibility. We can also react against the guilt and decide since we can't do enough, we just won't do anything.

Excess guilt makes us overly scrupulous. The guilt controls us, especially when we do or say something that may hurt someone's feelings. We project our guilt at others and 'guilt them.' The spirit of our own guilt continues and deepens. Guilt sets us up to feel like victims and martyrs, arrogant and defensive. If everything we do feels like a mistake, then hide all mistakes, admit to nothing. We tend to take fewer and fewer risks in relationships, for fear of being found out. We can't trust others for fear that we'll get caught.

We may do penance—decades of self-denial. We practice self-denial as an art form yet we can never find true restitution. In our childhood, uniqueness and preciousness were denied. We exist for others and must do what they say and become what they want us to be. This legacy of guilt continues as we project it on to those we purport to love.

Guilt can be disguised as love and become all the more potent in this cloak. One can be raised by parents who appear to be saints—Saint Mom and Dad—who, of course, are good, nice and do so much for their children. They would never fight with each other in front of the children. They would never show excess anger or be cruel, mean or vindictive, although one of my favorite quotes from "Wonder Years" is "Even parents who will not yell at each other in front of the children will yell at the children in front of each other." We cannot hurt St. Mom and Dad; that would be too mean. What would hurt them is if we don't do exactly what they want us to do, which is to become like them, become what they want us to be, or become like they couldn't be, *instead* of becoming ourselves. This is not love. This is guilt. Love is when you help someone become the best person they can possibly be. Guilt is when you make them what you want them to be.

In the process of having these wonderful parents, we learn that we cannot have ourselves. We cannot be ourselves and we cannot find ourselves. We must always be reactive and live up to other people's expectations of us.

Shame

Shame also becomes a controlling factor in our lives. Many of us become shame-based. A codependent has a veneer of guilt and an interior of shame. We judge ourselves through a jury of shameful feelings. Shame requests hiding but the childhood abuse *forces* the hiding of our shame. It is further hidden by the continuing self-disintegration. The internalized shame becomes an identity of self-hate, a belief system of inadequacy and incompetence which often controls our other emotions. It becomes an encapsulating sensation, filling each cell with a sense of worthlessness. We project our shame as blame, we protect it with defensiveness—we hide our shame and *we* become hidden.

The shame creates a fear and resistance to criticism or evaluation. We feel blamed and excessively criticized. When someone tells us that we made a mistake, because of the internalized shame, we hear we *are* a mistake. It empowers addiction since we are *denied our right to depend on others* in healthy ways. Shame fosters dependency problems, dependent relationships and denial of dependency needs. We become overwhelmed with the hopelessness of meeting these needs.

Shame originates in broken relationships with survival figures in our lives. Any time a parent is emotionally unavailable, abusing or using the child, the child learns they cannot really depend on the parent. This denied dependency is the key aspect of shame. The child also feels they are worth less than the parent. The worthless feelings become a belief system.

In the denial of our dependency we may become overly dependent and needy, independent or coerce people to depend on us. All these postures are fueled by shame. Shame is not codependency but repressed shame becomes its fuel. In becoming ashamed of needs and vulnerability, we consistently *appear* stronger than we feel. We cloak, hide and wear many masks, each one hiding a part of ourselves.

If shame creates the hiding, the hiding intensifies the shame. The shame, our own felt sense of flaw, differentness, badness and worthlessness reinforces itself. As we hide, we lose what we are hiding. It's as if the document is hidden so well we cannot find it. It is lost. It is the document of our birthright. In the hiding of us, because of shame, our document of humanity and value is lost. We *hide* us and subsequently *lose* us.

Our good feelings come from externals—looking good, young, thin, beautiful; being rich, powerful, successful; our children, home, clothes, faces, friends; our ability to work, serve, volunteer and our verve for winning. We become more and more competitive, addictive, insatiable, to keep the "good" feelings alive. We must now *prove* our worth in the face of our vast reservoir of worthlessness. Our teams, our town, our company, our ideas *must win*. Our arguments, our brands, our geography *must be best*. Our "good" feelings now come at the expense of other people. We become judgmental, arrogant, critical and overly competitive in an attempt to cover our poor self-worth. If we beat them at tennis, golf, talk, money, business, politics, religion or what other games we choose to play, the shame is abated. Our worth must be assured. We become embedded in competitiveness, which is an attempt to feel better at the expense of others.

Ever so fleeting are these hard-earned, bitterly-fought victories. Similar to a cocaine high, they give us a moment's pleasure and then with the sunset we are left to face our emptiness and shame. The "good" feelings that come from externals are worn like a cheap cologne, nauseating to others and soon wears off. Only building good feelings from inside, from within, has staying power. The feeling that comes from integrity, self-awareness and spirituality.

Our shame empowers our addictions, our problems with dependency. Addictions become our fixes, ever spiraling into further self-disintegration and greater shame. Shame intensifies with each broken relationship. People avoid us because of our arrogance and needlessness, or are driven away by our dependence and neediness. Shame originally came from our broken relationships with parents who used us or abused us. It is then recycled with each relationship that recreates abuse, being used, abandoned or neglected—whether it is us doing it, getting it, or imaging it. Shame is reinforced through reenacting abusive relationships.

We lose self-worth and love, our preciousness as human beings, but we also lose the gifts that a healthy sense of shame can give us, the loss of shame as a guide in our life. The shame controls us, but we lose what it has to offer us. In this repression and hiding of shame we operate with a sense of 'shame*ful*ness' but, perhaps even more damage is done when we function with a sense of shame*less*ness. The arrogant, shameless behavior that comes from hidden shamefulness is possibly a larger problem in our lives and in our culture.

Shameless behavior is the ability to act without looking at the consequences. It is a loss of the reality that there is bad person activity and behavior. It is a belief that one can do no wrong or evil. Whatever we do is OK and we are always *right* in the pursuit of power, our short term goals and our instant gratification needs. This is a major cultural issue because people with power act more and more shamelessly, rolling over others, rolling over our planet and our ecology.

We can hurt others with our lack of emotional boundaries. We can destroy the environment with our lack of noticing of consequences, a disregard for the preciousness of life. We troll for converts to selfishness, often pretending to be helpless, but extracting such a price for offers of help, a price of bondage, servitude, intrusiveness, using, abusiveness, destructiveness and insensitivity. This is also the "stuff" of codependency, not just the innocent, naïve, victimized, helpless, giving posture. In the meandering of a lost childhood, one can remain on the path of perpetual suffering and victimization or be motivated into a path of abusive and using destructiveness. The journeys both begin with the child's loss of childness, with the internalizing of the natural response to abuse, which is to feel bad about oneself, ashamed. One child continues to receive and internalize; another learns to project and offend. One identifies with victimization and postures of the victim, the other with the aggression and postures of the aggressor. Some of us may shift back and forth between the two roles. Those who do the hurting in our culture are the siblings of those who get hurt—both began life without the protecting and affirmation needed for sensitivity and gentleness to self and others.

The path back from the pain and destruction is to embrace, feel and share the sense of shame, to feel it, not repress it; to share it, not hide it; to embrace it, not get rid of it. In the shame lies our vulnerability and in our vulnerability lies our path to intimacy. In our shame is the gate to our humanity, honor, guardianship, spirituality.

Shame is not the problem—it is a key part of the solution. We need our shame, just as we need our anger, fear, sadness, guilt and joy. Our feelings are interwoven and to be rid of our feelings spells personal disaster. To not deal with each feeling affects our ability to deal with the others. It would be a strange child that would not feel shame when a parent hurts the child. It isn't the hurt, the abuse, or the shame that creates the life long problem. It is the denial of the hurt, the abuse, and the repression of the shame. When the shame is expressed, the child finds vulnerability, healthy dependency and healing. In expressing and sharing the shame and how bad we feel about ourselves, we are learning to depend on people. By expressing and embracing the shame, the child learns to act responsibly with a sense of shame, a sense of honor, and a sense of guardianship.

Recovery is not a process of "getting rid of shame" or "reducing shame," or seeing shame as "toxic." Our recovery is a process of learning to share our shame, listening to it, embracing it and using it as a guide. The Latin word "Pudor" means shame and honor, together at the same time. You cannot have honor without shame. The larger problem in our culture is with shamelessness which may come from hidden repressed shame, but it is denial of the shame and an inability to use it as a sense of guardianship. Shame is a felt sense of our capacity to do harm to others, to our planet and to ourselves. Codependency is *not* shame and shame is *not* codependency. Shame is a feeling that most of us have a difficult time embracing or dealing with, so we repress, ignore or detract from it. Some of us self-judge through shame and others will act shamelessly and roll over others. The more power a person or group has in our culture, the more shameless they tend to be, the more likely they are to abuse other people or the planet. Corporations, in their insatiability and lack of boundaries, will act with shameless behavior in rolling over and dismantling other corporations, not looking at the consequences of corporate decisions and behaviors and how they are effecting community, planet and employees.

Shame accesses our spirituality because it is a felt sense of our incompleteness, that we are not perfect. This felt sense of incompleteness creates a craving. When the shame is repressed, the craving becomes a need for a fix through addiction. In the embracing and sharing of our shame, the craving becomes a need for completeness through spirituality, through a sense of higher power, through meaning and the integration of our path in the process of creation.

Pain

We create a lifestyle which causes pain, but we are not really very good at suffering, even though we do so much of it. The problem is, we do not know *how* to suffer, to feel bad, to grieve. The inability to complete our grieving prevents us from moving on. We can't let go of the pain because we can't embrace it. Scott Peck, in *The Road Less Traveled,* said the only path away from our suffering is to embrace our suffering. This is true of all feelings — pain, guilt, shame and fear.

Drug dependency — the search for the fix, the high, the better life through chemistry can be more about an inability to feel bad than the inability and need to feel good. Pain and sadness are a part of life. When we experience pain we usually try to fix, distance, avoid, change or get rid of it. Our addictions serve that purpose. Recovery is learning to hurt, to feel bad, rather than continuing to seek the fix. Feeling bad isn't a great time. It's just an important aspect of life that if avoided, tends to snowball into isolation and self-destructive behaviors.

Our suffering is worn like a badge we've earned, or we avoid it like the plague. Either direction is the inability to embrace and move through our pain. Our sadness is a healing feeling and when avoided the healing doesn't take place. *You can't do the healing without having the feeling, you can't do the leaving until you complete the grieving.*

Sadness is another one of those sources of our vulnerability which is so important to achieving intimacy. Our sadness is a form of self-intimacy. When we hide or avoid it, we often become hard, non-empathic and invulnerable. Children who are hurt seldom are allowed to express the feelings of the hurt. The sadder we are, the more vulnerable we are and in our vulnerability we may get used and hurt more. We then avoid the sadness and tie it in with being used and hurt. Sadness enables us to do our grieving, move through our losses. How many of us, when we were children and our best friend just hurt us or betrayed us and we are sitting on our back step sobbing, got what we needed? We needed to know that what we were doing is what we needed to be doing. We needed someone to walk up to us and label and affirm our pain, so we could learn to do that for ourselves and others. We needed someone to say, "I know you're hurt, honey, and it's OK to cry about it. And if you want me to be here, I will stay and if you want to be alone, remember I'm available."

How many of us received that? How many of us have had our feelings of sadness affirmed? It seems so simple and it happens so seldom. Generally, we are talked out of our feelings, made to feel bad about being sad. We get ignored, teased and made fun of. Sometimes we just get told not to cry, don't worry, everything will be OK. This still denies our healing, our vulnerability and blocks our future intimacy.

Our sadness is the key part of our grieving process. The one constant in life is change and all change involves loss and all of loss requires grieving. Our ability to have our sadness can be our ability to move from the old to the new, from loss to gain, from relationships past to new intimacies. *All recovery is about grieving,*

61

because all recovery is about dealing with loss. *Grieving fuels the forward movement in our lives.*

Reenactment

Much of our adulthood is a reenactment of childhood experience. This may be based on a need to recycle circumstances that support or continue our unresolved feelings. If in childhood we lived around careless, violent or scary people, we learn to live with fear. We don't notice it's fear since we feel it all the time. The ability to distinguish a feeling gets lost or diminished. Out of this repressed fear may come a need to escalate, live on the edge, intensify experiences so the fear can have substance and it can be attached to something immediate. It feels crazy to have a feeling, even one we don't overtly recognize, that isn't attached to anything. A lifestyle of chaos, crisis, crime may help us feel the fear that is really about our childhood. In relationships with people who threaten abandonment, who are crazy, addicted or abusive, we can bring up the childhood fears. It can actually feel less crazy to live with this because our fears are attaching to something real. If we are in a safe environment and we still feel the fear, we tend to feel crazy.

The opposite of everything is also true. As I described earlier, 180 degrees from sick is still sick. The complete avoidance of scary situations or any risk is appealing because we have so much fear within us. Any excess fear might make us feel like we're going over the edge and we can't handle it. Living with violence may set us up to continue to live with violence to feel the way we've always felt, or it may set us up to avoid any kind of confrontation, any aggressiveness.

The same may be true for sadness. If we were abandoned in childhood and not allowed to grieve or feel the pain of the abandonment and sort out the experience, it is likely we will reenact the abandonment or avoid relationships and intimacy so the sadness can be experienced in the present. We can attach pain to our current relationship problems. This relationship will be the cause of my pain, not my parents' unavailability, not the adoption, the father I never knew or my parents' marriage that broke up. It's this relationship here and now; I won't have to go back and look at any of the original pain which is now connected to the present situation.

Shame from childhood becomes low self-worth or self-hate. It is the felt sense of our low self-esteem. If repressed and undealt with into adulthood, no matter how well we function, it can't erase the low self-esteem and self-hate. We may have a good job, a truly caring relationship in our life, a nice family and good friends, but we still hate ourselves. This feels so crazy that one of the ways not to feel crazy is to mess up, to blow it in some major way, then we really know why we feel bad about ourselves. The shame can then be attached to the mess we are presently in rather than to the painful childhood realities. Many of us will hang onto our shame so our parents don't have to feel guilt. The shame makes our present family problems and self destructive behaviors feel like there is something wrong with us. Shame keeps resurfacing in the consequences of our shame-based behaviors, recycling itself.

The 180 degrees rule also applies. We may become extremely perfectionistic as a way of not facing or exposing the internalized shame. Let's make everything look perfect in an attempt to fool ourselves and others.

Abandonment

Many of us have been abandoned in childhood. The abandonment by parents running away, a parent dying, never knowing one's father, being adopted out, a broken bond, divorce, separation, broken homes. The abandonment also gets reenacted, the feelings of the abandonment keep reattaching to relationships. Because of the original abandonment we:
- get into relationships with people who abandon us,
- feel abandoned even when we are not,
- abandon others before they abandon us,
- don't get close so people can't hurt us again,
- avoid relationships altogether,
- join the cling-on race, hanging onto an inappropriate relationship, or
- become one of the people who love too much.

We may stay in a relationship no matter how bad it is, for fear of the abandonment. Unless we look at the original abandonment, grieve it, express the feelings and embrace reality, the abandonment keeps becoming recycled in our lives.

Some of us don't recognize abandonment in our childhood because our parents were present. They didn't leave, they didn't divorce, we weren't adopted, we didn't lose a parent, we know who our parents are. Some of us were raised in alcoholic families, work-addicted families, or families where the parents were not emotionally available and we experience the same abandonment. For some of us the abandonment was repetitive. Every time the parent got drunk, disappeared for a week, worked a second or third job, closed themselves off in their room with migraine headaches or depression, we were abandoned. The repetitive and more covert abandonment can have a more profound effect than being left. It also gets recycled in the feelings of isolation and loneliness, the unavailability of the people around us in our adult lives. Abandonment is the therapeutic "first thing" in the quote "First things First."

Guilty As Charged

Guilt can create obsessive reenacting which reinforces the guilt. There is a constant wondering if we've made mistakes, said something wrong, weren't careful enough. The guilt can be produced by obsessing about doing everything right or by hurting others or not living up to our values. Excessive guilting of a child creates an anxious guilt ridden adult, who often becomes guilting toward their child. Scrupulousness can recycle the guilty feelings. Did I do it right, say it nicely, hurt anyone's feelings? Guilt can be a function of shame and is reenacted by being around guilting people and systems, by self-doubt and questioning or by · inappropriate behaviors. Guilt demands expression just as fear or anger does. We need to acknowledge and embrace what we are guilty of and what guilt has been projected on us.

Anger Always Makes Me Mad!

Anger gets reenacted by hanging around angry people, creating angry responses by our behavior or raging at those around us. If a person has grown up with a parent who was angry openly or covertly, the tolerance level for an abusive relationship becomes very high. We have an altered baseline tolerance level for anger and violence. We learn to live with alcoholic rages, passive aggressive sarcasm, put downs and cutting remarks. It's as though we become accustomed to this kind of treatment. The only immunity is in the noticing or being outraged by it, or effectively taking the appropriate action to end it. This requires dealing with where it began. As codependents we didn't have much self-esteem to start with and we don't notice it while it is being eroded. We didn't develop a sense of trust and confidence so each cutting remark slices off a little bit more of what we could have had. In the phenomenon of codependency, the victim of anger is clearly codependent. The bonded relationship to the abusive person fits our image of codependency. The most difficult part of this to see is that the offender is often acting out of their own victimization issues, low self-esteem, absence of boundaries and their inability to express their emotional reality in appropriate ways. The angry offender is codependent as well.

It may be possible for an offender to be anti-social and socio-pathic to a point where the codependency doesn't apply. I believe most of our offending behaviors are the absence of identity. We reenact our own abuse and the bonding with aggressors in our lives by abusing and forcing others to bond with us in unhealthy ways. We need to see codependence where it exists, not where we think it belongs.

4

The Choiceless Chapter
Addictions

"The most common recovery for addiction is addiction."

Some people consider codependency an addiction. Others recognize that it involves compulsive and addictive behaviors. It is frequently called an addiction to destructive relationships. Historically, codependency was seen as the enabling process and support system of an active addict. The addict would need an enabler and vice versa. This theory really doesn't fly since the enabler is usually an addict—and the addict is an enabler. Remember, you scratch an addict and find a codependent. The addiction is an expression of the codependent's dependency problem.

Addiction is a pathological, recurring relationship with any mood-altering event, experience, person or thing that causes major life problems. The addiction isn't *because* of the substances, experience, person or thing. It is the *relationship* with the substance or experience that goes awry. There is nothing wrong with banana cream pie, sex or alcohol. The *relationship* with these is what becomes pathological. Most of us would choose to stop using something that causes problems. *Addiction is a process of decreasing choice.* The consequences of the use increase and the ability to make choices decreases. Addicts hang on to these problem producers.

The entire concept of addiction in our culture is changing. It is gradually becoming more generic but if one were to introduce themselves as an addict, the immediate response would be, "Must be drugs or alcohol." For some reason we separate drugs and alcohol. The fact that alcohol is a drug seems lost in our culture. I think ignoring this fact enables us to have a war on drugs that doesn't include waging war against alcohol. Mostly it has been a *war of words on drugs*. We choose to ignore the two drugs that kill more people than all of the other drugs combined—nicotine and alcohol. This enables us to give the double message to our children of "Just say no," which is an arrogant concept if the child is addicted, since an addict really can't "Just say no." At best, it's dishonesty, and a double message to be modeling the behavior that we instruct our children not to do. As long as we have an adult drug-using culture we will have an adolescent and child drug-using culture. A major part of the developmental process of youth is to do what adults do.

The campaign to have a "drug-free America" is also fairly innocuous and dishonest. Some of the most powerful corporations and members of our culture are in the drug business. The likelihood of putting drug pushers out of business is nil, especially since the two leading fatal drugs are nicotine and alcohol. Making them illegal wouldn't matter much either. Prohibition doesn't work. Having a drug-free America has about the same chance as having a drug-free White House. It's not likely to happen.

One facet of cultural codependency is the public dishonesty and enabling by the impossible and ludicrous anti-addiction campaigns. It is a societal enabling through dishonesty, double standards and double messages. Form, but no substance, like political slogans and product salesmanship—catchy but insubstantial. The whole process of having some drugs illegal probably affects the crime rate much more than it affects drug use, especially since drug use has little to do with drugs anyway. Drug use is about feelings, isolation, hurt, shame, rage, poverty, abuse, greed etc.

The narrow concept that addiction is only about drugs primarily developed in the 1900s through the 1950s. Prior to that, addiction was more of a generic concept. We have been getting back to that broader concept since the 1970s.

Stanton Peale has been instrumental in helping us find our way to an appreciation of the many faces of addiction. His book in 1974, *Love and Addiction,* broke much of the ground of acceptance for the addiction model to be applied to self-destructive behaviors other than drugs. Gamblers Anonymous, which began in the 1950s, made even earlier inroads into our awareness.

In the 1950s the addict was the down and out alcoholic or the mainlining heroin user as depicted in "The Man With the Golden Arm," starring Frank Sinatra. This model of addiction had a focus on one aspect of some addictions. It was based on the physiological need that the use of some substances created in a person. The criteria for addiction was that if you didn't get whatever it was you needed, you became seriously ill for a period of time and went through physical withdrawal. The body craves the fix, the brain craves the drug. This led pharmaceutical research toward the direction of finding non-addictive mood-altering drugs, drugs that would be non-physically addictive but make people feel better: less anxiety, no pain, relaxed.

In examining a Physician's Desk Reference, one can find a myriad of these non-addictive drugs that thousands of people have become addicted to. This narrow view of addiction, based on physiological need, misses most of what addiction is about.

Feelings

The real addiction is not to the drug, but to the high. The real addiction is not physical, but emotional, the psychological dependency, the belief in the need and continued use in spite of harmful consequences. *Anything that removes or alters unwanted feelings— anger, pain, fear, sadness, anxiety—can become an addiction.* The process of addiction is reinforced by the fact that the more we use—whatever vehicle we use to relieve the feeling—the less ability we have to deal with that feeling, so the more we need the addictive activity or substance. For example, I hate anger, it always makes me mad. Whenever I have a conflict, I tend to eat. In fact, I watch refrigerator the way some people watch TV. I open the door, the light goes on and I watch things grow old and mold, I watch things disappear. While I'm watching refrigerator, the conflict is escalating while my ability to deal with the conflict is decreasing. This means I need to *use* food all the more to deal with the anger. My tight jaw now becomes a munching jaw. My tight gut becomes a full stomach. I lose the physiological connectedness to my anger. Food has enabled me to deny and disconnect from my feeling of anger. At the same time, the unwillingness to fight, to deal with the conflict, escalates the conflict.

Passive Aggressive

This unwillingness to deal with the conflict might even become the conflict. This "eating at someone" when we're mad may be called passive aggressive. It's a very common posture. We don't get mad; we get even. We do this by withdrawing, by using our drug of choice, going away physically or emotionally. Leaving often causes the other person to become aggressive-aggressive, even out of control, raging, or bitchy. The passive aggressive posture is a controlling posture. We shut down, go away and leave our anger with the other person to deal with, along with their own anger and their rage about our leaving. We keep our anger inside. Passive aggressive is like a big dog with its paws on your shoulders, licking your face and peeing on your leg at the same time. You don't always know you're getting it, but you are.

In families, there is no passive. Sometimes we think we had one parent who was a raging lunatic or angry, aggressive and hostile. The other parent might have looked gentle, quiet or withdrawn, but in reality the gentle quietness is often passivity. In relationships and families there is no passive, there is only passive aggressive. The withdrawing, the quietness, is punishing to others.

Addiction is a process of decreasing choice, a compulsion is like an urge that limits choice. The repetitive acting out of compulsive behavior eliminates choice. Addicts *seem* to have choice; occasionally they can choose not to act out their addiction or to limit their use. Even periodic acting out without choice that results in harmful consequences is addiction. Sometimes we act out with food or alcohol for a period of time to cope with stress or crises. This may not be addiction, it may be a release or trade off or meeting needs and we don't hold on to much denial about it. It may not be repetitive or cause major life problems.

Addictions are primarily about feelings, a need to alter, avoid, or distract us from our feelings. Some of the questions that are raised include:
- Why do we need to do this?
- Why do we need to medicate our pain to distract ourselves from our emotional reality?
- Why do we protect our addictions?
- If these addictions are feeling diseases, then where do we learn about our feelings?
- What did we learn about our feelings?
- How did we learn to express them or repress them?

In childhood we find out whether or not our feelings are OK. Feelings are part of the flow of life. They are present, expressed, affirmed and then go away. We pass through them on our way to new feelings. Feelings that we don't express, that don't get affirmed, become repressed and acted out. Addiction is one of the more common ways that we act out the feelings we can't express. With feelings, we either talk 'em out, work 'em out, or act 'em out.

70

Addiction involves a set of compulsions, highs, habits, fantasies, rituals, settings and beliefs that become repetitive, designed to produce a desired goal. If we can't do the addiction, we can do the ritual or we can seek the setting or fantasy.

Our model of addiction has become too rigid. Addictions are like Hong Kong suits. We don't tailor make us to suit the addiction; we tailor make the addiction to suit us. We find that people addicted to the same things look very different. Anything said about a group of addicts some addicts within that group will prove wrong. The addiction gradually begins to tailor make us to fit the addiction. As addiction intensifies, addicts tend to look more and more alike.

Rituals

Heroin addicts who volunteer to participate in hospital-based heroin programs often leave after a short time. Even though the heroin may be free, readily available and good stuff, the high isn't the high. The mind set creates the high. A heroin addict needs the settings, intensity, illegality and the street scene to find the high. Addiction is a set of urges that creates obsession and preoccupation. The rituals contribute to the obsession and the high. The settings become important parts of the high.

One alcoholic I helped get into treatment came back from treatment and was attending ninety meetings in ninety days—a twelve step meeting each day. He was very high on the process and the program, he was bringing friends to the meetings. Two weeks after leaving treatment, he received his first paycheck. The place where he always cashed his check was the local bar, whereupon he would get drunk, come home late and half broke. This time he knew he wasn't going to drink, but the bar was the best place to cash his check. He walked into the bar, said the same things he had always said to the bartender, sat at the same table he'd always sat at, around the same people he always sat around, and began to order the same drinks. He proceeded to get drunk and went home early Saturday morning, half broke. He didn't go into the bar with the intention of drinking. It wasn't that his program wasn't working for him. It was that he got caught in one of the rituals of his old behavior. Smokers frequently start using again because of their ritual behavior. We have to deal with these addictive rituals as a part of recovery from addiction. We have to learn new behaviors, rituals, patterns of life, socialization skills, and seek new settings in our recovery.

71

Adolescents, especially those who lack identity and socialization skills, tend to find that the rituals of addictive behavior help them socialize. The drug-using groups often provide a place for the adolescents to socialize when they lack socialization skills. When an adolescent has enough consequences, they end up in treatment. Since adolescents are good at rituals, they go through the rituals of treatment quite well. They learn treatment talk, group talk and the rituals of recovery talk. When they leave treatment and go back into their own settings where the pain, the abuse, the neglect is still going on, where they still have the problems of socialization, they tend to lose their sobriety very rapidly. The rituals of treatment don't work anymore, so they go back to the rituals of the drug-using group again. I think that adolescents in treatment need to deal with the settings and the rituals. They need to deal with the context of their lives. They need to deal with their family and learn coping mechanisms and survival skills. *Adolescents need to learn how to socialize with others as a key part of recovery.*

The preoccupation and fantasies of the addiction may be the high. When they are not the high, they enhance the high and become a set up to act out the addiction. We have to change what we think about. Our beliefs, our mind set, creates, enables and enhances the high.

The hallmark of addiction is a loss of control, marked by attempts to control. Addicts are very controlling people and very controlled people. They control feelings, the people around them, and try to control their addiction with repetitive, futile efforts. In some ways, the healthiest part of their lives can be their addiction because it's the one part of their life where they're out of control. If someone comes up to an alcoholic and says they can no longer drink, oftentimes they're taking away the one chance they have to let go of control, to be out of control. Sometimes the alcohol itself is how they survive, how they cope. It's the relief they get from all the controlling they do. Even though the alcohol may serve a function, eventually, it will destroy them. In recovery we have to face powerlessness—that we cannot control. The first step of the twelve step program is accepting that our lives have become unmanageable, that we are powerless.

The paradox of addiction is what we think we need the most of is really what we need the least of. We think we need to *get in control* and we try to control the addiction. *The most common recovery for addiction is addiction* because when we try to control the addiction that we have, other addictions tend to break out.

Our tendency in this country is to *treat symptoms rather than the issues.* People tend to move from one addiction to another, or they control an addiction until it resurfaces. The ability to control the addiction is often seen as the reason or justification that they aren't an addict. The alcoholic who is able to quit drinking or cut down is not proving that they're not an alcoholic. Why would they need to quit or cut down if they don't have a problem in the first place?

A friend of mine tells the story of his drive through life. He was a great driver. He could drive over obstacles, around obstacles and through obstacles. He was driving so well that he had a fine home in the suburbs and was one of the youngest partners in a major law firm in a large city. He had a condominium at a major ski resort, a wife and family. His wife decided to leave, she took the kids and the house. Shortly after that he lost his condominium and his partnership in the law firm. This gave him pause to reflect, so he opened his car door and walked away from his car. He looked at the car he'd been driving through life and he saw what he'd been driving was a Fischer-Price kiddie car where the steering wheel isn't even connected to the front wheels. All the control, all the driving that he'd done, had been an illusion.

Some of us believe that we're in control, yet we're careening through life without any connection between our steering wheels and our front wheels. This is the journey of addiction.

The hallmark of addiction is loss of control and the sustaining force is denial. Denial isn't necessarily of the addiction, but of the expanded impact of the addiction in our lives. I can admit that I have an eating disorder and that I gain weight when I use food to avoid feelings, but do I really look at the fact that after a workshop I go home and the first door I open seems to be the refrigerator door? That I might graze through or watch refrigerator for half an hour and then close that door, at which time I'm stuffed? I'm feeling a little bit down on myself and my kids want to play. My impatience gets projected at them and I don't feel like playing. I push them away gruffly and take a nap. I miss soccer practice or an important business meeting or phone calls or children's time. After my nap the kids still want to play because they haven't made any connection with me and they want to be noticed. Instead of noticing them, I notice it's their bedtime and send them off to bed gruffly, because now I'm really down on myself for having wasted my evening. The next step is to stay up late and watch TV, grazing through the Tonight Show and munching through the late show. Everyone else is in bed but I'm distracted, not tired. I feel unsettled. There's distance in my relationships. Staying up late may cause tiredness the next day and affect work. To those of us raised in alcoholic families, this may sound like the alcoholic system. It is the same system without the alcohol.

Addictive Systems

Before we can see the impact and break the denial of our addictions, we have to look at its effect on all areas of our life. Addictions are systems that affect all other systems. In systems theory, what is affected in turn affects each other part of the system. One of the things I've done with adolescents is have them draw a circle with the name of a self-destructive behavior in the middle of the circle. Around the circle, other circles are labeled with all the other important aspects of their life, their bodies, relationships, social system, family, primary relationship, work or school, community, spirituality, sports, interests and hobbies. Next we draw a line from our self-destructive behavior and see how it affects each of these systems. How can overeating affect relationship with family, spouse, work and body. How does it affect us socially and spiritually? From each one of those things that is affected we draw a line to each of the others to see how it will in turn affect the others.

Breaking denial is more difficult because much of our denial is delusion and self-deception. Delusion is sincere denial. We distort reality. Addicts tend not to see reality the way other people see it. As addicts we confuse reality. Our defensiveness is present, it goes back to our shame and fears. Dishonesty that becomes a part of our life protects the addiction.

Dependency

Why do we protect an addiction? Why do we hold on to an addiction even though it may be destroying our lives—killing us—even though it's keeping us from those things and people that are most important to us? In a dysfunctional family, children learn not to depend on people in healthy ways because no one is dependable enough to depend on. The child learns not to be vulnerable. The very ability to depend on others in childhood is *survival*. In lieu of dependency on others, we learn to depend on our addictions, highs and fixes. The dependency on the addiction begins to take care of the feelings and fears of survival. The addiction is misplaced dependency. To give up the addiction we need to go back into those feelings and fears of survival, of childhood. We start to fear for our own survival. The addiction that stems from our unmet dependency needs is now what we depend on and we can't give up. It's too scary. It is doom, death, and feels like the end. We hang onto it as if it were our survival.

Enabling

Addiction also requires enabling systems. We manipulate the people around us to enable, cover for us, help us, protect our addictions, to not confront, to not deal with their own feelings, even to become addicts with us. We find codependents that don't have enough ego strength or boundary sense to leave or demand change. Our culture is an enabling system. It teaches that happiness is outside of ourselves, that we have the right to be happy all the time, a belief in the quick fix, a denial of feelings, a fear of vulnerability. We learn if we own the right things, have enough of something, live in the right place, use the right products, if we have the right relationship, if we have the right looking family that uses and does the right things, we will be happy. Happiness comes from outside of ourselves rather than from within—that's the message of our culture and the message of addiction.

In our families we learn to deny feelings or medicate them. Addiction is modeled. Addictions stem from these modeled behaviors, our biochemical propensities, genetic predisposition, opportunity, emotional denial and denied dependency needs. The particular kind of addiction that we find often depends on our body's ability to process, use or react to the addiction and its highs. Some of us have endorphins released while we run. Others feel more of a rush around excitement, adventure or danger. Some react to alcohol in certain ways; for others it's sex. Our physical makeup affects what addiction may work for us. *In spite of our "biogenetics," modeled behavior and opportunities for addiction, the real cause of addiction is what we learn about ourselves and our feelings as children. It's about violence, the pain of neglect, the losses and traumas of our childhood. Addiction comes from despair.*

Many of us can use chemicals now. We can have a beer with dinner, or a glass of wine. If we were in another setting, if we were around violence, if we were in the ninth month of a ten-month tour of duty in Vietnam at the end of the war, we would not be able to use chemicals in moderation. We would have to medicate the pain, fear and trauma around us with whatever chemicals we could find available. *It is very difficult **not** to be an addict around meaningless violence.*

Addictions are sustained through our *distorted memory systems.*
The mechanisms to distort the system include:
- blackouts,
- selective memory,
- euphoric recall,
- false memory,
- brain damage,
- inability of our brain to develop dopamine and endorphins on its own,
- living with trauma, past or present,
- numbing of emotional memories of neglect.

Addictions are also sustained through our *rational defense systems.* These include distortion of reality, projection, minimization, grandiosity, intellectualizing, rationalizing and so on (see Chapter 2). Many of the defenses become addictive processes themselves.

Addicts constantly present us with things we can't control, make us feel crazy, challenge our own sense of reality and make us feel inadequate, responsible and shameful. It is similar to living with an adolescent! There are five criteria that make a "good" addiction:
- Euphoric—if it makes us high, it will be more addictive.
- Readily available—food, nicotine are readily available. Crack is more addictive than other forms of cocaine because it is cheaper, therefore more readily available.
- Fast acting—Wine is fine, but liquor is quicker. The faster we see the fix, the more we cling to it. Crack is faster acting than other forms of cocaine.
- Unclear cultural guidelines—cultural double messages, ambiguous values around gambling, drugs, sex, food and work.
- Tolerance changes involved in its use—the more we use the more it takes, until a little bit sets us off.

Not all addictions will meet all five of these criteria. Sex, banana cream pie, and cocaine do. All three of those in the same evening will just about kill anybody!

Euphoria

Some addictions are not euphoric. There is no extreme high involved in its use. The addictions that aren't euphoric are still mood-altering by being mood-distracting. They change how we feel or they distract us from how we feel. Vacuuming is an example. People who vacuum are not stoned, spaced out and high, but some people's lives *do* revolve around their Hoover.

Vacuuming is the distraction. I have a friend who went to rent a basement apartment while attending graduate school. The owner, who lived upstairs asked my friend, "Will my vacuuming upstairs bother your studying? I like to vacuum and I do it a lot, in fact I'd rather give up my husband than my Kirby." My friend couldn't imagine that the vacuuming would bother her so she moved in. Three months later she moved out! The women upstairs vacuumed incessantly from the time her husband left in the morning until he arrived home at night.

For many people, work can be obsessive, addictive and life-destructive, but it isn't necessarily euphoric. Workaholism can be a means to the end for engaging in another addiction or it can be an addiction itself. Work can provide a high in the overtime pay, being noticed or feelings of a job well-done. Even though work is not always euphoric, it does fit the other criteria. It's readily available—we can work anytime—there's always work to be done. It's fast-acting: as soon as we work we're distracted and we don't feel as much. We do have unclear cultural guidelines about work—on the one hand, we extol the work addicts as the movers and shakers of our culture and write about them with pride. On the other hand, we see them as Type A, stressed out, hyper tense individuals that are ruining their lives and their families. There are tolerance changes involved in the use of work. I recently had a client who said that several years ago he could work anybody under the table; now, he does a little bit of work and starts to fall apart.

Food fits all of the five criteria above. It feels good, it's readily available, fast-acting, it has unclear cultural guidelines and can have tolerance changes involved in its use.

Addictions vary a great deal. Some are very hard to quit. Alcohol is difficult because of the denial. Anorexia also has an intense denial system. Gambling and smoking are tough to quit. Food and sex addiction are more difficult in terms of understanding what sobriety involves and maintaining it.

There are many fallacies about certain addictions. Cocaine addicts believe they have a very different addiction that is much more difficult to quit because of the constant craving. In working with cocaine addicts, many of us in the field have concluded that cocaine addicts don't have more problems with the cravings than many other addicts. The same used to be said about heroin and even marijuana. Everyone wants their addiction to be unique, and the cocaine addict lives in a fast-paced, intense culture which frequently involves a bit of arrogance about the addictiveness of the substance.

Many of us have multiple addictions, even more than one primary addiction. Addictions tend to form helixes with each other. An attempt to treat one without treating the other usually results in failure, with little sobriety time in either. There is a Fischer-Price toy with a bench and a mallet. You hammer pegs down in the bench; when you hammer one down, another one pops up. This is the way our addictions are. There's a new arcade video game that involves a mallet and a platform with little holes and knobs that pop up when activated with a quarter. They pop up rapidly with no common sequence. The goal is to hit as many knobs as we can with the mallet in the time allowed, receiving points for a direct hit. For some of us, our addictions in recovery are much like this. We clobber one and another is already popping up. This is the reason it's so *dangerous to treat the addiction rather than addictiveness.*

A person addicted to rage and to alcohol may go to treatment for the alcoholism, but if the rage isn't dealt with, the alcohol use will eventually return. If only one is dealt with, the double helix tends to reform itself. The "rageaholic" will go back to using alcohol and again set up a pattern with the rage where it looks like one is about the other. They may be related, but they are still separate issues and both must be dealt with.

Gambling, eating disorders, drug abuse—all tend to form helixes with each other. They become interwoven. One of the major problems in treatment is the tendency to treat one addiction rather than the addictive process. Addiction is a symptom of denied dependency needs, lack of boundaries, an inability to express feelings in healthy ways, lack of intimacy and identity. Primary disease can also be symptomatic.

Expanding the concept of addiction to include more than drugs is a controversial process. It's important because accepting the self-destructive behavior that one has as an addictive process enhances the possibility of recovery. The concept of addiction is diluted some, but providing others with the process of recovery that was founded about fifty years ago by the alcoholics is more important than protecting the insularity of the concept of drug addiction.

Some people are involved in the controversy about whether certain behaviors are self-destructive, compulsions, addictions, absence of impulse control or diseases. I'm not overly concerned

with what label is used as long as treatment and recovery are offered and effective. I believe that addiction fits the criteria of disease for the following reasons. Addiction has:
- A definable onset—one can usually trace its origin which is rooted in powerlessness and inability to manage.
- Identifiable symptoms—there are specific earmarks of each addiction
- Predictable outcomes—the results of the addictive behavior, mental, physical, social, spiritual, sexual and so on.
- Primary—it is not a secondary result of another condition, although there are many key contributing factors. It is also primary in that other life problems are difficult or impossible to deal with until the addiction or the addictive behaviors are addressed.

Addiction is:
- Progressive—it tends to get worse in our lives.
- Predictable—we go through stages.
- Pervasive—it affects practically everything in our life.
- Permanent—we don't get over it, we work an ongoing recovery program.
- Terminal—eventually, without treatment, it will kill us.

This disease concept model applies to more than just drug addiction. Whether one calls this a compulsion, impulse control or disease is less important than that we *recognize* the things we do repeatedly, that adversely affect our lives, and from which we can find recovery. We need to see that the addictive behavior is symptomatic of other things that have gone on in our life and that our efforts to recover include an ongoing commitment to dealing with the addiction as well as looking at what has contributed to this addiction.

Recovery is a lifelong process. If we don't work the program, take care of ourselves, go to our meetings, and share feelings, we go back into the stasis of the disease, dry-drunk or wet. The same is also true for a codependent. Once we stop working a recovery program, don't take care of ourselves, share, find intimacy, balance, and continue self-discovery, we return to the stasis of codependency—the dysfunction, control issues, emptiness, depression, anger, shame, and guilt. Alcoholics who are committed to recovery from alcoholism need to do the same for their codependency. Most recovering alcoholics neglect this and often end up drinking again or sober but alone—sort of high and dry.

Stages Of Addiction

There are six stages of addiction. Stage one is *learning*. We discover an addiction as a survival skill, a coping mechanism. Often, this discovery is made in childhood. Some addictions aren't discovered until adolescence or later in life. We find some way to distract us from our pain, something that helps us survive or cope with the emptiness of self, with our fears and anxieties.

After learning how to distract from this pain we move into the *seeking* stage. We establish a trust, a relationship, a belief system that the addiction will work for us. We establish patterns and begin the rituals of addiction, seeking it and looking for new experiences with it.

The third stage is *harmful dependency*. The addiction has escalated, the rituals have become elaborate and rigid. Preoccupation becomes obsession and trust becomes a blind faith that the addiction will take care of us. The high of the addiction is now an attempt to cope and feel normal. Harmful consequences come in this stage.

Stage four is the *controlling* stage. We try to reduce the addiction and its impact on our lives. We cut down, we make decisions to stop, we go on diets, we quit for Lent or we change the relationship. In this control stage, we often switch to a new addiction. Quit smoking and start shopping. Quit drinking and start abusing food. Quit gambling and start spending or overworking. We may concentrate on one addiction and ignore the others. We usually control our addictions for a time, but go back to the harmful dependency.

Eventually we hit the *acute* stage. We lose important things in our lives and our priorities are affected. We may suffer a loss of family, friends, health, self-respect, money or job. We lose our values, spirituality and sexuality.

Finally the *chronic* stage of addiction is met when we've lost all of the above. We've truly hit bottom. In our culture we have a belief system about when we can intervene with an addict. We believe we have to wait until the addict is completely broken and they have to want to help. An addict who has hit bottom often has nothing to recover for. There is so much despair and helplessness that they do not want help and sometimes can't be given help.

Categories of Addiction

Intensity addiction is possibly the truest of all addictions. We enter an altered mood state immediately. Intensity can be part of the addiction to activities, people and substances. Included in this category are addictions to crisis, chaos, crime, fear, work, rage, danger, risk, adventure, newness, aggression, gambling, spending, power, sports, heroics, religion, various eating disorders, love, prayer, sex, suffering, conflict and violence—to name a few.

Distracting activities which may or may not be intensity include TV, video games, busy work, cleaning, hobbies, computers, volunteering, ritual, spectator sports, shopping, misering, music, reading, school, talking.

Thoughts that seem to fit an addictive process include obsessing, worrying, fantasy and destructive thought talk.

People/relationship addictions include obsessive or destructive relationships, love addiction, over bonding with children, hanging on to abusive relationships.

Substance addiction includes nicotine, caffeine, other mood altering drugs, food—eating disorders include anorexia nervosa, bulimia, over eating, obsessing and dieting. Collecting and hoarding are substance addictions as well.

Interventions

The process of breaking the addiction cycle is called intervention. We cannot wait for an addict to become chronic before intervening and we don't have to wait until they want help. We need to look at earlier interventions, breaking the process of the addiction before a person has had too many major life losses. If we are going to impact addiction in our culture, we need to go back to the beginning, back to the learning stage of addiction. Look at where the addiction began, where the need for an addiction was set up in our lives. That happens in CHILDHOOD. It happens with what we learn about our feelings, our survival and our dependency needs.

Many people working in the field believe addiction is primarily about biochemical makeup and there are genetic predispositions for specific addictions. Some of us because of our physical make up are more vulnerable to certain addictions. This biological propensity means we will find an addiction that works for us depending on what we can respond to. Unfortunately the real issues are not addressed. Some things go beyond a physical craving or the brain's inability to manufacture endorphines or dopamine on its own without the addictive stimulant. We need to address why we must change how we feel, why we don't ask for help or refuse it when offered, why we continue addictive substances or activities. Why don't we find balance in our lives?

Addictiveness is effected by our biological chemistry, modeled behaviors, opportunity, cultural messages and personal beliefs, but the real set up for addiction lies in childhood. Our addictiveness is initiated in formative years and is concurrent with our codependency. Addictiveness is initiated by the lack of developmental needs, dependency needs, boundaries, trust, identity and emotional appropriateness. The primary causes of addiction are abuse, abandonment and enmeshment which are discussed in later chapters.

5

Stuck, Lost And
On The Wrong Path
Enmeshment

*"There are no secrets only denial.
Denial is the only dysfunction, the rest
are problems."*

Enmeshment is a result of boundary violations and a lack of
boundaries. It is the absence of differentiation and autonomy.
Children in dysfunctional families get enmeshed in the pathology
and they are unable to individuate. Enmeshment occurs developmentally, socially, cognitively and emotionally. It is an aspect of
system theory. In the analogy of the mobile in family systems, the
bond holding the mobile together becomes enmeshment in an
unhealthy family. Enmeshment is the internalization of another's
reality, problems, feelings, beliefs, hopes, suicidality, rage and so
on. Enmeshment develops from family mythology, beliefs, rules,
roles, premises, denial, protectiveness, loyalty, rebellion, projection, expectations and threats. It stems from inappropriate modeling, mixed messages, over or under bonding, abandonment,
neglect, physical, sexual, spiritual or religious abuse.

Enmeshment may be expressed in attempts to resolve dilemmas
from childhood, so we keep repeating them. It can be an attempt
to explain our fears, anger and shame—so we keep creating
angry, fearful, shameful events and processes around us. Our
enmeshment is sustained through denial. It usually happens
covertly. Enmeshment is the single most important place that we
get stuck in our journey toward intimacy and self-esteem. It is the
vehicle for the intergenerationality of family dysfunction. If we

were to do a list of our top ten problems—a David Letterman list, so to speak—our list may include:

A LETTERMAN LIST
1. compulsive behavior around food and nicotine
2. high level of impatience or intolerance
3. working too hard
4. not caring for ourselves physically
5. unable to say "no" to excess demands, so we over commit
6. difficulty reaching out to people we care about.
7. little or no intimacy
8. fear of being a failure or feeling like one
9. feeling lonely
10. withdrawing when things go wrong

Whatever the problems are, if we create a geneogram, a family history, and break all the denial going back several generations in our families, what we would find hanging on most of the branches of the family tree would be our list of problems in one form or another. We may have gone 180 degrees from some and added a few, but essentially our list would show up over and over again. Denial sets up the problem to be acted out intergenerationally. Children get enmeshed in the denial and the family problems continue to be problems in their adulthood and future generations.

Enmeshment is the primary basis of codependency, isolation, spiritual bankruptcy and addiction. Enmeshment is what codependents mistake for intimacy, the over involvement of one person in another's life, the over involvement of children in parents' lives, problems, fears, losses and inability to resolve conflicts. Enmeshment in dysfunctional families is the opposite of freedom. Freedom is the right to become us, the right to choose. Enmeshment keeps us from us and choice. Enmeshment happens overtly and covertly. In a low functioning family, children are often used, the objects of parents' needs, affections, meaningfulness, companionship, pride. The child becomes an extension of the parent. I worked with a man who was clearly enmeshed with his dad's reality, an extension of his father. He was an attorney, he wore his father's suits, had his father's name, attended his father's law school and worked for his father's law firm. Somewhere within, this man existed. What he had to do was move through the enmeshment to peel off what was his father to find himself.

Sources of Enmeshment

Enmeshment can come from guilt disguised as love. The second family I worked with in the early 1970s was a family with five children. I worked with three of the children, who all talked about their parents as saints. St. Mom and Dad were wonderful; they didn't fight with each other in front of the children and they were kind and loving. Four of the five children were chemically dependent and one child had suicided. I figured there must be something wrong somewhere. It seems that the pathology was in the very sainthood of Mom and Dad. They were so nice that they gave a very clear message—we are nice, we are good, we are caring, so you would never do anything that would hurt us. What would hurt us is if you don't become exactly like us or be like what we want you to be and do what we tell you to do. The five children were so enmeshed in the parents' reality and needs that they couldn't make choices of their own or lead their own lives. The emptiness within themselves was the primary cause of their chemical dependency. They tried to fill, numb or anesthetize the emptiness. I believe the suicide was a reaction to not being allowed to be alive, to be oneself.

Enmeshment also comes from children's survival needs. As a child I was able to survive by reacting, noticing, over-involving myself in things that were beyond my control—my parents' marriage, my dad's alcohol use or my mother's depression. Enmeshment comes from the unmet needs of the family. Many of the roles in families are enmeshment roles. We get enmeshed in the need for parenting the younger children, the need for the family to have mediating, guidance, pride, humor, fun, leadership, spirituality, spousing. These role reversals of our childhood involve getting enmeshed in a need of the family that should have been taken care of by the adults.

Roles, Roles, Roles

Dysfunctional family roles are multiple, dynamic, and changing and all involve the loss of identity and choice. The roles are assigned, prevent us from self-fulfillment, help us survive and continue the sickness. They also have a residual impact on our lives even after we leave the role. Some roles we never leave. Following is a list of enmeshment roles:
- Little parent
- Family mediator
- Orphan, lost child

85

- Victim, scapegoat
- Little princess or prince
- Surrogate spouse
- Parent's best buddy
- Extension of a parent
- Family hero, overachiever, star
- Family oracle
- The General
- Mascot, clown, tension reliever
- Mom's mom, dad's dad, mom's dad, dad's mom (or a parent's parent)
- The tramp, lady killer, etc.
- Spiritual leader, religious one
- The nurturer, the loving child, caretaker
- The rebel
- Brat!
- The _____ one — fill in the blank with dumb, pretty, ugly, smart, weird, crazy, self-destructive, sensitive, strong, fragile

There are roles based on gender, scripting, bonding, physical characteristics, birth order, and the needs and peculiarities of the family. There are healthy roles and unhealthy roles. The unhealthy roles are examples of enmeshment. In order to leave the role or its impact in our adulthood, we need to accept the role and the resulting feelings and behaviors.

Sometimes we are enmeshed in the inappropriateness and dishonesty of the family. Through our compensatory loyalties we try to make up for stuff. Four years ago I was working with a client who was completely burned out. She had spent the last ten years voluntarily working with handicapped, learning disabled and mentally retarded people. She refused any pay for this. She was working sixty to eighty hours a week and trying to raise her own family. In discussing the family that she came from, it turned out that she had a mentally retarded younger brother who she felt very jealous and resentful of. Her parents eventually moved him to a home. She, in acting out her guilt and the family guilt, began to volunteer. The volunteering wasn't the problem, it was that she could never do enough, she was burning herself out, she couldn't take care of herself. She could never quite fix or make up for what she thought was the family's and her failure toward her brother.

If spirituality is the process of becoming the person we were meant to by our creator, then enmeshment is essentially spiritual abuse. The opposite of spirituality is enmeshment. We are all on a path to becoming ourselves—that's what we're here for, but many of us get pulled off the path. We may get beaten off the path or neglected to the point where we wander off the path. Many of us get pulled off the path by being what someone else wants us to be, what they couldn't be, what they expect us to be, we lose the ability to become ourselves. We get enmeshed in the expectations and the realities of others.

Several years ago I received a call from a young woman who was feeling suicidal. She was in medical school. In talking with her, I discovered that she didn't like medical school, she couldn't stand the sight of blood, gross anatomy grossed her out and she didn't want to be a doctor. I suggested that she drop out or at least take some time out. I thought it might be better, in fact, than suicide. She thought that even though it might kill her to stay in, it might kill her mother if she left. She was in a bind. We brought Mother in, Mom was very clear about what her goals in life had been. She talked about how, after high school, she knew she was going to go to college and after college, drop out of school for awhile and become a flight attendant, I guess because she had seen a movie about how much fun they had *(Airplane II)*. She had decided that after two or three years of seeing the world, being playful and spontaneous, she was going to go to medical school, become a doctor, get married and have two children. Instead of doing all of the above, she managed to get out of high school, get married and have two children. She married an alcoholic and decided to continue living through her children. One was in medical school and one was (you might expect) a flight attendant, but she never made it that far. At the time I was involved with the family, the second daughter was 18 years old and had been through chemical dependency treatment twice. When she was 12, Mom would say, "You should be having more fun, you should be socializing and dating." By the time she was 13, she was sexually active; at 14, chemically dependent; at 15, in treatment the first time; at 17, in treatment the second time. Mom kept telling her, "You shouldn't be doing this, but tell me more." Mom had two extensions of herself in her children. One was the doctor, the serious side, the professional. The other was her "dark side," the side that wanted to act out and enjoy more of life. Neither one of these young women had been able to choose their own reality. They were set up to act out the two sides of Mom.

Scripting is enmeshment. Many of us have been given scripts to follow, often written by parents and passed on from previous generations. Scripting keeps us from making choices. We may choose the same career that Dad or Mom had or wanted. If we have choice, we are still on our path and use choice to express talents and interests that we learned in our families. When we don't have choice, it is enmeshment. Learning is not enmeshment, but learning a dysfunctional approach to life when we don't have choice and learning within a dysfunctional system, creates enmeshment.

There are no secrets in families—only denial. We get enmeshed more in the denial than any other aspect of family. What is denied always gets acted out. Virginia Satir used to teach the family systems concepts through the use of a mobile. She would hold a mobile in front of her, hit a part of the mobile and the whole thing would move. She would say, "Tension in one part of the mobile affects the entire mobile. The same is true for families." Tension in any part of the family sets up the rest of the family to react to that tension. If I had the mobile in front of me and I hit part of it and then grabbed the part of it I just hit, not letting it move at all, the rest of the mobile would still be moving. Now the mobile is not only moving, but it's feeling crazy because no one knows why it's moving or what it's reacting to. This is how denial works in families. We react to it, but we can't see it. We can't figure out what it is that's setting us up to act out and to react. Children always know enough about what is going on in a family, even if it isn't talked about, to act it out, but when the family dysfunction is denied, the children feel anxious and crazy.

I once had a client who was referred to me by the courts. He had been busted for exposing himself. He was motivated, he joined a 12-step program right away and really wanted to stop the behavior. His acting out was an aspect of his sexual addiction. Two weeks into his recovery, his brother heard about what had happened to him and wanted to come in and talk. In the session with the two of them, the brother said, "I've been exposing myself, too. I haven't been busted yet, but I need to deal with it." Neither knew that the other had been exposing himself. Now this may have been coincidence, but a few months into their therapy, they started talking about Dad and wanting to do some healing with Dad. They had a lot of fear about this because Dad was rigid, moralistic and judgmental. About four months into recovery, they invited Dad in for a session. Sitting in my office, they're scared, in fact, I'm scared. Dad sits down and he is rigid, moralistic and judgmental. I find myself apologizing for his two sons exposing themselves, as if it were my fault. Halfway into the session, something changes. Dad sort of slumps over, rolls off the chair, is lying on the floor sobbing—deep convulsive sobs—and within his sobs, we hear the words, "I've been exposing myself for over thirty years." At this point I thought I was no longer working with a coincidence. It looked to me like Dad had a secret and two of his sons were acting it out.

When I was working with adolescents in the early 1970s I was getting many referrals for shoplifting. The interesting thing is, the first family that ever came in when the son was caught shoplifting, the Dad had also been shoplifting. From then on, I decided to ask questions about the family. Where I was able to obtain information, whenever a child got busted for shoplifting, I found there was some level of either stealing or dishonesty in the family, whether it be cheating, embezzlement or some other type of major boundary violations. I suspect acting out is really an acting out of what we learn, but can't choose or process. If someone comes up and says, "Your father steals," you may be able to make a choice about stealing. As long as it's covert, there is no choosing. It can become a true compulsion.

In working with children and adolescents, I've seen many families in which one member attempted suicide. Suicide is the second leading causes of death among adolescent males. In families where there was either a suicide attempt or completed suicide, I usually found that Mom or Dad had a death wish that they hadn't resolved or dealt with. I don't believe that child and adolescent suicide is all about children's and adolescents' lives. I believe it's more about enmeshment in parents' unresolved conflicts, their hopelessness. The children act out what the parents don't deal with. Even the parent's death wish may have been enmeshment in their parent's lives, hopelessness or suicidality.

This is also true for sexual affairs. Many people who are dealing and struggling with affairs came from families where there were affairs. The denial sets up the absence of choice. The things that we deny the most are the things we are the most ashamed of, the acting out behaviors. A person drives downtown, has an affair in the morning, exposes himself to the noontime crowd, shoplifts through the afternoon and feels like driving into a truck on the way home, doesn't walk into the house and explain everything that is going on. They may say, "Boy, have I had a busy day." Then, follow that up with "all I do is work, work, phone calls, demands" and the family believes he's obsessed with work, but they feel something else. One of the children at some point may get arrested for shoplifting, another one might end up in a relationship where there are affairs, another may end up feeling suicidal and another may be exposing himself. They could all be in therapy and each therapist would say, "What's your dad like?" Each of them would respond, "My dad would be really shocked to find this out, really hurt; my dad is a very good man, but he works too hard, he has a lot of pressure on him."

How do we know to act out what we don't know? It seems almost unbelievably that we could act out things which are so covert. Some of the reasons for the enmeshment and why we are able to pick up on the hidden, denied behaviors include:

- Eighty percent of communication in families is non-verbal. It's not what's said, it's how it's said, where it's said, the context of what's said, the emphasis and what's left out.
- Communications involve feelings. Sometimes the feelings are denied but we always know. We sense how others feel around us, even if we don't know it consciously. If, in the family, there's a lot of paranoia—you've got to get them before they get you—then everybody acts out the paranoia, possibly by stealing and 'getting' others. If there is rage at the world—the world's a horrible place—why not rip it off? The rage creates the same behaviors intergenerationally.
- We also learn through the premises about life—you can't trust anyone, get yours while you can and we act out accordingly.
- We follow the rules and get enmeshed in the dysfunctional ones. Many rules are overt, but many are covert, hidden rules—rules about sex, feelings, property, ownership, touch, weight, food, socializing, parties. We follow the rules of our families, stay loyal to those rules, even though they didn't work for our families. Many times, it's because we don't recognize it as a rule. It's hard to break a rule until you know it's a rule.
- Much enmeshment comes from what is projected on us. If a parent feels phobic and anxious, they will project their worries and fears. What if someone steals your bike at school? What if you have a flat tire and won't be able to get home? Maybe you'd better take the bus. The child becomes more anxious and soon enough will be saying the same to their child.
- Mythology in families causes us to be enmeshed in the things the family believes. A family myth is a story told or related that

may or may not be true and it's purpose is to keep us from noticing or doing something else. We might be told that we're stubborn and we get enmeshed in the mythology of our own stubbornness. We may be told we're stubborn to keep from noticing that we need to get stubborn about taking care of ourselves. Many people who are stubborn do a lot of caretaking of others. The scenario may go like this: You've been babysitting 22 nights in a row and your parents say, "You'll take care of the younger ones tonight, won't you?" You say, "But tonight's senior prom. I have a formal/I've rented a tuxedo; we have a limousine. This is the biggest night of the year." They'll look at you and say, "Well, do it your way. Of course, you're always going to do it your way. You're the stubborn one." Whether you stay home and baby-sit or go to the senior prom isn't the issue. It's that you believe that you're stubborn when you decide to do something that you want to do or take care of yourself. The expectation is you are there to serve and take care of others. Another myth might be the independent myth: "You were a hard baby to hold, you were too squiggly, you're always on your own," which is the myth that keeps you from noticing that you never had anybody to depend on. It doesn't mean you are or you are not independent; it just keeps you from noticing what you need to notice to have real recovery and learning healthy dependency.

- We get enmeshed in the modeled behavior, the messages, the abuses of the family and the bonding. We become rebellious as a function of our enmeshment and in our rebelliousness become controlled by what we react against. We get enmeshed in the unpredictability, insecurity, inconsistency, chaos and relationships in the family.
- Life scripts can be a set up for us to become enmeshed.
- Double messages and dilemmas enmesh us.
- Loyalty to the family system may become enmeshment.

I have had clients who are extremely rageful and they didn't know why until they started looking at the rage one or both parents held, sometimes covertly and other times overtly. We get enmeshed in that rage and we act it out. During a workshop a person asked me a question because they were a little upset. They had done much family work. He had healed his relationship with his father, dealt with his mother, but he still felt like he wasn't going to get there. He had been in recovery and working hard at it, but it didn't seem to be working for him. I said, "It seems like you're feeling hopeless and like a failure." He said, "Yes, that's exactly how I feel." Out of the blue, I asked, "What's your father like?" He said, "Well, I've worked on my father; I've dealt with him, forgiven him." I said, "No, I don't mean about your relationship with him. What was he like?" He said, "You mean, did he feel like a failure and was he hopeless? He wasn't a failure, but I think inside he always felt like one. And yes, he did feel hopeless about his life." My suggestion was that maybe he has dealt with his father, but what he hasn't dealt with was his enmeshment with his father's attitude or his posture toward life. He was living out his father's feelings of hopelessness, helplessness and failure. This is another example of enmeshment.

In the same workshop, someone asked a similar question about impatience. Since I was on a roll, I asked, "What's your father like?" It turned out that father was impatient about everything. Someone else in that workshop said, "OK, you and everybody else are always telling me what's wrong, this is the problem, that's the problem, this is enmeshment, etc. But what do I do about it? I want to know what I can do about this stuff." I asked if the family she came from is the family in which you learn you can do anything you decide to do as long as you decide you can do it. Just go out and do it. Was she from a family of a lot of human doings rather than human beings? She said, "Yeah, did you meet them?" My suggestion was that she had gotten enmeshed in the very doing and couldn't embrace the being. Whenever she heard something that may or may not be true, she wanted to know what to do about it instead of being able to be with it, to grow out of it, to move through it. The only path away from our suffering is to embrace our suffering. We have to be there with it before we can move through it. She accepted this, she looked at me, and said, "That's sounds right, but what do I do about it?" At that point, I said, "Well, grasshopper."

It was at this same workshop that someone raised their hand and said, "What do you do if your childhood is a blank, if it's empty, if you don't remember it?" I asked if possibly the blankness was the memory of your childhood. At that point, a little tear rolled down her check, and she said, "Yes, I think you're right. Both my parents were chemically dependent. Their lives were empty, the family was empty and my childhood was empty." She got enmeshed in the void, in the the emptiness and carried it within.

I once had a client whose father had a severe pain in his stomach. He went to the Mayo Clinic, local hospitals, different physicians. He tried everything, but no one could locate the source of the pain. His father lived and died with that pain. My client was at the funeral, watching his father being buried when, all of a sudden, he started to feel a pain in his stomach. He went home, ignoring the pain for a period of time. Then he started going to doctors, to local hospitals, to the Mayo Clinic. No one could find the source of his pain. The only way we could find to deal with his pain was to go back to the funeral site and to symbolically bury it with his father. As he left the funeral site the second time, he was relieved of the pain.

We get stuck in our enmeshment because it doesn't belong in our lives. What doesn't belong is hard to deal with. If you're living your own life on your own path, your problems will fit for who you are. They'll be resolvable. But our problems become crises because we can't resolve them when we're on someone else's path, when the problems come from outside of us, when they're someone else's issue. Our problems become crises when they don't fit, career crises, vocational crises, sexual identity crises, intimacy crises, mid life crises, marriage crises. Crises are a symptom of the enmeshment. Recurrent, unsolvable problems are a symptom of enmeshment. I've worked with many addicts who can't seem to find recovery. They can't seem to get better or work a program. Invariably, one of their parents was an addict who never got better, could never quite stay with a program.

For most of my life I felt an emptiness that I might have been able to live with, expecially knowing that many codependents feel empty, but it was an emptiness that wasn't a quiet or peaceful emptiness—it was a noisy and clanging emptiness. It made me uncomfortable, restless, fidgety. Several years ago I attended a workshop on imagery. On the way back from the workshop, a friend of mine and I were doing images and sharing them with each other. I did an image of my parents' relationship. What I envisioned was a plain in the winter and a tree alone in the middle of the plain. The tree had no leaves and there was a large branch hung low to the ground that had two strings tied onto it. An empty tin can was tied to the end of each string, just a couple of feet apart. There was a cold winter wind blowing across the plain, blowing against the branch and the tin cans on the string. As the wind blew, the tin cans would bang against each other and clang. The image of my parents' relationship was the emptiness and the clanging of the two tin cans. As I said this, I realized I wasn't just talking about my parents' relationship; I was also talking about the feeling I had inside myself for most of my life, the emptiness and clanging. It was also the feeling I was beginning to reenact and put into my own relationships. As a child growing up, the most important thing to me was my parents' relationship. I used to come home and talk to my mother, entertain my mother, counsel her and let her cry on my shoulder so that she would be OK and stay in the relationship. I used to try to talk my dad out of drinking, distract him, entertain him, so he would stay in the relationship or not drink so much that my mother wouldn't have to leave. I tried to mediate their fights. I was so invested because it felt to me like my survival depended on their relationship. I ended up getting so mixed up in their relationship, in their emptiness and loneliness, their anger and their clanging that I carried the felt sense within me. It became my reality and my feeling. It was a feeling I couldn't deal with until I realized what it was about. Nothing changes until it becomes real. I had gotten enmeshed in something that wasn't about me, but it was controlling me, my life and my relationships. I had internalized it.

Memory and awareness do not give us recovery, but recovery does give us awareness and memory. The awareness facilitates our continuing recovery, the process of discovering us, of sorting out what is of us, what has been done to us, and what belongs in our life. With awareness, we can leave behind that which doesn't belong. We may get enmeshed in others' emotional reality and relationship problems, but we can't give it back or get rid of it. We must embrace it, feel it, share it. We must have our feelings rather than our feelings having us, wherever they come from. The symbolic sending back to parents what is of their lives is symbolic work only. The reality of the work is in the recognizing, embracing, and sharing with others. The symbolic work can have a profound effect, but it is in the embracing of our reality that we find recovery.

I can write to my parents, call them, do a role play or sculpture and let them know the pain that I felt because of their relationship problems, how enmeshed I got into their relationship issues. I can tell them they hurt me by using me to take care of their needs. This will help, but it doesn't fill the emptiness or calm the clanging until I change how I relate to others, until I let love and care and affirmation into my own life, until I fill my life, discover and find myself. The antidote for enmeshment is identity.

94

6

Look, List and Learn
Earmarks of Dysfunction

"You can't do the healing without the feeling, the leaving without the grieving."

Much pathology is a pattern of learned response, a reaction to modeled behavior while living in addictive systems. Some of the behaviors can be altered simply through insight, education, awareness and decision. When the behavior is repetitive and not altered, even after we are aware and decide to change, it falls into the compulsive, addictive mode.

Codependency is made up of several compulsive disorders. It fits the addiction model and is best treated within that model, it overlaps and responds to other approaches and treatment modalities. There are several paths to building self-esteem, identity and boundary sense. Many of the learned aspects can be unlearned, but the addictive aspects require a support system and a treatment process.

Problems, Problems, Problems

We view life as a problem to be solved, becoming addicted to control. The lack of ego strength, fear of helplessness, fear of powerlessness and the defensiveness create a need for control. To maintain control a person must head off each possible uncontrollable factor at the pass by anticipating, planning strategies and avoiding. The hurt adult begins to view each day in terms of the problems to be solved and the methods a person must maintain to not lose control. More and more we become problem oriented. We make lists of problems and check them off. This problem orientation builds toward many of the phobias and anxieties that travel with codependency. The more control we need the more we can fear being out of control. The more control we have, the more likely we are to become out of control. We overreact to anything that may produce a loss of control—flying, storms, ski lifts, driving on freeways, shopping in crowds, elevators, heights and other fears. We fear the panic attack that may happen when we feel out of control, when we're in crowded places or our feet leave the ground.

We often quit doing the things we enjoy because they look too hard. Physical challenges are avoided. When traveling we expect to be pampered, taken care of and get impatient and controlling with the people we meet. Flight delays, hotel mix-ups are an affront to us. We no longer notice people and places. We live for the next foul-up, the next problem, the next place to attack. We may act positively and friendly but the steam inside builds up. If our lives are a problem to be solved, we can no longer see that *life is a mystery to be embraced, a process to be enjoyed.* We lose a sense of time, of the preciousness of the moment and a connectedness with others. We perpetuate the myth of our control. We think that we have control. Our control is an illusion. It's insatiable. We are controllers and sometimes the control appears to be the healthiest part of our life. The irony is that giving up control and accepting our powerlessness leads us to recovery.

We try to control our feelings, other people, the world. It's like a pressure cooker with no release valve. We will and do explode. Sometimes our addictiveness provides the release—the nicotine, food, sex, spending, gambling and obsessive relationships. In our attempt to recover from the addictions, things get worse. New addictions take the place of the old. Our codependent relationships become more and more troubled. We switch, trade, go back and forth among the many addictions we have without ever dealing with control.

It's no coincidence that the first step of Alcoholics Anonymous or any other twelve step program deals with powerlessness. We keep trying to prove we can control the compulsions we have, as if that is going to prove we don't have a problem. We often can control it or think we are controlling a compulsion by stopping it temporarily. This is a pseudo control since even if we do end up controlling, it is the difference between sobriety and serenity. The addiction isn't really the problem, the control is. We control the symptoms but ignore the codependency.

Mission Control

Control is the most addictive process of all. Our control falls short of our expectations. Even people who know they can't control addictions, people that work in the field of alcoholism, go on diets. What is a diet but an attempt to control a compulsive overeating problem or an obsession about body shape and size? No wonder only a small percent of diets have a lasting, positive impact on people's lives. Strictly behavioral approaches to the systems and issues don't work, or they may seem to work but only for a short time.

The paradox of addiction to accept that we are out of control enables us to find manageability in our lives. Food management may be a part of a recovery program, but it's never all of it. The management of our time and our decisions may be a part of our recovery program but never all of it.

Spectatoring—The Watchers

We become reactive to externals and lose the capacity to be introspective. The spectating is a process of watching how other people are doing and feeling, looking for flaws, mistakes and conflicts. We get jealous when we watch success, righteous with others' faults, arrogant about their mistakes. If we make mistakes it's because we were watching other people so they wouldn't screw up too badly. We often watch people as their guides, coaching them and cheering them on, but sometimes secretly hoping they will mess up. As watchful as we become, we learn selective vision, selective hearing. We see and hear what we want. Our relationships are ongoing battles about what the other said, each always clear with perfect memory, but with different perceptions. The fights are often over details, exactly what was said, how they said it or what they left out. Our watchfulness becomes so intense our vision is blurred. We become picky, but no longer notice the small and wonderful things. We have lost the childlike awareness of noticing, the way a child walks down a sidewalk, looking at the cracks, the lines, noticing, wondering, asking, looking at what's in the cracks. We notice the cracks in the sidewalks and worry about the tax bill for the city repairing the sidewalk or the liability issues if someone should trip. There is a new insurance policy for codependents called "my fault" insurance!

A line in the movie, "The Color Purple," says, "God gets angry if you walk by a field with the color purple in it and don't notice." We often can't read poetry because we don't recognize nuances. We don't notice the hues, the beauty or the processes of life. We simply don't notice, losing the childlike wonder necessary for spirituality.

My son Dan always notices the color purple. I realized how much he notices when I took a walk with him. He started pointing out geometric patterns, colors, the balances of the things around us. I believe this is his spirituality. Possibly many of us don't read poetry because we can't let it flow over us. We try to catch it, contain it and control it. Even if we successfully dissect it we can't enjoy it.

The Art Of Fine Whine!

In our critical, complaining and whining style we learn to use problems and spectating to bond with others. It's a negative bonding that builds around what's wrong with everyone else, the world, the church. We criticize and dissect, we figure it all out and analyze everyone we know. The real connecting is done through our negativism and whining. Our best friends become people who complain with us. Others we drive away with our intellectual arrogance and complaining postures. We wonder why our kids are negative and complaining, but modeling is the most powerful form of teaching. We nitpick and expect them to be able to be happy and relaxed. We become obsessive and phobic around them. We teach them our control and they control us. We focus on them and they sabotage us. We obsess them and they ignore us.

Individual Traits

A list of common characteristics of codependent individuals follows. For each characteristic mentioned, the opposite of the characteristic may also be true, since 180 degrees from sick is still sick. It's on the same line and it's usually indicative of the same problem. I've listed 100, although I am sure there are more, I just like round, *big* numbers!

1. **Self-doubt** Question and doubt thoughts, feelings and behavior. The opposite is excessive self-assurance to the point of arrogance.
2. **Poor Self-image** We miss the precious, valuable person we are. Nothing is enough for us to decide that we look or are OK.
3. **Difficulty Caring For Oneself** We take care of others, not ourselves. We practice self-neglect as an art form. The opposite is a total self-focus, an addiction to self.

4. **Burnout** The mark of later stages of our illness, at work, as parents, as a spouse or with community involvement. We lose our energy. We have nothing left to give and collapse.

5. **Living With Stress** Stress to a codependent is like water to a dolphin. We can exist outside of it, but just barely. We swim through it, play with it, steep ourselves in it. Only, unlike water, it doesn't provide us with buoyancy and sustenance. It becomes a short-cut to burnout. We drown in it.

6. **Poor Body Image** We experience dissatisfaction with our appearance, body shape and size. It is easy to get caught up in feeling ugly, too short, bald, fat, tall, skinny, flat chested and thick thighed. Physical shame sets up isolation and the self destruction of fad diets, unnecessary surgeries, expensive treatments, narcissistic body shaping and resort pampering. We attempt to change our external being through clothes, hair colors, make overs, tanning salons, cosmetics, jewelry and labels.

7. **Feeling Like An Imposter** We feel like we are fooling people, believing that if we get found out they will know we are inadequate. The opposite is feeling smug about who we are and what we do.

8. **Excess Social Discomfort** Social situations can produce extreme anxiety. We avoid certain social settings and use alcohol or externals to gain power and control. We may choose to socialize with people we can control easily. We can also use seduction and charm as a way of controlling and manipulating.

9. **Compulsive, Addictive and Self-destructive Behaviors** Using externals to fill the emptiness, avoid pain and numb feelings. The dependent part of codependent.

10. **Being Controlled By Children** Always reacting to, trying to fix or being obsessed with our children is common. Our lives revolve around *their* needs—education, illness, struggles. The opposite is to ignore and neglect children or have them take care of us.

11. **Giving More and Receiving Less** We keep doing more and more for others and receiving less and less in return. We get into the triangle of being the rescuer, finding the victim and then getting kicked in return and become the victim, then needing a rescuer and doing the kicking.

12. **Losing Ourselves In Causes** We get so obsessed in someone else's pain, need or cause that we lose a sense of self. It is

starving ourselves for world hunger. Ignoring the needs of others and social issues is the opposite.

13. **Unsatisfactory Relationships** Our relationships don't quite fit our lives or needs. They never live up to our expectations. The other extreme is to pretend our relationships are perfect, when in fact they are empty or falling apart.

14. **Feeling Isolated, Unloved, Unwanted, Unappreciated and Unnoticed** People can't fill our emptiness; they can't give us enough. Our own lives don't provide what we need to feel like we fit.

15. **Distrusting Self** We do not trust our instincts, feelings, thoughts or ideas and believe other people know more than we do or have the answer that we don't. We have little confidence. The opposite is being overconfident in our ideas, never doubting ourselves and our feelings and instincts. We tend to go along with other people's ideas even when we know it is wrong.

16. **Underachieving** Many of us are underemployed, work at jobs that are below us, or believe that what we're doing is below us. The fear of challenge, fear of putting our talents to use or fear of success controls us. The opposite is working at levels beyond our competence.

17. **Perfectionistic** We attempt perfection and become compulsive to hide the broken self and our broken integrity. We hide behind the image of being "altogether." The opposite is to screw up most of what we do, goof off and set up others to expect nothing of us.

18. **Problem-oriented** Our view of life is a problem to be solved. We create the problems faster than anybody can solve them. The opposite is to ignore problems altogether.

19. **Dissatisfaction** We are in constant churning, emotionalism, we can't do it right. There's no resting and very little letting go. The opposite is to act complacent, have a flat affect and no movement in our lives.

20. **Being Driven** Sometimes it seems as though there are external forces that drive us in unfathomable directions. We act as though we have goals, but the drivenness is from behind or within and never toward anything real. Having the opposite—no goals or plans with nothing to motivate us—is equally destructive.

21. **Time Mismanagement**   Poor scheduling, excess tension woven into our days is a result of not understanding time, its value or our relationship to it. We don't understand our limits. The opposite is being obsessed with the clock, time, schedules and guarding it too jealously.
22. **Sleep Disorders**   We either toss, turn and don't get enough sleep or we use sleep as our avoidance.
23. **Feeling Disconnected**   We dissociate, feeling spaced out, crazy and unreal. We use the dissociation. It becomes a primary defense pattern, but we fear and don't understand it.
24. **Fears**   Fears become worries, obsessiveness, anxiety and phobias. The absence of a feeling of safety in our lives keeps us from really being ourselves. We become so reactive to the fears that we seek fear or we begin to fear nothing.
25. **Energy Swings**   We have fits of fitness and energy and then periods of exhaustion where we are wiped out to the point of illness or emotional depression. We become a whirlwind of energy, accomplishing more in a day than most people can in a week and then we lose our energy, our batteries die, our machinery winds down and we fade out.
26. **Depression**   We have a tendency toward depression and turn things inward, we beat up on ourselves. Our listlessness becomes a symptom of the energy demands of our fight with self, our battle with our own thoughts and feelings. The opposite is blaming outward, accusing, beating on others and paranoia. Paranoia is feeling my editor is *out to get me!* My older brother has reverse paranoia, he thinks he's following someone. I know I've always followed him.
27. **Accident-prone**   Our distracted lifestyle causes us to not notice where we're going, what we're doing or what's around us. We hurt ourselves. We become walking disasters. We continue the self-destructiveness through accidents. The other extreme is being over cautious and never taking any risks.
28. **Somatic Illness**   Our feelings become physical pain and illness. We have a lessened boundary sense, a lessened immune system. We become vulnerable to allergies, stress-related illness, asthma, viral infections; whatever is going around we'll catch.
29. **Nasty Mood Afflictions**   Our anger and resentments sweep through us and out toward people around us. We project much of our bad feeling about ourselves on others and our

own inadequacy gives rise to noting inadequacies in others. The opposite is a *pretend* passivity.

30. **Tolerance Breaks** We have a high tolerance for intolerable behavior, marked by tolerance breaks. We seem so passive around inappropriate behaviors of others. Then suddenly we break down and we say, "Now I can be a jerk. You've been a jerk long enough," and we fall apart and become inappropriate ourselves.

31. **Work Addiction** We use work as a way of having worth, avoiding our personal lives and getting people to need us. We can't say no. The opposite is a refusal to be productive or a fear of losing uniqueness if we work.

32. **Constant Chaos or Crisis** As long as we are in a whirlwind, nothing can touch us. Our problems are too big, but we feel truly alive as long as we're in a state of intensity. The opposite is to avoid any stress, never making waves. Crisis-oriented: career crises, mid-life crises, relationship crises, spiritual crises, sexual crises and a continuation of unresolved problems.

33. **Enabling Relationships** We become disrespectful in our relationships with others by enabling the people we are with to continue their crummy behaviors. They do the crime, we pay the fine and do the time. We remove the harmful consequences of other people's inappropriateness. The opposite is to take no risk, involvement or responsibility in any relationships.

34. **Passive Aggressive** We don't get angry, we get even. We get sideways. We go away. We withdraw. We shut down emotionally or physically, while punishing the people around us.

35. **Scrupulosity** We constantly judge ourselves and are controlled by excess guilt. We wear our guilt as a veneer, as a suit of armor. Each move we make we mark against the judgments, the injunctions, the self-imposed inhibitions. We deny our uniqueness. We're controlled by our self-judging guilt. The opposite is no conscience, no sense of our impact on others, no guilt.

36. **Shamefulness and Shamelessness** We feel terrible about ourselves and cannot acknowledge these bad feelings, so we act shamelessly. Our behavior either becomes a shameless manifestation of our repressed shame or direct projection of this shame. We blame shame and destroy others or the

environment out of shamelessness. We need a healthy sense of shame.

37. **Martyrdom**   We believe we are going to achieve sanctity by sacrificing ourselves for others. We may believe we are being sacrificed for the causes of others. We practice martyrdom and we're proud of our saintliness. The opposite is never sacrificing for anyone or anything or set up others to sacrifice.

38. **Lack Boundaries**   We don't have boundaries intellectually, physically, emotionally, spiritually or sexually. We often don't notice, recognize or respect other people's boundaries. When we develop boundaries we often use them as a club, becoming rigid and isolated.

39. **Counterdependence**   We defy authority, rebel and sabotage systems and relationships.

40. **Sexual Dysfunction**   Sexual abuse, fears, shame, sexual compulsion, sexual problems, poor sexual identity, sexual shame, sexual relationship issues and disorders of desire may surface.

41. **Sex Role Rigidity**   Messages of what it is to be a man or woman become restrictions on who we can be, on what we expect of others, how we see others, our ability to have friendships, relationships and acquaintances with the other sex and same sex.

42. **Religious Problems**   Religious addiction, spiritual confusion and religious vulnerability lead us to become bait for religious extortionists and religious exhibitionists. We become victims of religious exploitation and hide behind a cloak of religiosity.

43. **Mood Swings**   Codependents may experience emotional ups and downs. Highs become manic and lows follow. We lack evenness of temperament. Things are either great or awful. We move from grandiosity to self-hate.

44. **Disordered Eating**   We use food to medicate our pain and hurt. We obsess food or ignore our need for food. Our relationship with food becomes distorted. We struggle and battle with ourselves and over-focus on our body shape and size.

45. **Suicidal Feelings**   Self-destructive flashes, feelings of wanting to disappear, wanting to end it, that others would be better off without us may be pervasive. We believe things would be better if we didn't exist.

46. **Lacking Life Balance**   We work on one area of our life and neglect other things. We work on our spirituality and we ignore our recreation. We work on our recreation and we ignore our need to be productive. We work on our need to be productive and we ignore our relationships, our nutrition, our sexuality or our social needs. We improve our lives but only on one track at a time, never quite getting it all together.

47. **Repeatedly Being Used**   We are vulnerable to people who use us. We have fast friends that take us for short rides and drop us off after they've gotten what they need from us. We have a Pollyanna, naive attitude toward life and toward relationships. This is also marked by being excessively suspicious or cynical, believing that everyone has a motive or reason for anything they do or give. We also use others.

48. **Eternal Optimism and Minimizing**   We ignore the reality of our problems until they've reached crisis proportions. We pretend that everything is OK. The opposite is eternal pessimism. Everything looks like a problem. Things are all going to hell in a hand basket. We can no longer see the positives in our lives.

49. **Manipulative**   We do things round about and control covertly or indirectly. We take the side approaches rather than directly noticing and dealing with issues.

50. **Secretiveness**   We keep secrets. We ask others to keep secrets. We get people enmeshed through the covert and hidden aspects of our lives.

51. **Defensive**   Our defensiveness pushes people away. We do it out of a need for self-protection, but instead it leads us into more self-destruction. We can't acknowledge making mistakes because we feel like we are a mistake. We can't accept criticism because we believe that people are breaking off or abandoning the relationship. The opposite is never defending ourselves, we won't stand up for ourselves.

52. **Indecisiveness**   Every time we make a decision we second-guess it. We fear the consequences of our decisions. We look at what we decided against more than what we decided on. Sometimes we get frozen into immobility because of the confusion and fear of alternatives. At least I think that's true, maybe it's not.

53. **Hypervigilance and Spectatoring**   We become wary, constantly watching, guarding against unspoken attack. We keep watching how others feel, what they need, losing the

ability to see ourselves. The opposite is not noticing anyone but ourselves; self-absorption.

54. **Invulnerability** We feel too vulnerable, so we try to act invulnerable. Being ourselves, being real, being close means we can be hurt, so we try to keep control, a safe distance, denying all of the things that might penetrate our armor. The opposite is being too vulnerable.

55. **Delayed Recovery Syndrome** Whenever something happens to set us back, we crash. We are delayed in recovering from illness, injuries, lost relationships or jobs. We can no longer regroup our strengths, forces or efforts to get back on track. We wallow in our pain, our illness; we have a fear of being hurt again, or getting sick again, or losing another job. We avoid going on, getting well or finding another job. We obsess and fear injuries and coddle ourselves. The opposite is ignoring the injury which exacerbates the problems or we minimize the illness or loss.

56. **Hypochondria** When our feelings can't be dealt with we convert them into imagined physical pain. Our illness isn't real but the pain is real. We obsess our bodies, we obsess and fear illness. We constantly worry about whether we are sick or what's happening to our body or whether we're getting cancer, etc.

57. **Constantly Seeking Answers** We bounce around from one program to another. We read the latest book by the latest author. Please note this is the latest book by the latest author—better late than never!

58. **Instant Gratification** What we want, we want now. If we want to feel good we want to feel good now. If we're hungry we have to have it right now. We lack the ability to delay our needs. We look for the fix. The opposite is *always* delaying or avoiding gratification.

59. **Belief In Suffering** Believing that through pain we find sainthood. Suffering will make us good people. Our pain proves our moral superiority to others and will give us a higher place in the afterlife.

60. **Money Problems** The insecurities of our lives, relationships and childhood become concern about financial survival. We hoard, miser, and become compulsive. We can't spend money on ourselves. We try to control what the people around us spend. We become compulsive about spending or obsessive about our finances and financially irresponsible.

61. **Acting Childish**   We try to regain our lost childhood by becoming childish rather than embracing childness. We pout, throw tantrums. Our playfulness doesn't involve consideration of others, it becomes mean or vindictive. We act cute for attention, approval, or to manipulate. The opposite of this is pseudo maturity, never playful or spontaneous, denying our childness.

62. **Judging Ourselves**   We judge ourselves through externals, appearances, wealth, by how others see us. This is a no-win situation since we are usually our own worst critics. Nothing we can do will ever satisfy ourselves. Nothing we can own will ever be enough to make us feel successful in other people's eyes. The opposite is to not care at all what others see or feel about us.

63. **Lack of Emotional Fluency**   We don't affirm our feelings or others, we don't speak in the language of feelings, we have a hard time processing feelings, we don't embrace feelings, we try to get rid of them or distract from them. When we talk about sharing feelings, they usually come out as thoughts. We say, "I feel that . . . or I feel like . . ." Anytime "that" or "like" follows the word "feel," it's not a feeling that's being shared, it is an idea, thought or observation. We become shallow, lack substance and don't look for depth in other people. The opposite is emotional fluency as a way of controlling others or processing feelings ad nauseam.

64. **Feeling Empty**   We're not empty, we just *feel* empty. We can't seem to get enough in our lives. We become insatiable. Nothing is ever enough. Not enough to go around.

65. **Fear of Intimacy and Abandonment**   The fears cause us to withdraw in relationships. We feel abandoned even when we're not being abandoned. When close, we fear the intimacy. When distant, we fear the isolation.

66. **Being Critical, Whining and Complaining**   This is a posture toward life that keeps us judgmental, negative and pushes people away. We negatively bond with people through our complaining.

67. **Practicing Sentimentality**   Some of us become sentimental rather than being emotionally appropriate. We can cry when a loved one leaves for a weekend but we can't be tender and sharing or supportive when they're with us through the week. We can talk longingly of things we care about, but we can't share the care in an appropriate setting.

68. **Inability to Complete Tasks** We've become addicted to beginnings, the excitement, but after something has begun we can't stay with it. This is true of relationships, projects, works, pets, interests, hobbies. The opposite is we get compulsive about completion or avoiding the joy and excitement of beginnings.

69. **Lacking Privacy** We talk too much. We gossip. We share too much with people who either don't care or wouldn't be respectful of the information.

70. **Not Trusting** We can't turn ourselves over to somebody else's care. We get overly suspicious, cynical and believe everyone has an ulterior motive or our trust is inappropriately placed and we behave naively.

71. **Lost in Details** We quibble and argue about insignificant things. We get stuck in the little data while missing the larger issues. The opposite is to ignore details to the point of insensitivity.

72. **Inability to Let Go** We have to complete everything perfectly. Everything has to be done a certain way, no sense of surrender, no acceptance. Worrying too much to is how we look like we care.

73. **Being Competitive** We have to beat others to feel good about ourselves. We can't just do the best we can, we have to win.

74. **Judging and Comparing Ourselves** We judge our children by comparing them to other children. We judge our house by comparing it other houses, the things we see in magazines and on TV. We judge our relationships by how we see other people's relationships. We judge ourselves without mercy.

75. **Ritualistic** We have an *over focus* on tradition. We become rigid, not bending. Our lives are controlled by sameness and ritual.

76. **Defiant** We become defiant to authority or tradition. We refuse to allow any patterns in our life. We operate totally on impulse. We won't accept direction. We break the rules for the sake of breaking rules. We feel like the rules are impinging on our freedom of expression, that traditions, the old way won't work for us. We despise scheduling or having to be somewhere.

77. **Excess Fear of Authority** We are easily intimidated. We seek and create gurus, put leaders on pedestals, often sabo-

taging their leadership. The opposite is to shame, bully and intimidate others. We force other people to perform according to our will. We will be the ultimate authority on everything.

78. **Filtering Sights and Sounds** We filter what is said to us and what we see to fit our model of what we like, to fit what we believe. We only follow paths that are familiar. We avoid the new, what might change our mind and have selective vision and hearing.

79. **Helper Role** We adopt the role as helper but we can't ask for help ourselves. We have to be the helper. It gives us more control. We are always the listener, we're always the one with the advice. Many people can come to us, but we go to no one.

80. **False Identities** People don't know us. They view us with exaggerated descriptions—the best mom, smartest person, greatest athlete, biggest traveler, biggest ne'er do well. We become known for what we do rather than who we are.

81. **Inability to Delegate** We can't defer. We have to do it ourselves as a way of maintaining control and maintaining the exaggerated view of how other people see us. It must be done our way.

82. **No Team Work** We either have to do it ourselves or back off. We can't do one part or take our responsibility. We either feel completely responsible or not responsible at all. We sabotage or try to control everyone's efforts. We must be the star, the leader *or* the screw-up. We can't be a team player.

83. **Blaming and Projecting** When things go wrong we can't take responsibility, so we blame and project. It must be someone else's fault. When things go well we want the credit. When things go wrong we deliver the blame.

84. **Harboring Resentments** We have a hard time getting through our anger. Our resentments eventually fester until they become apathy and boredom. We don't forgive. The opposite is never standing up for ourselves, forgiving by forgetting, forgiving too easily.

85. **Pretending Things Don't Bother Us** We become blasé and glib. We show a flat affect while our stomachs are churning. We believe that detachment means that we no longer have feelings.

86. **No Sense of Humor** We lack the ability to laugh at ourselves. We lack the ability to be spontaneous and laugh with

others. The opposite is excessive reliance on humor as a way of avoiding our pain or the seriousness of things around us.

87. **Belief in Punishment** We believe in the *cosmic balance scale*. We believe that we must make up for the sins and mistakes of others, of our parents, of our past. The tragedies of our lives or of those around us must be some kind of reparation, punishment or balance due. We punish ourselves and other people, losing gentleness in the process.

88. **Self-Deprecation** We sometimes take on a self-put down posture. If we are the ones to first criticize ourselves, maybe no one else will. If we put on the act of humility, maybe people will try to cheer us up or notice us or not expect too much from us.

89. **Impatience** In our impatience we can't teach others, and it's difficult to be taught by others. Obsessions with the externals, with the details causes us to want things to move too fast through our lives. We don't take enough time with our children, their projects and questions, with our friends, to really care or be there. We become impatient with ourselves. We expect us to be perfect. We expect us to get better right away.

90. **Learned Helplessness** We pretend incompetence. The more helpless we can show people we are, the less they will ask of us, the less they will expect. If it turns out we do something well, they'll be surprised. The opposite is to pretend we can do anything.

91. **Not Seeing Consequences** We don't notice the consequences of our behavior. We become obsessed with the short term. We miss the long term impact of our lives, of our actions. We can't create long term goals for ourselves. The opposite is we get so concerned about consequences we can't function at all.

92. **Missing the Forest for the Trees** We can't see the connectedness and the relatedness of events and reactions. We can't see the relationship between our feelings and things going on in our life. We don't recognize the relationship between our behaviors and feelings or relationship between our losses and illness or the connection between our thoughts and our actions.

93. **Overly Adaptable** We try and adapt to our surroundings by looking and acting sane in crazy systems and settings.

Oftentimes we adapt and fit the pathology of those around us. The opposite is the inability to adapt because of rigidity.

94. **Pretending Crazy Places Are Normal** We seek crazy systems and set ourselves up to look normal but to gradually fall apart because of the setting or the relationship. We find settings that match how we feel inside, that match our own fears, inadequacies, insecurities, and craziness.

95. **Over-explaining and Fear of Being Misunderstood** We rationalize, talk too much and editorialize, constantly worried that people will not fully understand our positions or sympathize with us.

96. **Overcautious** Avoiding risks, fear of not looking good or making mistakes. We act out our worries by smothering others.

97. **Independence** This is compulsive avoidance of depending on others, seeming always strong, separate and capable. Fear of getting close because we lose too much of self. This is the independent codependent.

98. **Denial and Self-deception** We deny, distort reality. We deceive ourselves into believing ours or others' lies.

99. **Hopelessness** We believe nothing will ever change. We despair, give up and can look sicker than we are.

100. **Projective Identification** We project our issues on others. We read this list and see how it affects everyone but us. (Editor's note: "I hate to admit it, but that is exactly what I did while editing this list!")

Relationship Traits

Codependent relationships, whether with heterosexual, lesbian or gay partners, have many peculiarities and particular earmarks. Following is a list of fifty traits (each trait is about a relationship between two people so if we multiply each trait by two, it really is like another list of 100 traits; I still like *round, big* numbers!):

1. *A fast track relationship,* a relationship made in haste with too much too soon.
2. A relationship **based on sexual intensity** and early sexual experiences.
3. *Feeling owed,* a feeling of staying in to get yours because the person owes you after all that you've done for that person.
4. *Improbable partners,* too much difference in background, age attitudes and values.

5. *Arrogance* about the relationship. The same rules don't apply to us. We're different. The other person is too brilliant. People don't understand. We have a different kind of relationship than other people.
6. *Exaggeration* in the relationship, obsession with the other person, expecting the same level of feeling in return. "Do you think of me as much as I think of you?"
7. *Little spontaneous playfulness,* excess rituals, excess reliance on tradition.
8. Too many *fixed requirements and objectives* to the relationship, lack of spontaneity.
9. *Lose individual differences* or don't value those differences, attempts to achieve sameness.
10. *Imbalance of time for the relationship.* A shortage of time for the relationship or too much time for the relationship, rather than a sense of balance.
11. *Lack of conflict resolution,* never seem to resolve things, constantly obsessing conflict and problems, little progress, things don't seem to get better. *The disease is the same damn thing over and over and recovery is one damn thing after another.*
12. *Self-control and censured feelings,* careful about who you are and what you say, no sharing of feelings and vulnerability, walking on eggshells.
13. *Verbal put downs,* defensive behaviors or glib jokes about the person or the relationship, cruelty, nasty mind games.
14. *Fear of exploring* different things in the relationship, in our lives, lack of experimentation, lack of risk.
15. One or both partners have a *myth of their own perfection* or the other's perfection.
16. A sense of *one down or one up* in the relationship, the good partner, the bad partner, the smart one, the dumb one.
17. *No talk rules,* talk less and less about what is going on. Too many taboo subjects and sacred cows.
18. *Excessive defensiveness* about relationship problems, feelings, self and very little openness.
19. Belief that the *other person defines who you are,* how they dress, what they say, how they look, who they hang around with makes people judge you, that your partner is an extension of you. This doesn't mean other people's behavior won't embarrass you or cause you feelings and discomfort. Codependents get defined by others and look to them for validation and worth.

20. Over *cautious about making commitment* in the relationship or regretting the commitment you have already made.
21. Entering a relationship with the idea that you can *change the other person,* that love conquers all, it won't be like that after we're married or together.
22. Being *preoccupied* with the other person, obsessing them.
23. Unresolved, *unspoken sexual issues,* sexual dysfunction, hurts or shame, sex isn't a shared respectful process, no playfulness with sexuality.
24. Unsuccessful *struggles to maintain intimacy.* We mistake the struggle and enmeshment of a relationship for intimacy. This is the earmark everyone sees as codependency, although it is mostly a symptom. Struggling to maintain intimacy can be a convoluted way to avoid intimacy. The opposite of struggling to maintain intimacy may be the independent posture of seeking no intimacy at all.
25. A relationship that is *tumultuous, chaotic,* a roller coaster, ups and downs, close and far, highs and lows.
26. *Sacrifice outside things* for the relationship, such as old friends, interests, hobbies, travel and privacy.
27. *Using substitutes to avoid intimacy*—drugs, sex, food, TV and different sleep patterns.
28. Undue nurturing and *caretaking* instead of shared intimacy, it is an adult and child kind of relationship.
29. *Threats of abandonment or violence* in the relationship.
30. *Rigid sex role expectations.* A good woman does this. A man should be doing that. Men are supposed to be . . .
31. *No sharing of interests,* no sharing of the world outside, no sharing of literature, hobbies, games, spiritual process or pastimes.
32. *Relationship based on control,* based on naivete, based on power differential such as a doctor/patient or teacher/student or naive innocent/worldly wise partner.
33. *Absence of common beliefs* and long term goals. The journey isn't a shared one.
34. *Excessive differences regarding children;* whether or not to have children, how to deal with or raise children or using children to avoid intimacy.
35. *Constantly covering for the other person,* making excuses, hanging in there because he or she "isn't really like that."
36. *Distorted relationships,* similarities are maximized and differences minimized.

37. *Doing for the relationship and the other person what you will not do for yourself.*
38. Caring in the relationship means *being responsible for and not to.* You feel just a little bit above the other person.
39. Putting more *emphasis on how the relationship looks* than how it really is. Appearances must be kept up.
40. More and more *spectating* in the relationship, watching what they're doing, if they're making mistakes or how they feel and less and less on ourselves.
41. *Social isolation,* absence of common friends and excess socializing to avoid intimacy.
42. A gradual *increase of tolerance for intolerable behavior* in the other person, marked by tolerance breaks.
43. *Financial issues* and money used to control, financial disagreements, dishonesty, economic dependency and fear.
44. *Setting up a partner to look bad,* hoping they'll screw up or get caught out of our anger.
45. *Boredom, apathy, no fight or passion,* flat affect about the relationship.
46. *Clingy,* overly affectionate, excess physical affection as public displays.
47. *Jealousy,* ownership, constant concerns about exclusivity, excess watchfulness about other relationships.
48. *Niceness,* always being nice, never fighting; one partner gives up who they are for the sake of the other; there will be no waves, peace at any price.
49. *Over productive* and constantly working. Relationship built around a joint career or the job of raising children or maintaining a home. Little shared intimacy outside of being productive.
50. *Empty threats* and ultimatums that do not get followed up, about leaving, counseling, divorce, separation and treatment.

Family Traits

Each family is made up of individuals and a multitude of relationships. The traits of the codependent individuals and relationships outlined above pervade and there are numerous traits regarding the family unit itself. Fifty of the traits are as follows:

1. **Rigidity, Fear of Change** People are always trying to maintain the status quo, no fluidity, a break-don't bend approach. Lots of rules about how it ought to be, trying to live up to the

image. A lost sense of who we are. What doesn't fit doesn't belong. An authoritarian approach, often patriarchal systems.

2. **Unpredictability** We never know what's going to happen, something occurs producing a certain reaction one time, but the next time in the same setting, a totally different reaction occurs. Discipline is random, relationships are up and down. Erratic emotional and physical reactions. Plans are made and then dropped. People are constantly leaving and coming back. People are angry one moment, happy the next.

3. **Emotional Problems** Feelings are denied or projected and get acted out rather than shared. Feelings are not affirmed. It's not OK to have feelings. It becomes difficult to sort out whether one's feelings are about what's happening to oneself, what's happening in the family or what's happening to someone else.

4. **Triangulation** Twosomes are not allowed to work out their *stuff*. Parents get into the kids' fights and vice versa. They can't let go of other people's relationships in the system. People are mucking around in other people's business.

5. **Judgmentalism** Differences are not tolerated. Anybody that is different gets shamed, criticized or teased. People with different ideas are made to feel stupid. People outside of the family are put down because they live in different communities, go to different schools, different religions, dress differently, live in different countries, have different beliefs, different politics. The judgment includes an arrogance about our ways, beliefs and religion.

6. **Denial** No talk rules and a conspiracy of silence are common. It requires denial to build codependency. Denial is the family dysfunction. It's the elephant in the living room. No one must notice. We don't get to have our feelings about it. We lose a sense of trust between what is said to be true and what we feel to be true. The denial is crazy-making. We deny the problems, and its impact on our lives, our feelings about the problem or major aspects of the problem. Denial is what perpetuates the problems, the reason the problems become intergenerational in families. Denial is what sets up most of the enmeshment. Collusion is learned—enabling postures are taught. Euphoric recall supports denial. Family members invent or focus on good times and ignore the pain, emptiness or abuse.

7. **Shame—Lack of Support** We learn not to depend on people because they won't support us. We don't get enough affirmation or positive feedback about who we are. There's physical and sexual shame, shame about our behaviors, shame about what we like, shame about vulnerability, needs and feelings. Shame is used to control people. Parents get afraid of kid's dependency needs on them so they bring up shame as a way of controlling and staying in control. The parents' codependency, their bad feelings about themselves get projected onto the children. It is a shame/blame system.

8. **Focus on Doing the Right Thing** Very often, the right thing isn't explained or the right thing is impossible to do. The expectation that someone should do it is still there.

9. **Covert Rules** Rules about touch, sex, food, weight, feelings, men, women and relationship. These rules can't be broken because they remain undefined and hidden. These rules are double binds because they are impossible to follow.

10. **Limited Affirmations** There is little recognition of personal strengths or uniqueness of individuals. The denial of personal strengths keeps everybody in a one-down position. Family members are shamed for their uniqueness.

11. **Little Recognition of Family Strengths** We can't fall back and use the resources of the family even when present.

12. **Success is Shared, Failure is Blamed** If you do something well, it's about the family, but if you do something wrong it's about you.

13. **Lack of Awareness About the Past** It's part of the denial. We don't know what parents are really like, their goals, aspirations, dreams, feelings, losses and past. We don't understand the history of our families or the childhood of the adults. The past is often mythology and falsehoods. Sometimes we know one branch of the family and not the other.

14. **False Premises About Life** Belief systems that don't work, that are not true and can control us. Examples: All men are no good. All religious leaders are crooks. Never show affection in public. Don't ever tell anybody you love them, just show it. Men don't cry. If you're vulnerable you'll get hurt. Never trust anyone outside of the family. *Better dead than bald.*

15. **Addiction or Compulsion** Self destructive behaviors are the primary way of dealing with feelings. Medicating pain is the modeled behavior.

16. **Certain Family Members Count More**   Some people are more significant than other people. Certain children are more valued and parents are more important or one parent counts more over the other.
17. **No Forgiveness**   There is no way to make restitution, no way back into the good graces of the family or the relationship if you make a mistake.
18. **Objects Count More Than People**   Wealth, money and the things we own are more important than the relationships or individuals in the family. Money isn't everything but it can buy everything. You can't have everything—where would you put it?
19. **Absence of Freedom**   Choices are limited and rights are minimized. Few decisions are allowed. All the judgment is external and the rules are already set.
20. **Excessive Reliance on Discipline and Control**   There is a belief that children are the property of parents and the primary goal of parenting is to control, make children respect, and keep children disciplined.
21. **Family Loyalty**   Loyalty to family is more important than the individual needs, choices, health, or happiness. If the family needs us to be in a certain place, regardless of what it does to us or our present family, you must be there. A loyalty to the family may involve taking over the family business, taking care of family members, keeping the family secrets. This is more important than the individuals. Disloyalty means guilt and is often punished.
22. **Secrets**   There are secrets everyone knows but no one talks about that makes everybody feel crazy and shameful. Secrets that very few know, but everybody acts outs. Intergenerational secrets that affect the entire system. Secrets become crazy-making. The bigger the secrets, the larger the family dysfunction. The secrets often breed dishonesty and lies. The secrets are boundary violations. *A family is only as sick as its secrets.*
23. **Role Reversals**   The parents act more like children and the children learn to act like adults, take over responsibilities, do the parenting, become surrogate spouses, become providers and make the family look good in the community. The child loses their childhood, pretends to be an adult, but can't be because to be an adult you have to have been a child. This is where *adult children* come from.

24. **Abandonment and Neglect**   Parents separate, leave, divorce, run away, use addictions, are emotionally unavailable, get so enmeshed in their problems in relationships or work that they ignore the needs of the family. Abandonment is the physical or emotional withdrawal or the breaking of a bond with one to whom there is a legal, moral or emotional commitment or connection.

25. **No-talk Rules**   Children don't talk about their needs or feelings. They don't notice the pathology of parents. The family system is a system where things can't be discussed. There is a conspiracy of silence about the problems.

26. **Marriage Problems** don't get resolved. The marriage partners can't relate to each other or themselves. We maintain distant, empty, enabling or hostile relationships. One partner may give up who they are for the other.

27. **Enmeshment**   People have a hard time sorting out who they are and separating from who other people are. Identity is lost; individuals get enmeshed in the needs, wants, pathology and feelings of other family members.

28. **Comparisons and Competition** are set up among family members where things are said such as "Why can't you be like your brother?" Or "Let's see if you can beat him now." Parents compete with children and vice versa.

29. **Little Shared Leisure Time**   We have little or no spontaneous playfulness or laughter. People go their separate ways, laugh their separate laughs and have their fun at the expense of each other. If you can't laugh at yourself, laugh at someone else.

30. **People are Objectified**   They are not respected but are objects to be used and manipulated or they exist for the gratification of others. Personhood is lost.

31. **Sexual Problems**   There is repression, acting out, shame, dysfunction, sexual innuendos and lack of healthy sexual boundaries, affirmation or information.

32. **Scarcity**   An ingrained belief that there isn't enough to go around. Some get and some don't which results in hoarding and competing for what there is.

33. **Religion Without Spirituality**   Families are involved in empty shell religion with no sense of gratitude, prayerfulness, noticing, awareness or awe. No felt sense of the harmony, balance and becoming of creation.

34. **No Accountability** There is little follow-through, everything has to look OK, but there is a lack of real encouragement and parental involvement. Consequences are removed or made into punishments.
35. **It's Not OK to Love Yourself** Being gentle with oneself is met with derision. You're supposed to be tough and hard on yourself. You're told you are feeling sorry for yourself when in fact you are feeling sorrow for self.
36. **Absence of Information** You can't ask questions or make mistakes. It is difficult to find out where to get information and often when information is given, it's false.
37. **Absence of Community Involvement** Family feels isolated and separate from social functions and community, political functions, church involvement. The opposite—over involvement may also be true.
38. **Inability to Leave** In some families you can leave geographically, but you can't really leave the family, live out your own life or make your own choices about relationships, career, raising kids. In some families you can't even leave geographically.
39. **Socialization Problems** There is little influx of healthy friends or people in the system but many abusive and angry relationships without boundaries exist. The inappropriate people coming into the system act abusively either emotionally, physically, sexually or intellectually. Healthy social process is unknown.
40. **Violence and Abuse** Children are beaten under the guise of discipline; emotional violence, violation of feelings, put downs, etc.
41. **Denial and Minimizing Abuse** If things blow up or explode, the witnesses to the violence—or the children if they are victims of the violence—are not able to respond or show a response to the violence. They have to pretend to ignore it, the shock prevents reaction. Parents minimize the effect of any family trauma on the children. Altered baseline tolerance for abuse and violence is developed.
42. **Children Used For Family Status** Children become the front for the family, their successes, niceness, shyness, athletic prowess and giving all become justification for the family. There is an excess focus on the family, not enough on individual achievement.
43. **Jealousy Regarding Outside Involvement** Restrictions are placed on extra curricular activities. Members aaren't allowed

to stay with or travel with friends or get involved with other families or church functions. Parents get jealous if children bond with other adults or talk about them in positive ways.

44. **Fear of Vulnerability** Children are beaten to *toughen* them up. The more vulnerable members are hurt more often and get less. People bond with and protect the person who seems to have the power.

45. **Boundary Problems** People are not allowed their space, privacy or feelings. Boundary violations create most of the problems in these families.

46. **Broken Promises** Commitments go unmet, promises to change are made and then forgotten and the letdowns become commonplace.

47. **Threats of Abandonment** Conform or get out. "I'm leaving" is used to control behavior.

48. **Selfishness** Rather than service to others we become overly self-serving, accumulate and give only to our own. There is an absence of balance in giving to charities and volunteering—too much or too little.

49. **Crisis Oriented** It is through chaos and crisis that we experience a false sense of closeness and aliveness. A crisis is the only time people are allowed to have feelings.

50. **Hopelessness** A belief that nothing will change while trying to maintain false fantasies. This leads to depression and despair.

Cultural Codependency

Our personal and family issues overlap into our societal, political and cultural issues. Most of the problems in our culture can be traced to hurt and despair coming from low functioning families and living self-destructively. It may appear over simplistic to say the major problems of our era all result from child abuse, but if a person follows the process from personal to family and through community, the culture will reflect codependency. Specific earmarks are outlined below:

1. *Dishonesty* Dishonesty goes virtually unnoticed until it breaks into a scandal in politics, religion, government or business. Scandals create a media flurry and most of the dishonesty is denied. Those who are prosecuted end up on the lecture circuit, charging enormous rates for a short talk about their part in the scandal. There are scandals in politics such as

Watergate and the Iran Contra scandal. Scandals are often buried—the meetings of federal officials with drug cartel members. The are religious scandals, sexual, financial mismanagement which affect millions of people and billions of dollars. There are business scandals—insider trading and embezzlement. Our culture is codependent when it is no longer appalled by the dishonesty, when it expects it and finds those who get caught amusing. A culture is codependent and enabling when the major perpetrators of the dishonesty not only continue to profit but become arrogant about it. Even the agencies founded to help others such as HUD become self-serving, greedy and dishonest.

2. ***Denial*** Denial can be about wrong-doing or mistakes. This is reflected in government's inability to admit wrong-doing regarding Agent Orange and harming their own soldiers and the country in which they spread it. It is the denial of wrong-doing in escalating the Russian shooting down of the Korean jetliner. The U.S. officials knew it was a mistake, but used it as a propaganda process. Even after it came out that they had done this, there was no apology, no public acceptance of wrong-doing. There is denial of the covert manipulations in the Middle East, Central America, in most of the hot spots in the world that we continue to be involved in.

3. ***Inappropriate Behaviors*** Politicians don't behave according to moral guidelines. In our culture, people tend more and more to behave according to what they believe they can get away with. The more outrageous the behavior, the more media attention, and the more the person is seen as eccentric and charming. Possibly, with inappropriate behavior, you can be an American hero—Oliver North—commit a crime, write a book, lecture, get rich and keep protecting the higher ups.

4. ***Lack of Boundaries*** People come and people leave, but there are no boundaries in the sense of who can come and who must leave. We tend to get involved in places where we can't impact and ignore where we can. We muck around in other people's business that we don't have an invitation for or vested interest in. We have borders that are very restrictive for some people; others cross over by the thousands. We have an immigration policy around our boundaries that doesn't make sense and doesn't work. We invite people in, ignore their needs, give some of them a check and let them be victimized without the opportunity of integrating. We expect our sovereignty to be

respected reaching way beyond our borders but we regularly violate the boundaries of others, periodically picking a small country to invade (if you're going to invade a country, a *small* one is the best choice).

5. *Sexual Repression*   There are sexual double messages, sexual acting out, but little open and healthy sexual information or expression, lots of sexual ignorance and fear. We have a great deal of sexual misinformation and very few healthy sexual teachers, leaders and informers. Sex is either made to be trivial, power oriented, secretive or denied. There are many double standards and double messages regarding sexuality, lots of sexual repression which tends to create sexual obsession which tends to support the sexual acting out, sex role rigidity, rape, sexual abuse, sexual dysfunction. Sexual compulsion and addiction are widespread with little recognition and recovery. Sex addicts, victims and offenders are the identified patients of a cultural sexual illness.

6. *Violence*   There exists rampant violence in our cities, streets, communities; rape, burglary, murder as well as violence against other countries. This is one of the most violent nations on earth. We also maintain a codependent posture of being appalled and focusing on the violence elsewhere, rather than focusing on it in our own front and back yards. The other codependent posture regarding violence is to blame it on a conspiracy, whether it's a drug conspiracy, a foreign conspiracy or racial conspiracy, rather than taking responsibility that the violence is built into our own system. The violence is the codependency of imbalance of power and wealth, it is about despair, poverty, hopelessness, and family abuse. We deny, minimize and collude with the violence in our culture. The victims continue to get victimized by the system, while offenders get protection within the system. Even if the offenders don't get protected, the offender system still exists since offenders are sent to places that maintain and increase the offender system. What right do we have acting as an independent country to invade any independent country that is not threatening us in any significant way? Our country is frequently run by war criminals; we go to war too easily.

7. *Unpredictability*   The inability to know where we can take a stand, what we're supposed to believe, what the next move will be. One minute in a crisis, we're doing nothing. The next week we may invade an island and go to war about it. The next

month we're making threats and shortly after that we're being very reasonable and doing nothing again. We have leaders with hair trigger responses that often seem to be asleep at the wheel.

8. **Fear of Change** Change may disrupt our rigid, controlling and manipulating system. People with far-reaching ideas, whether they be political, mechanical or social tend to be feared in a codependent culture. Any idea may upset a power structure, a lobby, an industry. Our goal is to rigidly maintain and defend the existing structures we have. Look at our beleaguered auto industry. This involves a great deal of control by business of the political processes and lots of manipulating people who vote. Much of the maintenance of the status quo is done by setting up a focus on the conspiracies outside of us—the projecting and blaming part of codependency. We look for a scapegoat so we can maintain a belief that we are pure.

9. **Wealth Imbalance** There *seems* to be not enough to go around. Some get and some don't resulting in extreme wealth and extreme poverty and an increase of both. Most wealth is in a few families. Power and money become a game of accumulation with no limit and no limitations on how the accumulation is done. The accumulators love the game, while millions of other people suffer as they play it.

10. **Fear of Vulnerability and Worship of Power** We ignore the weak, the newcomers, children's health, infant mortality, the vulnerable, we have a disdain of vulnerability and obsession with power. We focus on the rich and famous, while we ignore the down and out. Some people are more important than others in codependent systems. In our culture, it's easy to see who's more important, simply compare the Defense budget with the Health and Human Services budget.

11. **Little Respect of Life** The cherishing of life seems to be only rhetoric, symbolic gestures to spend hundreds of thousands of dollars to save two whales trapped in the ice while we are threatening the lives of so many species. In the United States we are destroying plant and animal life daily by polluting our air, water and land through car exhaust, the lumber industry, manufacturing, waste disposal, mining, the Civil Corps of Engineers and their attitude and approach toward our rivers, through the overuse and mismanagement of wilderness areas, to name a few—all in the name of progress. Above all,

122

pollution is about our blatant over consumption, our individual gluttony and greediness of consumer goods, whether it be clothes, toys, food, cars, gadgets, electronics, beauty aids, household goods and on and on — *all the **stuff** we **think** we need to be happy*. The bottom line is, the less each one of us consumes, the less we draw and destroy from our magnificent planet to satisfy our selfish needs and ultimately the less garbage we dump back into our Mother Earth. Codependency is about irresponsibility — irresponsibility to self, each other, our families, our homeland and our planet. We must each begin to live in a responsible style, to recognize, own, embrace, and *change* our part in the destruction of our planet.

12. ***An Ineffective Education System*** Our education system works for a few. A rigid system that doesn't allow for people who learn differently, have a difficult time learning or have special needs. While programs are implemented, they're underfunded, understaffed or the staff is under trained. A codependent culture makes sure that everybody *participates* in education but very few *get* an education. It goes something like: put in the time, look like you're doing it, whether you are or not doesn't matter, make sure the appearance is there — that we have an educated population, when in fact most of our population knows virtually nothing about geography, history, math and many can't read or write. Teachers are often under trained, underpaid, and seen as social outcasts or the bottom of the professional ladder. Kids are failing because we are failing the needs of teachers.

13. ***Absence of Spirituality*** There is a national focus on religion but an absence of spirituality. We accept religious exploitation, extortion, threats and dishonesty. We need gurus and religious heros that aren't accountable, who use their power and influence to accumulate wealth and act out sexually to feed their addictive need for power. You can burn a cross but not a flag. National *symbols* are sacred, *values* are not.

14. ***Detached, Arrogant and Dishonest Leadership*** Our country's leadership continually reflects how out of touch they are with the reality of the lives of most people. The most popular president of modern times was a severely acting out sex addict and it seems to have gone down from there, possibly including a sociopath, a non-recovering adult child and a president who doesn't have a relationship with his own children. The most real and honest of our recent presidents couldn't get re-

elected. Our past "president actor" was so disconnected from his own presidency, his own staff, his own country, that he could well be the most detached leader we've ever had. His affability was probably a cover up for his deafness. He spent most of his presidency confused or not wanting to deal with any of the issues. Our present president speaks of gentleness with barely concealed rage, a former leader of the CIA who acts tough, talks of gentleness, operates covertly and doesn't seem to understand or be willing to deal with the problems for what they really are. He operates secretly with a very small group of advisors. He reflects a willingness to wage a "War on Drugs"—or even drug pushers and ignores the people who suffer from drug related problems. He will invade a country to arrest a drug dealer, one who is difficult to prosecute since there was a hidden involvement of the drug dealer with the CIA our president directed.

15. *Defensiveness*   We've spent approximately two trillion dollars on defense in seven years. That's a tad defensive. Political art has become the process of being able to defend one's position, denying reality and pointing fingers.

16. *Arrogance*   This includes a puritan approach that the evil must be outside of us. Let's find a scapegoat. If it's not going to work to have the Communists as scapegoat this year and Gays have already been scapegoated and so have Blacks and we have laws against that type of discrimination now—then let's find the drug pushers and make them the scapegoats, but only pushers of certain drugs.

17. *Secrets*   There are many things that everybody knows and no one talks about. Secrets that few people know, also abound. What was our president's involvement in the Iran controversy or in Central America? We act indignant and even arrogant about the Russians' promise to reduce chemical warfare stockpiles, the possibility of a chemical plant in Iran that may be used to manufacture chemical weapons. We know and don't talk about our country having recently waged the largest chemical warfare in the history of mankind. Did you know our country has repeatedly refused to sign a "no first strike" agreement regarding nuclear warfare?

18. *Projective Shame*   The more shameful our own culture's behavior, the more shameful is our behavior toward other cultures and the more we need to point out all the atrocities and human rights violations that other cultures are involved

in. We do this to distract from our own shame and abusiveness, from our shameless position of arrogance. Our cultural shame is stored in underground silos.

19. *Fiscal Irresponsibility, Economic Unpredictability* Corporations become insatiable, powerful and roll over other corporations. They become uncontrollable. It is a basic economic system run amuck. Corporations are leveraging and buying other corporations and using the assets of the other corporation to pay for their purchases. The dismantling of corporations, the firing and the trimming of employees of the corporations, corporations that look at profit before pollution, before honesty or loyalty. A federal concept of spending that puts our entire nation into debt. Insatiable, greedy, reckless, partisan spending of most elected officials in our country. Hence, the consequence of increasing debt. The government behaves like a compulsive shopper with too many credit cards. Loaning money to countries that can't possibly pay it back, that can't even pay back the interest on the loan. Rather than finding ways to help these countries to become economically stable, we put the countries in debt to us and then we try to take over and use these countries as markets for our industries. The HUD scandals and the Savings and Loan Debacle are further examples.

20. *Enough Is Never Enough* Consumptive economics, insatiability, planned obsolescence and a need to feed greed all fuel cultural codependency. Happiness will come from outside of us. Spend. Buy. Own. Nutrition research in our country is focused on the development of food that when eaten will not give us a sense of fullness. You just get to keep on eating, but receive little nutritional value. The packaging may be more nutritious than some of the food itself. Our marketing and manufacturing networks require a nationwide addictiveness. Our greatest talent is our ability to sell *things* to each other.

21. *Chemical Dependency* Most of our drug problems are virtually ignored by focusing on smaller issues. Ignore alcohol; look at cocaine. Ignore nicotine; be concerned about marijuana. Waging a war of words on drugs or a war on users, putting people with a health problem in prison, focusing on symptoms rather than looking at the issues is how we are *"dealing with drugs."*

22. ***No-talk Rules*** Pretending our drug problem is about drugs. No discussion of what's happening to immigrants in our country; no discussion of what's happening to Native Americans; no real acceptance of why people in poverty areas form gangs or end up addicted to substances. There is no discussion about the lost war on poverty nor talk of crime addiction.

23. ***Double Messages*** We continue to give our children and ourselves double messages about addiction, wealth and respect for life. We tell our children "Just say no to drugs" as we use drugs. There exists a pretend separation of drugs and alcohol. Many double messages exist about sex, gambling, honesty, freedom, other countries and social responsibility.

24. ***Little Respect for Environment*** We are unable to look at consequences, to enforce safeguards against increasing pollution. We have corporations that won't put double layers of steel on the bottom of tankers because it's supposedly not needed. Now after an 11 million gallon oil spill into Prince William Sound, probably nothing has been done about the other tankers. (I can see running into something—even with a ship—but the state of Alaska, now that is a tough one not to notice!) Our nation ignores alcoholism and then has a public uproar about the possibility of alcoholism being the cause of the accident. We are outraged by the spill of the oil without any real awareness that the only worse place for the oil than in the sea around Prince William Sound would have been to burn the oil and put it in the atmosphere. Lip service is given to recycling, but no real funding, education or insistence is in place.

25. ***Punishment Rather Than Treatment*** Protect the offender system by incarcerating them and teaching them to be better offenders, or ignoring them if the offenders are parents. Punish people with mental illness by letting them live without homes; punish people that don't learn by failing them because they're not learning the way we teach.

26. ***Blame Posture*** A codependent culture is blame-crazy, lawsuit-crazy. Insurance companies own a great deal of our nation because insurance companies sell protection—protection against people who are ready to sue at a moment's notice. Many people can no longer function because of the cost of liability. Attorneys in large firms are forced to find billable hours to maintain the salaries and the investments of the firm.

27. ***Unavailable Health Care***   Health care for the rich. Health care is too expensive. Some of the providers become extremely wealthy and others suffer along. Health care relies on the insurance system, is selective in who it treats and will turn people down with needs. A codependent country is obsessed with health, where most of its members are dying of disease of lifestyle due to poor nutrition choices, limited physical activity and basic health care virtually unavailable or unknown by a large percentage of the population.
28. ***Prejudices***   Homophobia, agism, fatism, racism, sexism, exconism, classism and all other 'isms' against differently abled, special learning, crime and trauma victims, less privileged and vulnerable people.
29. ***Supporting Offenders***   This is an offender protective society. Rapists are seldom prosecuted, offending parents are protected, we enable offensive and oppressive leaders and groups in other countries in exchange for short term political benefits or tenuous alliance, for example Noriega.
30. ***Buy Friends, Purchase Loyalty***   Favors are granted and expected to be returned. This occurs in trade agreements, pouring money into countries without knowing where and how it is used, we payroll groups to support or ignore our covert operations. We feel betrayed when we financially support a country or leader and they won't enable our policies and aggressiveness.

In summary, our country is similar to an alcoholic family. We are defensive, ignore children, buy off spouses, lie, deny, blame and break promises. Leadership is chosen on the basis of wealth, TV image, script writers, false fronts, trading favors and power backing. To gain leadership a person must compromise too often, cannot be in recovery or honest about feelings and values. Potential leaders are not allowed to make waves or rock the boat even when it is sinking.

Each one of us is affected by codependency, either as individuals, in relationships, families and certainly in our culture. It permeates our existence on all levels. We cannot avoid it or ignore the effects. It takes so much energy to repress and deny how it affects each one of us. Rather than fight the term, codependency, let's celebrate having a name to represent this breakdown of integrity and use the term to assist us in defining and finding recovery, identity and wholeness.

Codependency is a painful and difficult subject. So, on the lighter side, sit back, relax and play with this quiz below.

Codependency Quiz
Multiple choice:
1. Codependency was first discovered in
    A. Children of alcoholics
    B. Spouses of alcoholics
    C. Helping professionals
2. Codependency was first written about in
    A. Nineteenth century poetry to dead virgins
    B. Country western music
    C. Greek mythology
3. Alcoholics are
    A. Married to codependents
    B. Have codependent children
    C. Are codependents
4. Codependents are usually
    A. Alone
    B. In a relationship they obsess
    C. Run in packs
5. Codependents seek
    A. Happiness and recovery
    B. Misery and pain
    C. Information
6. Codependents need
    A. Treatment
    B. Valium
    C. Continuing education credits
7. Codependents depend on
    A. Everyone
    B. No one
    C. Anyone
    D. Everyone depends on them
8. You know you're codependent if
    A. You're writing someone else's autobiography
    B. You're drowning and someone else's life passes before your eyes
    C. Your birth certificate has an expiration date
    D. You peel away who you are not and there's nothing left
    E. Your kids demand room service.
9. The best place to see a codependent is

A. Your neighbors
B. The mirror
C. Your spouse
10. Codependency is
   A. The fine art of never giving up
   B. The fine art of always giving up
   C. Not a fine art at all
11. Codependents who avoid relationships are called
   A. Anti-social
   B. Extraterrestrial
   C. Independent
12. Codependents
   A. Watch evangelists
   B. Send money to evangelists
   C. Become evangelists

Notes On Treatment and Recovery

The key issues are a lack of identity and self-esteem, control issues and denial. There are many struggles with treating these issues.

The primary problems in the treatment of codependency are:

1. It's easier to see in others than ourselves. We become spectators, focusing on what is outside of us rather than what is within.

2. It's usually treated by untreated codependents. The helping profession is a magnet for codependents. We can work with others to ignore our own needs, just as the alcoholic spouse can focus on the alcoholic to avoid their own pain and emptiness. Professionals can deal with others' pain and vicariously experience the healing but often neglect our own pain. We become enablers, give too much, model poor boundaries, and frequently burn out.

3. The focus on relationships of codependents is codependency. Therapists often have codependents talk about, look at, and work very hard on their relationships. Therapists themselves get caught in the relationship problems and try to resolve these issues, rather than seeing that the relationship problems are really symptoms, and codependency is primarily the absence of relationship with self, a lack of identity and boundary.

4. We confront the kindness and caring, so instead of treating codependency, we may be killing spirituality. Confronting kindness and caring has become a fad in our culture. When someone

does something for someone else, picks someone up, bring cookies to the meeting, they get confronted about being codependent. If we could cure all codependents of their kindness and caring, who would be left to do it or teach it? Codependency isn't about kindness and caring. It just happens that a lot of people who are codependent also do many of the kind and caring things in our culture. John Powell once said that spirituality is self-forgetfulness. You cannot have what you don't give away. Both of these sound like codependent postures. We come close to spirituality in that it seems like they're being self-forgetful, but we cannot forget ourselves until we know ourselves. In achieving spirituality, we are trying to forget ourselves before we know ourselves, before we've remembered ourselves. Codependents are trying to give of themselves before they truly have themselves. We can only truly give of what we have and out of what we know.

5. We are given education and information but not therapy. This came about with the discovery of codependency in the alcoholic family. We discovered that the spouse had a lot of the earmarks of the disease. We knew this was a family disease, so we decided to treat the spouse. The addict was still given the thirty days, six weeks, six months or two years of treatment, whereas the spouse was given a lecture series for a few evenings over a period of a few months or a few days. They were given information rather than therapy. Lip service was paid to the family disease concept.

6. Codependency is thought to be about alcoholism, thus it is a limitation of terms. Due to its name, it's intrinsically related to dependency issues. The name affects how people receive the concept and how they see it. Codependency is the first word we've had to describe what happens to children in dysfunctional families who have their dependency needs denied. People outside of the addiction field have a hard time adopting or using the term. There have been efforts to change the concept to "affected family syndrome," but I believe the term "codependency" is what we have and we might as well stick with it. It does describe a key aspect of the issue. Most of us have a problem with healthy dependency or interdependency.

7. Codependency itself is a nebulous term, possibly applying to nebulous people, people without identity. The lack of clarity and constantly defining it through symptoms makes it more difficult to treat.

8. Codependency is a childhood disease that gets acted out in adolescence and not treated until adulthood, if at all. I believe that

childhood is the place that we need to start looking at codependency issues. It's essentially an absence of childhood. Codependents are people who missed basic developmental processes—nurturing, trust, autonomy, industry, integrity, identity—things that enable us to move into adulthood. Most of the acting out begins in adolescence or before. It begins with drugs, relationships, underachieving, boredom, anxiety, rituals, the stress of trying to be what people want the adolescent to be, trying to be too mature and over reactive to others. It's interesting to me that we have adolescent drug treatment and adult drug and codependency treatment, but adolescent codependency treatment is nearly nonexistent. This may be the primary treatment need for young people. We need to recognize and start dealing more with children in dysfunctional families and provide real treatment for each member of the family. Our adolescents need identity formation and treatment can provide it.

9. Codependents tend to run in packs and enable each other. We give too much advice that is often conflicting. Sometimes we tell people what to do rather than support and listen.

10. Codependency is supported by a codependent culture. The culture teaches us sex role rigidity. It teaches women how to take care of everybody, give up their own needs. It teaches men how to be stoic, unemotional, protective and always adequate. Culture dictates the denial of our vulnerability and provides messages that support our addictiveness and insatiability.

11. Codependency is different for different people. It's hard to describe as a syndrome. Anything you say about a group of codependents, there will be some members of the group doing the exact opposite or not involving themselves in the issue at all. For example, all codependents have relationship problems. This isn't true, because some of us totally avoid relationships because they lose too much of themselves in a relationship. All codependents give too much. This isn't true because many can only take.

12. Codependency is easily overlooked, and dealing with it may mean other things are overlooked. The fact that one is codependent doesn't mean that they aren't something else as well. A person can be manic depressive, anxiety-ridden, phobic as well as codependent. The other issues may be by-products of the codependency or they may not be. It can exist with other mental health issues.

13. Codependency is always viewed through our own background. Our own approaches and framework become limitations

in how we treat it, what we write about it and how we view it. Physicians will focus on the stress-related illness; a person with a developmental orientation will look at developmental issues and ignore the relationship problems. A marriage counselor might not deal with the childhood issues at all. A minister will focus on the spiritual bankruptcy.

14. Codependents are problem oriented. We try to fix the codependent by fixing the problems, but the therapist's focus on fixing problems is the therapist's problem orientation, codependency, and need to fix. We will create problems faster than anyone can solve them. Some problems we have to let solve themselves; some problems we need to let remain problems. Some problems we can deal with, but life isn't a problem to be solved. We have to avoid the problem lists as we start out each day and begin to see the miracle of living.

15. There is no real recovery from codependency, no fix. The recovery process involves a tremendous risk and work. It involves grieving and pain. Since problems become the homeostasis of our lives, recovery is an ongoing process. Recovery involves taking risks, learning to suffer and embracing the pain as well as learning joy. There isn't a fix. It is a handicap but we can achieve a fulfilled, wonderful, happy life when we commit to a lifelong process of change and support. Recovery is a journey with no destination.

16. We have spiritual recovery but no sexual recovery. Addiction and codependency are seen as a process of spiritual bankruptcy. Our spirituality is the core of our being and we find it in recovery, but we also need sexual recovery. Sexuality is the core of our identity; it's our relationship with ourselves as men and women. Codependency and addiction are processes and symptoms of sexual bankruptcy as well. It is the *absence* of a healthy relationship with ourselves as men and women. We have very little sexual recovery available, unless we have identified specific sexual abuse or addiction.

17. Codependency is different for men and women, thus the treatment process and what we are taught must also be different. Some of the differences between men and women are exaggerated since codependency is more about what happens to children in dysfunctional families and men and women come from the same families. Primarily, it seems that women's codependency is power through powerlessness; men's is powerlessness through power.

What we face and work on in recovery has to be dealt with somewhat differently.

18. Recovery involves looking at the hurt of childhood, it is a painful process. Recovery involves learning to grieve, suffer, feel the fears and go through the pain of childhood. This makes it rather unappealing. The pain and fears are only part of the recovery process. Recovery has to do with knowing oneself and establishing identity.

19. There is an excess focus on childness and not enough on adulthood. The separation of adult and child is a dissociation, a split off of self. We don't have a child within, a precious child, an inner child. We don't even have a brat. We are children. Real recovery involves integration of childness and adulthood, and accepting that we are both. In becoming an adult we don't give up our childness to gain adulthood. Separating our child gives us insight and acceptance of the child aspect of self but recovering is the *integration* of the two.

20. The focus on shame as a bad feeling can make us ashamed of having shame; we miss its healthier aspects, shame as vulnerability, guardianship and spirituality.

21. Oversimplification which leads to denial. A family of four children, we are taught, has four roles—the hero, mascot, lost child and scapegoat. If we accept that we are the hero, we might miss that we were lost for a period of time, that we were the surrogate spouse of a parent, that we were the little parent to the other children, that we got enmeshed with Dad, became an extension of him and lived out his self-destructive lifestyle. We might miss that we had to father our own father, that we were the mediator, caretaker, or other roles in the family. So much of systems and addiction theory is oversimplified that it misses the dynamics of the changing roles and issues. Families grow and change; so do we as children.

22. There is a narrow view of violence and abuse. This causes us to miss the fact that we are victims of physical, sexual, emotional or spiritual violence. We miss that all abuse is sexual abuse because it breaks down our relationship with self as men and women. All abuse is spiritual abuse because it keeps us from becoming the person we were meant to be by our creator. Abuse affects our ability to relate, to notice, appreciate and have a sense of gratitude for creation. We miss that the absence of information may be sexual abuse, relocations physical abuse, and so on. We don't understand the continuum of violence.

A More Positive Note

Finally we have a name for a disorder that has plagued so many people for so long—codependence. It is positive that it was spotted in the addiction field, because the one thing the addiction field has given to mental health is a very powerful, effective and inexpensive recovery program as an ongoing process. We do get better with information and education. Codependents fooled the people that were treating the addicts and just giving the codependents information, because we took the information and made significant changes in our lives. It seems that we would often rather get information than recovery. There's a cartoon that's been passed around for some time. It shows a sign that says, "Heaven" with an arrow pointing to the left. There's another sign that says, "Lecture on heaven," with an arrow pointing to the right. All the codependents are lined up for the lecture on heaven.

Codependency has been responsible for much of the information explosion in the mental health field. We now have physicians, psychiatrists, psychologists, social workers and therapists giving families and individuals tapes, recommending books, readings and doing a lot of teaching. They now support and put on workshops and programs.

Codependency may be different for men and women, but, the bottom line is the same. Both men and women need to establish identity, learn to trust and depend on others and love ourselves.

Though recovery involves suffering, grieving, fears and pain, most of the recovery process is joyful. It's a process of self-discovery, of becoming childlike and integrating that into adulthood. It's like finding a soul mate, a best friend and falling in love. In our recovery we discover the selflessness, self-forgetfulness and true spirituality. We begin to establish our sexual identity by creating a relationship with ourselves as men and women.

7

My Mother, My Father, Myself
Parenting and Dependency

"Play is the work of children, we are all children.

"We can appreciate our children when we appreciate our childness."

Healthy parenting enables the child to flow through the developmental stages necessary to be "whole." Children learn to depend on parents who are available, nurturing, and affirming. Children need to learn from parents who have integrity and know how to take care of themselves. Children in our culture are often viewed as extensions of parents, a method to give meaning to one's life, a reflection of the parent, a way to achieve immortality. Parents use children as a patch to repair broken self-esteem or to fill the emptiness of their lives. In our culture families revolve around children; we worship youth. At the same time, we have a culture that seems to fear and hate children. Families become obsessed with children's activities, moods, whims and accomplishments, but children are not really respected. Children become the object of parental rages, resentments, frustrations, jealousies and needs. Children are used to meet affectional needs, companionship and nurturing needs of parents. Children are used to fill in for empty marriages, a fill up for empty lives, a salve for loneliness. Children are "taken from" under the guise of being "given to." They are used to raise other children, to give the family pride in community, and sometimes they are used as a bridge between the parent and the world.

Parenting is seen as a process of providing discipline, control and limits to children. These limits are often enforced by adults who have few limits themselves. Adults who practice Spartan discipline in their lives often give children unrealistic expectations, unrealistic limits. Adults who are rigid and over controlled attempt to confer the same on their children.

One becomes a good parent in our culture if one can control a child well into their adulthood. If a child is good they react with silent obedience, become noiseless, over-functioning automatons capable of reacting to parents' expectations and able to be successful in school and sports, but not so successful that adult inadequacies are exposed.

Children can be the relief and distraction for an empty marital relationship. Children exist to meet parents' needs and live up to parents' expectations in reversal of role. Children's needs and expectations are often ignored or so focused on that the child is set up to be self-centered and narcissistic until they, too, have a child to focus on.

Narcissm

Children may become narcissistic when a parent focuses all their love, attention, and devotion on the child. The child can do no wrong. The child, in turn, focuses on self. Once the child becomes a parent, this narcissistic parent can only love their child as they see a reflection of themselves in the child. It is a false sense of themselves reflected that they want to love. The appearance of love is there, but the child has to be an extension of the narcissistic parent and will be set up to continue the narcissistic self-absorption. The child is only loveable as long as they reflect the parent.

Some parents will ignore any deviancy, aberration or vulnerability in the child. The child can do no wrong. Others will shut off the love when the child no longer seems a reflection of them, when the child shows signs of being a *real* and separate person and they get rejected. A person may be focused on self and still a lack identity and boundary sense, but the self-fullness doesn't look like codependency in the usual sense; it doesn't show up in a relationship form since the narcissistic person doesn't seem to get enmeshed with others, but is actually enmeshed and engrossed in self. It is self addiction.

The narcissistic person will need a partner in the relationship that will focus totally on them as a continuation of the unconditional and overwhelming parental love. This partner will usually have such low self-esteem that they become grateful just to be in the relationship with the narcissist. Their life has meaning through the mutual love they share for the narcissist. This relationship may last a long time, until children arrive. Then one partner may focus on the children, again to fill the emptiness. The narcissistic partner will either project self-love into the image of self they see in their children or the children will have to learn that everybody's life revolves around the narcissistic parent. Eventually, the children will act out and strain this tenuous bond, maybe exploding the family apart. Of course, it will be about some character defect in the acting out children or the influence of peers, school, or whatever—rather than the parenting.

An alternative relationship for the narcissist will be another narcissist. There is an attraction in someone else attracted to themselves. Two people, both in the syndrome, would have to be pretty far removed from reality, unable to grasp the possibility of making a mistake or the possibility of someone not loving them, for the relationship to work out. Usually, a relationship like this lasts only a short time and then a bitter fight over property ensues, including the children as property.

Another relationship for the narcissist is someone who is the opposite of the parent who gave the smothering love—or is like the non-loving parent. (Usually one parent smothers with love while the other is absent.) This relationship becomes emotionally and often physically abusive. Oddly enough, the narcissist may stay in a relationship like this for decades, almost as a cure or a punishment for the narcissism, although it really only forces a deeper internal focus of suffering that one can wallow in for years. If I can't find someone who loves me as I deserve, if I can't find 100% attention and devotion, I will find someone who will neglect or abuse me, and then I can whine and lick my wounds and know it's all their fault and have children who I will love to death, or who will love me as I deserve.

Narcissus and Echo

In the story of Narcissus and Echo, it definitely seems that Echo is a codependent—Echo, who is the compulsive talker; Echo, who falls in love with someone who can't love; Echo, who loses the ability to initiate conversation and pines away in misery, *seems* like the perfect codependent. Does our concept of codependency also apply to Narcissus, who is driven crazy by Echo, who has so little integrity and boundary sense that he can love no one, but falls in love with an image of himself in the pool and dies for this love? Is codependency about both? Do they both reflect the possibilities of the adult symptoms that flow from inappropriate parenting? Are they both perhaps examples of flawed identity and boundary sense?

Impact of Parenting

The symptoms of a wounded child will vary with the kind of dysfunctional parenting at certain ages of childhood. Early trauma, inappropriate bonding, no bonding in infancy, inability to trust because of parental dishonesty, parental abandonment or divorce, at three or at twelve—all have an impact. The impact varies.

It's difficult to say that because this has happened your relationships will be like this. In systems theory all pieces are interwoven and affected by other pieces. There are tendencies and some traumas are impacting enough to produce predicted results. There are certain periods in our lives that require certain developmental gains. If these are not met, there will be specific problems. Generally, describing systems is like describing the wind. We know what it can and will do, but its impact depends on how hard it's blowing, how long it blows and what it is blowing through, as well as the direction, consistency and predictability. The same wind in the desert has a different impact, a different description and sounds different than the wind in a city, a forest, the ocean. A hurricane is different than a tornado and a breeze in winter is different than in summer.

A parenting system will also produce different effects depending on varying factors and settings. I've worked with clients who have had similar experiences around abuse issues, both sexually molested by a close family member at an early age. The first client had voices that regularly appeared in her head, couldn't even fathom being close to a friend or in a relationship with a man, was very suicidal, dissociative, self-destructive, felt hopeless and damaged. The second client had difficulty maintaining sexuality and closeness together and suffered from sleeplessness with occasional startle responses at night. Both suffered from eating disorders, although the first client was chronically obese while the second slightly overweight and less obsessed with the problem. Both clients were able to identify the incest, although the memory loss was greater in the first, which is one of the factors why it so severely impacted her life. The first client believed that if she talked about it, she would die; she was threatened as a child. The second felt some impending doom when talking about it, but not the belief that it was a life or death problem.

I believe the key factor in the differences between these two clients, although other differences were present, was very simply that the second client had talked about it before as a child. She had confidants while growing up and the relationship with these confidants made her more resilient to the abuse itself. The first client had hidden everything, had stored all the secrets, all the realities away from others and even her own perceptions. The severity of the reaction of abusive parenting in controlling our lives depends on the:

- severity of the abuse,
- age it happens — generally, the earlier the age the more impact
- ability and opportunity to debrief, discuss and share it with people in our lives,
- frequency of and what we believe about the abuse,
- information we were told about it,
- reaction people give us and
- what we learned about the secret.

The ability to find confidants is a key variable in the recovery of abuse. Confidants can be friends, neighbors, parents, siblings or peripheral relatives. Although the stored pain makes it difficult to get close enough to talk about it with siblings, they can also be confidants. Other possible confidants can be counselors, teachers, ministers, coaches, and occasionally, but rarely a parent, the non-abusing parent. It often seems as though the parent is a confidant, but if we look closely we will discover that, in most cases, we were the parent's confidant. Our sharing with them had more to do with their need than with ours. If they were really our confidants, they would have done something about what was happening. They would have been more available. What we shared when and how we shared was designed to take care of them. They would have been protecting us from the abuse if it was the other way around. If the first sharing was soon after the abuse and prompted action, then they were acting as parents. Often we didn't even share the events in order to protect them. Collusive parents have blinders on, act naive, helpless, don't know what to do about it, or they're in on it. They are collusive with the abuse — active or passive. We keep the secret so they don't have to feel pain and guilt. This is the role reversal of the abused child.

Much of therapy is finding a confidant relationship, someone to share the details of our reality with, to listen to us, affirm us, help us know that we're not crazy, someone to be there for us. When children are needy, hurting and vulnerable, they are frequently abandoned, neglected and abused by the adults in their lives. They learned to despise their vulnerability. Some parents will keep slapping a child who cries until they stop crying or ignore or yell at a child to create a harder, tougher, even seemingly more mature child. Then this parent, especially one who is afraid of the child's dependency needs and doesn't really want to be a parent, can depend on the child more than the child depends on the parent.

Vulnerability

Our children represent the vulnerability that we fear and despise. When we have children, this inability to be vulnerable, this disdain and fear of our vulnerability gets projected onto our children. We do the same with other vulnerable people in our lives, whether they be handicapped, mentally ill, disfigured, physically ill, lost, homeless, impoverished, addicted, or grieving. We get uncomfortable and don't know how to respond, so we want to avoid them. This fear and disdain for vulnerability kills chances for intimacy. The disdain of vulnerability affects our environment. We practice a disdain for the vulnerability of our planet. We can't parent, we've lost the ability to be healthy guardians of children, of people, and our planet. We cannot give what we haven't received. Parenting when we haven't had parenting is like writing checks out of an empty account. We cannot parent ourselves either. When we feel vulnerable, hurting, lost, and needy, we use food, excitement, spending, drugs, we close down, get busy, get tough, get going. But we don't affirm, nurture and cherish our vulnerability.

Happy Holidays?

Our lost vulnerability is lost intimacy with self as well as with others. We reenact the childhood experience of adult abandonment. The abandonment of the vulnerable child we were, by the adults around us, is recreated by the abandonment of our vulnerable childness by the adult that we are. Working with adult children of alcoholics, I noticed that a great many despise, don't enjoy and even fear holiday seasons. Anxiety, frustration and tension increase as holidays approach. Depression for some seems to be a part of the season. Compulsive behavior escalates, avoidance runs rampant, and yet we do pretty much the same things in the same places each holiday.

Children generally feel expectations, excitement, and hopeful about the holidays. In an alcoholic family, however, this is frequently a time of serious acting out by parents with alcohol and conflict. The child's expectations aren't met, excitement turns to fear, hopefulness is crushed. Many of us retain the anxiety regarding the holiday season. There is adult abandonment of what the child needed. Though not necessarily intentional, the child is hurt and abandoned.

This isn't restricted to alcoholic families; it's just more overt and frequent. For most of us, there's still a wanting, a hope, an expectation for the holidays that can get mixed up with the old fear, anxiety and pain. We actually tend to recreate our childhood experiences emotionally. We even reenact the abandonment of our child needs for the wonder and fun, giving, receiving, loving and excitement. As adults we tell ourselves to not get involved, don't expect anything, it's too crowded, too busy, it's too commercial. We act out our addictions, we go where we were miserable, we practice many of the rituals we can't stand, we spend our time with people who can't affirm us, that make us feel crazy and act out. We recreate the holidays of our childhood. What if we really took the wisdom, experiences, guardianship, nurturing, affirming, and ability to make choices of adulthood and integrated it with the magic, the sparkle, the curiosity, the excitement, and the expectations of childness? What if, as adults, we affirmed our hope and needs, we protected our vulnerability, we planned, based on our experience and strength? What if we arranged the season so we could enjoy and be enjoyed, being with people who help us, who affirm us and care about us, enjoying the lights, music, and giving of the season?

The answer lies in grieving the loss of past expectations and dreams, accepting the reality of the abandonment of the needs, and plan future holiday seasons based on an awareness and acceptance of childness and vulnerability, the need to be with people and in places that support childlike qualities, childness, not childishness, but also act responsibly as adults. Of course, if we could do this during the holidays, there's really no reason we can't do it each day of the year. Integrating the qualities of adulthood and childness, not abandoning ourselves when vulnerable, we can provide enjoyable, safe, challenging places and people to be around. This is self-parenting, a decision to not reenact the abandonment of the child we were.

Getting Parenting

To be able to parent ourselves, the child we are, we must first let others parent us, the adult that we are. Those of us who did not find healthy parenting as children have dependency problems. Our child dependency needs were denied. Hence, chemical dependency, food dependency, gambling dependency, work, excitement, control, sex dependency and codependency. The human child is the most dependent creature on earth for the longest period of time. Children's dependency needs are insatiable, but it's not that a child needs so much at a given time, they need the emotional and physical availability of parents in an ongoing way. In the denial of dependency needs we develop stress, addictions, anxieties, and fears. Our addictions are insatiable because child dependency needs are insatiable. The addiction is trying to fill the emptiness with something other than what the emptiness is about. It's not a food or alcohol emptiness. It's a people emptiness. We become codependent, unable to depend on others or self in healthy ways. We may try to find someone else to fill the emptiness. In this, we get close to what the emptiness is about, but we can't fill it with others. It must be filled with self. We need to find the parenting that will help us find ourselves. *Parenting is the source of our lost identity, trust, boundaries, knowledge, awareness and safety. Parenting can teach us healthy bonding.*

Dependency Needs

Many of us have become codependent or independent and have never found what we need. People depend on us, but we don't receive what we need from others. We keep trying to give, and we burn out very quickly. We run out of gas because we can't refuel. We give more than we have. In searching for ways to meet our dependency needs, we try to find the fathering and mothering that we didn't get. The needs we get in touch with are our child dependency needs, which are, again, insatiable. We want someone to *be* our mother and father, and we can drive them away with our neediness. We ask for too much. We expect too much. We attach like parasite, sucking people dry. It's like the marsupial who wants to bounce around in someone's pouch forever, dragging them down, giving their pouch stretch marks. Someone notices us and we give up our feigned independence and can't seem to get enough from them. We keep needing more than they want to give. This drives them away. They chuck us out of their pouch at the first intersection. The child needs the parent's availability, noticing and listening in an ongoing way. The parent must be there. In our attempt to meet these child dependency needs, we demand the same thing. The problem is, no one can possibly be on call and always available. People have a great difficulty making that kind of commitment to their own children. They're not very likely to make it to us in our dependency needs. This makes us more ashamed of our neediness, our dependency, which sets us up to pretend independence, not need people, not being vulnerable and never asking for anything. It also sets us up for an attempt to fill the emptiness and erase the fear with addiction or codependent relationships. We will never find the parents we wanted or needed as children and will never have people available to us in an ongoing way, on call. These child dependency needs are lost and must be grieved. One must feel and accept this loss. We cannot go back to being children. We cannot find the love and support and nourishment of childhood. We cannot find our parents, but we can find parenting.

Getting Needs Met

Once we have entered the grieving process of our child dependency needs we can begin to discover our adult dependency needs. Adult dependency needs are different than child dependency needs. The difference is that child needs are insatiable. Nothing is ever enough. In our adult dependency needs we can let what is given be enough. If someone comes up to me after a lecture or workshop and says, "Thank you. Good information," and gives me a pat on the back, I don't follow them to their car and say, "What's for dinner and where do we live?" If I get advice, noticed or affirmed, I don't ask them to come home and live with me and teach me and care for me. I say, "Thank you." I let in the affirmation, noticing, advice and I let it be enough. This way we can get parenting without driving people away.

As adults, it's important that we not set people up to be parents or gurus, that we don't find fathers or mothers, but we find parenting, fathering, mothering, guiding, mentoring and teaching. If you meet the Buddha on the road, turn the other way. There are no Buddhas or gurus. There are many of us struggling in recovery, trying to find ourselves and intimacy. Some of us do workshops and teach others as we go along, and some of us sell tires and teach others. Some of us are too unsettled, afraid or feel it's too early to teach others. Eventually, the teaching and parenting of each other is another place we find our own recovery and each other.

People often attempt to make their therapist or a twelve step program sponsor their parent. They find someone at a meeting and latch onto them to be a parent. This transference of our child dependency needs on another person sets us up because we set them up. We put them on a pedestal. Whenever we put others on a pedestal, there's a tendency for them to fall off of it. Usually, they fall right on top of us, crushing us in their descent. (This transference in a healthy client relationship is normal and will be dealt with as part of the therapeutic process.)

When we find these new parents, we can experience the same rejection, the same not being noticed, remembered or cared about, the same let downs as when we were children with parents who couldn't be there for us. We may feel that way even when it's not happening because we do the transference of our child anger, our fears, and sense of disappointment. We often pick people who will parent us the way we've been parented, expecting it to be different. We can set it up so it can't be different, or we demand so much that they can't possibly meet these needs. We fall back again into being a disappointed child, lost and unable to meet the needs that we have. We feel ashamed of having needs. We try to meet them inappropriately, indirectly in sneaky ways, or pretending they aren't there.

It is important to parent and teach, but it's also important to learn and receive. Knowing things and running around and letting others know we know isn't recovery. It's just knowing and telling. When combined with recovery, combined with knowing ourselves, it's a spiritual journey. In the absence of knowing self and recovery, it's latent and often arrogant codependency, even when it sounds like recovery.

Receiving can be more difficult than giving. Accepting information is more difficult than sharing information. I've sat in many groups where people would be very free to give, nurture, offer advice, but when asked to ask for something, to receive from others, when asked to be vulnerable and need others, they freeze up. The hardest thing for some of us in the recovery process is to ask for what we need, to let others give it to us. Our shame tells us we can't depend on others. Our experience tells us we'll be disappointed. We know that we can't be vulnerable because in our vulnerability we've been hurt in the past. This is sometimes the key issue in recovery—allowing ourselves to be vulnerable, to ask and receive and when we receive, to let it be enough.

Threatened Relationships

Adult dependency needs can find many resources—friends, sponsors, groups, twelve step programs, therapists, those in recovery, as well as family and spouse. Even our spouse or primary relationship can give us parenting. They can give us the nurturing, but it's important not to set up our spouses to replace our parents, not to project the fathering or mothering needs on that person. We cannot look to one person to meet all of our needs. The more sources we have for support, the easier it becomes for someone to give us support. Our relationships often become possessive or jealous, so if they are to be the only source of our lives, ownership issues begin. From their emptiness and dependency, they may try to fill themselves with us, they may act out an addictive need to control. If we look elsewhere for our needs, they get threatened and on the edge of losing their monopoly over us, they may become abusive, punishing, distant, withdrawn and depressed. They may leave. As painful as it may be to see them leave, that pain tapers off and has an end. If they stay and we continue to be controlled by their need for our undivided attention, if we keep trying to fill their insatiable child dependency needs, the loss of ourselves and our pain goes on and on without end.

To Leave or Not to Leave

We don't recover from codependency by leaving the relationship, but hanging on too tight to some relationships can keep us from recovery. Recovery at best is extremely difficult, but it's important not to make decisions about relationships too early. Unless we're being actively abused, it's better to wait until we have more ego strength, more clarity of insight, more awareness of self and support in our choices.

Our recovery isn't entirely based on doing our own thing. It's not a cloak for narcissistic stardom. Many times we use our recovery to avoid compromise, being responsible or reasonable. With the little modeling some of us have had, it's very important to go slow. It's more important to not be abused, but we must make sure that we are being abused before dealing with being abused. Those of us who have been abused in childhood may feel abused even when we are doing the abusing, even when no one is abusing. The feelings of victimization may get projected out in our offensive behavior. They can also get attached to behavior in others that isn't abusive, behavior that we don't like or want to control, or behavior that happens to push a button or flip a switch in us that brings us back to old childhood issues.

In our networking, groups, and therapy we need to sort out if we are being used or abused or if we are doing it. This takes time because people around us tend to get our perspective only. As codependents we do run in packs and enable each other. If there is a pattern in our relationship, and we always end up getting used in similar ways or feeling the same way, it's very possible that it's us and not others. This pattern will often emerge in groups, social relationships, at work or in our recreation. It is a reenactment of the childhood experience or a reaction to it. This includes not letting what is given be enough, always having our own way, sabotaging other people's leadership, not able to be a member of a team, always feeling lost, let down, isolated, unnoticed, getting angry when there are delays or stalls, overreacting to indecisiveness in others and overreacting to the covert issues or feelings in the group. Under the guise of recovery, we codependent victims learn how to be offenders. In our recovery, we try to get even, we try to get rid of our feelings at other people and we become self-centered, selfish, and aggressive rather than assertive. We withdraw, punish, rage and manipulate as we storm through the feelings of what happened to us in childhood. We project those feelings around us at people who weren't involved, who do care. I have often thought that one of the missing elements of recovery was support for people whose spouses or significant others are in the recovery process. The need is present because of the projecting that can go on in recovery, particularly around abuse issues. Some of the spouses of my clients have taught me about love in their patience and acceptance of the anger, pain, mood swings and sexual or physical withdrawal.

Offending is Offensive

Often offender behavior was present before we began recovery, but in recovery we have a tendency to focus on the victim and survivor issues rather than how we have hurt others. These are tougher questions to ask, and they are tougher answers to give. The offender roles that we've adopted involve more shame. Many of us who have been hurt have hurt others. It may not have been in a primary offender role, but we certainly can turn our victimization into the destructiveness of other people's egos and the violation of their boundaries.

Parenting

In receiving parenting, it's important to acknowledge that it *is* parenting, that it is mothering or fathering. It's important to let it be enough and to ask for what we need. Codependents have the mistaken belief that if they have to ask, it doesn't count if it's given. This limits our relationship choices to psychics and mind readers. Most of us need mothering and fathering. Few of us received it appropriately or adequately in childhood. Finding this parenting is one of the processes of recovery. In our groups we are told to parent ourselves, but I don't think that works any better than when we try to parent our kids. You can't give what you've never received, to self or others. First we need the parenting. We must let others parent the adult that we are, and then we can parent the child we are. We can parent our childness, other children and other adults. Parenting is the guiding, noticing, labeling and affirming of child experiences, consequences and feelings. Parenting is the safety net for the high wire journey through childhood.

In giving parenting to our childness we need to accept that we are the only ones that will never leave us. We are the only ones who can give us all that the childness needs. If we spread our parenting needs around, if we find it in several differences places, find mothering and fathering, we can be available to nurture the childness in us, to give our childness what we need.

We can internalize and embrace the hugs, noticing, affirmation, teaching, modeling and caring from others. We can allow what we give to be enough when we let what others give be enough.

Same Sex—Other Sex Parenting

To love others, we must love ourselves. Love thy neighbor *as* thyself. The love of a neighbor is predicated on one's ability to love oneself. Love of self, not self-absorbed, self-centeredness, but a respectful willing and doing the good of self. The act of caring for self is part of loving myself. If we are to find self intimacy, we must love ourselves as men or women, as the gendered creatures that we are. To have a healthy relationship with self, we must embrace and love the gender that we are. This is our sexuality. Healthy sexuality is to love oneself as a man or a woman, at which point we have the potential to love men and women.

Other sex parenting is important in developing healthy sexuality, learning to feel good about ourselves as men and women, care about ourselves and to feel safe and respectful around men or women. We find nurturing, respect, safety, comfort with self and others in this relationship with the opposite sex parent.

Same sex parenting is critical to our relationship with ourselves as men and women. My love of self as a man is an outgrowth of having been loved by men. It is the result of healthy fathering. I learn my male identity from fathering. Women receive the ability to love themselves as women, the core of their identity as women, from mothering. If I don't receive healthy fathering, it affects my ability to have a relationship with self and from this relationship with self all other relationships flow.

When many of us leave families in which people were not dependable, we have an emptiness of self. We look for a member of the other sex to take care of that emptiness. I want to find a woman to help me love myself as a man. I want a woman to fix the emptiness, to give me a reason for living. Relationships *are* a priority for men—but we are taught that it will come to us if we work hard, are successful and good providers. In our culture, it is work and economic success that gives men value and attractiveness. A man can work in a garage and date, but to own the garage is to be an eligible bachelor. To own all three garages in town is to be one of the more eligible bachelors in town. By the time we own all three garages, we have probably worked so much on the garages that we've become work-addicted and unavailable for relationship. The relationship itself isn't developed. Or maybe we own all the garages in town and finally retire and find that those who we wanted to have intimacy with, that we wanted a relationship with, are long gone, because of neglect.

Intimacy

I believe men *do* desire, seek and plan for intimacy. We just are not sure what intimacy is. We are unsure of how to get it. In our search for intimacy we do things that keep us from getting it, that prevent us from finding it. Men have a few strikes against us when it comes to finding intimacy. We have been socialized to believe we get it through work and money. The most attractive men in our culture are attractive because of wealth, power and machismo. As men we are not allowed the vulnerability that is required for real intimacy. Vulnerability involves sensitivity, emotional openness and fluency. About the time people start thinking of intimacy, relationships or the other sex, men learn they are supposed to be hard, tough, macho, unfeeling and invulnerable. Our heros are passive, stoic, violent and distant.

Men are taught intimacy is sex. This gets reinforced in those early years of puberty, post-puberty, high school and early adulthood. In the hallway of a typical high school, a male student might be saying, "Hey, I met three girls last week and got laid by all of them," and all the guys will respond with oohs and aahs and ask for his autograph; he becomes the school stud, possibly also the school liar, but who cares? At the other end of the hall, if a female student says the same thing, "I met three guys last week and got laid by all of them," she's avoided, no one asks for her autograph, except maybe some of the guys, and she becomes the school slut.

If the next day at the end of the hall, some guy says, "Hey, I met this girl last week and we walked around town the entire weekend and just held hands," the guys say, "Oh, what a wimp. What's the matter with you? Couldn't you get any?" A girl at the other end of the hall that day, is saying the same thing, "I met this guy last weekend and we walked around town the whole weekend and just held hands," the girls will say ooh and wow and ask for her autograph. It becomes the romance of the year in the yearbook. Men get reinforced to sexualize their affectional needs. Women are reinforced to turn their sexual needs into affectional needs. Women are shamed for having sexual feelings, sexual needs, sexual thoughts, whereas men are shamed if they need affection, nurturing and if they don't find sex.

Men need to learn to let closeness be closeness, to let affection be affection without it becoming sexual. Women sometimes need to be reminded that when closeness or affection becomes sexual, that doesn't take away from the closeness or the affection.

Since men are born of women (a fact I noticed after 12 years of research), we have a survival bond to Mom. This bond is important, but as males get a little older they gradually react more assertively, sometimes angrily toward mom to break this bond. This makes them available to bond with dad and establish male identity. Men get angry at Mom, break the bond, but if there is no father to identify or bond with, they get stuck being angry at women and have no male identity. This seems to happen with great frequency—*no one I know, of course!*

Women who have been abused, put down, neglected or so overindulged by parents tend to thrive on *the* challenge. They are set up to be in a relationships with men who lack healthy identity.

Women who have been in the surrogate spouse role, having to take care of Dad as Daddy's little girl—especially if he has an anger toward women—will often find men who are disdainful, passive aggressive, unaffectionate and invulnerable. They may find a man to focus their anger on or to punish and control. This is a projection of the anger at Dad.

Even though men feel anger toward women, we will seek a woman to make us happy. We do not understand the covert anger within us. Men cannot find a woman to make them happy because we are going to the wrong store for what we need. Men need male identity, we need to love ourselves as men. Our place of learning this is through fathering. A man who lacks fathering seeks to find that fathering in his relationships with women. We seek a woman who will help us feel good about ourselves as men and we are destined to churn through relationship after relationship without finding what's we're looking for. We will be disappointed in the relationships we have until we get what we need to heal the relationship with self.

Fathering

Active, available, emotional, sensitive fathering has been a rare commodity in families in the past, especially to males. Fathers have had a tremendous fear that their sons will become sissies if they are gentle with them or if they hug or hold them close. Men are so homophobic that they tend to be too hard, too aggressive or too passive with their male children. Fathers get competitive and want to toughen up their sons. Fathers who haven't learned sensitivity, who are unavailable in their marriages model poor intimacy, invulnerability and the absence of feelings. Fathers without fathers can't father.

In recovery we must find fathering—not a father. We must find it in several places and to let what's given be enough. Find male mentors, teachers, sponsors, friends, therapists, men that we can chat and be with and befriend, men with whom we can share our recovery and practice rituals. Men have traditionally done a much better job of networking in the areas of sports and business, but women do much better networking in recovery, in family, in friendship. One of the most difficult things I ever did in my own recovery was to let a man hold me. It was in a men's group where I was paying $35 per session with no insurance. The absence of male nurturing in my life became apparent (no pun intended!). The group suggested I get some fathering. I said, "Sure, I'll work on that." In group talk this usually means they will let you off the hook but this group didn't. They wanted me to sit on a man's lap. Since I lacked insurance and didn't want to be in group forever I crawled up there. It wasn't something I went home and told my rugby club about.

While being held I was uncomfortable a great deal of the time. This wasn't something that men were supposed to do. Eventually, I started feeling small and safe. I kept worrying about whether I was putting this man's legs to sleep. The man who held me was the male therapist in the group. I set up an individual session with him expecting to have this new "father" all to myself. When I walked into the session, he hardly remembered who I was, what group I was in, if I was married or whether my dad was dead or alive. I realized at this point that I was trying to make someone my father and it felt just like the the fathering I had before—distant, cold, scary, empty and lonely. I eventually learned to find fathering from many men in my life through sharing advice, nurturing, talking sports, hanging around, sharing pain, watching a ball game, fishing or playing cards.

In addition I have learned I need to have men friends, some friends I call, some friends that call me more often, friends I just play tennis with, friends I can spill my guts to, friends in recovery and friends in my profession. It wasn't until after I grieved the loss of my child dependency needs for fathering, that I could accept fathering from other men, including my father who is an alcoholic struggling in recovery. Now occasionally my father and I run in the desert together and it feels like fathering, a bond I didn't have as a child. I am able to enjoy his fathering since many of my needs are being met by other men. *I can let what is given be enough.* Actually, while we're running, if the conversation turns nasty, I run a little faster. My father can't accept my being ahead so he catches up, all out of breath and it becomes quiet and feels like fathering again.

Women are taught to find the right man and you'll be happy. Men are taught that if they find the right job the right woman will find them and they'll be happy. Women are taught to be provided for. Oftentimes, women have been economically dependent in a relationship, which is a problem for women in relationships because you're not really free to be in a relationship unless you are free *not* to be in a relationship. You're really not free to say, "Yes" to something until you're free to say, "No." Besides looking for men to make them happy, women often are seeking a relationship to fill their emptiness. The same is true for women as men, that women have to love themselves as women, they have to have been loved by a woman, they need the mothering to be able to have a healthy relationship with a man. Men can't make them happy nor fill the emptiness.

A woman having problems in relationships with men usually needs mothering, the nurturing, affirmation and attention from women. Many women did not get this from their mothers. Sometimes moms and daughters can bond in the pain, regrets and anger, but mothers are often unavailable to their daughters as well as to themselves. Some mothers are too busy trying to make up to the sons what the son's father won't give the sons, and they ignore their daughters. The women and female children learn that their job is to take care of all the men and male children in the family. Some mothers are just too hurt in their marriages and lives, their self-esteem is too low. They can't transmit the affirmation and self-esteem to their daughters because they don't have it themselves. They can't take care of their daughters or love their children, because they can't take care of and love themselves. Some women participate in women-hate and do not value their daughters.

Women seek to fill the emptiness through their relationships with men, but men can't do it. Men can't give them what they need. Women go to the wrong store as well. Women need to find mothering to love themselves as women first. Men look for a way to feel good about themselves from women; and women look for a way to feel good about themselves from men. None of us can give the other what they're looking to us for. We are asked to do the impossible.

This creates specific relationship problems that partly stem from what women and men are taught about impossible jobs. Part of the relationship problem depends on how one deals with these impossible jobs. In our culture men are taught to never be inadequate. We're taught to be John Waynes, competent, always able to rise to the occasion. If a woman asks a man to make her feel good about herself, to make her happy and he finds early on that he can't do it, he can't give enough or be the parents or the mother that she missed, he shuts down, goes away, offers nothing and becomes passive.

Women are taught that if it's an impossible job, keep trying, never give up. Therefore, we have women who love too much, women who cling and try and sometimes die trying. This is the phenomena that's written about in many current books.

Avoiding Intimacy

Men are simple creatures, many of us simply avoid intimacy. We don't know what it is, we simply avoid it by avoiding it. Women sometimes avoid intimacy by looking like they're trying very hard to have it. Many of the books with the themes of women loving too much are not about love but about codependency. I'm not sure why the theme is love. It's several stories of women who cling onto inappropriate relationships, who obsess, worry about and strive to make these relationships work. The very obsession with the relationship itself is a way of avoiding intimacy because before we can have intimacy with someone else, we have to have it with self. Women may have abusive or obsessive relationships with someone else to avoid facing the absence of relationship with self and then are unable to find the intimacy they seek. A woman codependent relationship is a way of avoiding intimacy while men just avoid it.

Men need mothering to learn trust, to feel safe and respectful around women. Women need healthy fathering for the same reasons. It is an important part of our sexual development to have the opposite sex parenting. To have our gender and sexuality affirmed and to be noticed by both parents is essential to self love and sexual identity. Learning healthy sex roles comes from same and other sex parenting. Due to what men are taught about relationships—that intimacy is sex and that you work hard to find it—men are much more likely to become sex addicted or work addicted, addicted to power, heroism and wealth. Women, since they're taught to find the right relationship and be provided for to be happy, are much more likely to become love addicted and relationship addicted. Their style of codependency is to maintain relationships even dysfunctional ones. Men's style of codependency is to become more of a "human doing," the economic symbol, power object, expendable warrior, whereas women are back into being the sex symbol, beauty object and child bearers with limitations.

It's interesting that men's and women's codependency looks so different, that our relationship problems look so different. Sex role rigidity causes much of this difference, but underneath it all, our issues are similar. In eighteen years of hard, diligent research I've discovered men and women come from the same families (one wonders what the next 18 years will bring!). Much of what is written about men, women and relationships is a red herring, a distraction from the real causes of relationship problems. The intimacy problems are not about sex role rigidity and not about the relationships we get into, but about our problems with our-selves. In the families we came from there was little intimacy modeled, no one real enough to get close to. We didn't find the affirmation we needed. Children must learn to depend on others so they can then depend on selves—achieving interdependency. Since men and women come from the same families, this broken self relationship process happens to both of us. We've been hurt in the same way. We just act it out differently in our culture, jobs, communities and relationships.

In recovery we have to become like the recovering siblings we really are, that have been hurt in dysfunctional families and are looking for the parenting we need. Siblings in dysfunctional families are often distant and angry. They have a hard time being supportive of each other. When they leave the family they have only sporadic contact that sometimes ends up disastrously. The distance in the sibling relationships is not about the anger, it's really the stored pain that keeps us from being able to be close, supportive and intimate. Our pain is similar and it runs deep in dysfunctional families. When we look at a sibling and see the child they were, we know how they have been hurt. We see their pain, fears, emptiness, lost hopes and dreams. It also forces us to see the child hurts within ourselves. If we want to avoid the pain, we have to avoid the sibling—or keep enough distance and anger so we can keep the pain covered. In healthy and recovering families the siblings get very close and supportive, talk in connected ways. In recovery we notice the pain and childness in the other person and use it to access our own pain, so we can continue our healing. We can see our vulnerability, the child we were, by seeing the child in the sibling we grew up with. They help us touch the childness within us. Siblings holding hands in recovery is a beautiful sight. They use each other to facilitate the healing process. This isn't about gender—it's about sibling relationships and stored pain.

Men and women need to do the same as siblings. It is possible in our recovery to begin looking at each other as coming from the same family, with the same kind of dysfunction and hurts. In our recovery we can look at the other person and see the childness within them, their vulnerability and hurt, what they didn't get, how they were used, abused, neglected and set up. Seeing the childness in the other person helps us to see the child in ourselves.

We can start to hold hands with each other—men and women, men and men, women and women—in our recovery process in healing and growth. I've seen this happen repeatedly in therapy groups, mixed groups and twelve step programs, where the care and relationships aren't sexualized or romanticized, where the abuse and anger aren't minimized and the vulnerability and pain are shared. The group holding hands in recovery as brothers and sisters from dysfunctional families. The most powerful examples I've seen of this are in the adult children programs. We feel as though we are siblings going into these meetings.

Most of the progress we are making in the healing of gender differences—the battle of the sexes—isn't in the progress of holding hands in recovery. We are making progress in terms of sex role rigidity. Now men can become sex symbols and beauty objects. Men are being asked to take their clothes off on stage and women are tucking money in men's G-strings. Men are becoming centerfolds; participating in the ongoing beauty contest that women have been involved in for so many years. This is a form of progress. At the same time, women are now able to run and own corporations, to fight in wars, and we may even have serious women contenders for the presidency. What women are finding is that they can be power objects, they can compete and they can also die several years earlier like men have been doing. They can burn out, they can find that men's power is an illusion, men's codependency is powerlessness through power, men don't run and own corporations, men are owned and run by corporations. Men don't fight war—men die, get maimed, and lose their friends in wars. For men who are excited about the beauty contests, the excitement doesn't last long after 95% of us aren't asked to participate, that very few men get asked to take their clothes off on stage while women tuck money in their G-strings. Men also will find the emptiness and the objectification of the sex and beauty contest. *In the name of progress, what we're really getting to do now is participate in each other's pathology!*

In our recovery we can find both mothering and fathering, but I think we learn that there is a difference in the two. The difference is rather simple. Mothering is what is given by women and fathering is what is given by men. It doesn't matter what's given; it's who gives it that makes it mothering or fathering. A man teaches you to fix a bird's broken wing or fix the roof on the garage—that's fathering. A woman teaches you to fix a bird's broken wing or fix the roof on the garage—that's mothering.

Single parents cannot be both. They cannot be mother and father. A single parent can help the children grieve the loss of their dependency needs on the missing parent, especially if that parent isn't very involved in their life anymore. They can help the child grieve by noticing the pain, anger and feelings involved in the absence of the parent as it's happening. They can also, as they help the child grieve the loss of the child dependency needs, teach the child, at an early age, about adult dependency needs, which is to let what's given be enough. They can help the child find the fathering and mothering—not father or mother—in several different places, from coaches, teachers, Big Brother and Sister programs, and others.

When single parents get into a relationship and are about to get married, there is frequently an issue about whether the new relationship is going to be the parent of the children. There can be a lot of conflict over this issue, but there doesn't need to be. I don't think a person getting into a relationship with someone who has children needs to make the decision to commit to the relationship *and* commit to being a parent to the children. I believe if the children have gone through their grieving process and have learned about adult dependency needs, the new relationship can provide parenting without having to be "the parent." Oftentimes the parenting provided is enough. Sometimes the person can slide easily into the role of wanting to adopt the children if appropriate or be more in a primary parent role. What is important is being available, doing some parenting, but they don't have to do it all. They don't have to do all of the fathering or all of the mothering to be in a relationship with the other parent.

In summary healing is:
- loving self for who we are as men and women,
- finding same sex and opposite sex parenting,
- letting it in for what it is,
- finding it in several places,
- letting what we find be enough,
- grieving the losses of our child dependency needs,
- learning to self-parent,
- developing enough of a relationship with self to be vulnerable with others,
- stop looking to be taken care of, to be loved, and concentrate on being caring and loving, and
- make sure that we have people in our lives that refuel us.

8

A Chapter With Boundaries
Family Boundaries And
Boundary Violations

*"Children bond to survival figures,
even abusive and absent ones."*

Boundaries have become a key issue for people in recovery. The concept of boundaries has many meanings, but for the most part, it's a term that reflects limits. A boundary is a defining of borders or limits. A personal boundary defines our borders and limits. In looking at maps as a child, I was always relieved when a boundary was real, for example a river or an oceanfront. I had a difficult time with imaginary lines based on latitude and longitude. Most of the boundaries involved in recovery are not real, but they do depend on our limits. In physical objects, the boundaries are usually external, the extreme limits of the object. In our personal recovery boundaries are often visualized as external when they actually are internal. This is similar to the latitudes and longitudes, the imaginary lines, but even more imaginary because the boundaries come from what we imagine ourselves to be, the image of us that we carry with us.

In a sense, a boundary is another construct of identity. Where we focus on boundaries as external we lose a true boundary sense. We do set boundaries by setting limits and we cannot set our limits until we *know* our limits, which vary according to time, settings, persons, moods, and circumstances. We cannot know these changing limits until we know ourselves. Once we know ourselves, we have our limits and know our limitations, which is a key in codependency recovery. We learn what we need and what will help

157

us get there. We know the situations in which we are most likely to be vulnerable or hurt. Knowing this we can open up more to our support systems when we're in those situations. The more we believe in our own fragility, fear and vulnerability, the more rigid our boundaries become. The more we identify ourselves as victims, the more rigid our boundaries become. The more we identify ourselves as victims and the more we've been victimized the victim role becomes a part of our identity and our boundaries become rigid or absent.

The concept of boundaries, especially for people with poor self-esteem and victim postures, can often become a club wielded by the repressed anger, used to beat people up and keep them away. If someone gets in the way of our self-indulgent path that some of us mistake for recovery, these boundaries may be used destructively, as a weapon constantly lashing out at people who irritate us. We shame them and become isolated. In recovery we can develop an ego strength that allows flexibility of boundary and a gentleness in dealing with demands and needs of others, and the distractions from our journey. We do need the backup of our strength and assertiveness, and even the ability to become aggressive, to fight for our integrity, but most of our journey can be strong and flexible, firm and gentle, bending but not breaking.

Boundaries exist in various levels and aspects of our being. There are spiritual, sexual, physical, emotional and intellectual boundaries. The immune system itself is one aspect of physical boundaries. We have boundaries and limits on play, prayer, work, food, alcohol and stress. There are boundaries on how fast we can go, where we can go and how close we can get.

Rules are often boundary guides. Playing by the rules is an indication of healthy boundary sense. Sometimes rules are covert or inappropriate which create boundary violations. Not playing by the rules does the same. Covert rules mean you may violate boundaries without knowing it. Healthy rules are easily recognized and maintain healthy boundaries.

Breaking Boundaries

Violence is a violation of boundary and violation of rules. Incest, stealing, vandalism, cheating, dishonesty involve the breaking of rules. Addiction is a violation of boundary, of limits. We lose a sense of our limitations in work, food, drugs, relationships, sex. Healthy boundaries involve bringing rules and healthy limits back

158

into our lives and realizing a sense of balance. Recovery involves healing the wounds of violence, the violation of us.

Codependency stems from this violation of our boundaries. Violence creates the broken identity, the lack of individuation. Dysfunctional patterns of bonding are boundary violations that create disorders. Abuse creates inappropriate bondage, enslavement, enmeshment, lack of freedom and lack of choice. Broken boundaries become low self-esteem, overreaction, hypervigilance, loss of autonomy, industry, initiative and intimacy.

Our boundaries include the imaginary lines and the very real limits we set for our intellectual, emotional, physical and sexual needs and wants. Each person's boundaries may vary, healthy boundaries feel acceptable and appropriate for us as an individual and do not harm or intrude on other people. It frequently is easier to recognize healthy boundaries by identifying boundary violations.

Intellectual Boundaries — Intellectual Abuse List

When intellectual boundary violations occur, we feel less than and slower than others. We don't seek educational advancement or information, we don't trust our ideas or thoughts, we're excessively vulnerable to other people's ideas. The lack of intellectual boundaries is a set up for enmeshed relationships, being used, abused, underemployed and underachieving. It can be the basis for hidden shame and poor self-image which are the ingredients of codependency.

Intellectual boundary violations involve being:
• denied information,
• given misinformation,
• given too much information, too fast, too early,
• told what to think,
• told what you really mean when you have said what you mean,
• spoken for,
• made fun of,
• ignored,
• not listened to,
• constantly improved upon and having your thoughts altered,
• treated with cruel mind games that adults can play with children,
• called names, like "Stupid" or "Dummy,"
• unrecognized for special learning difficulties,
• tested in non-supportive ways,

- not taught in a manner or at a time we could learn it,
- pressured excessively to perform in school for grades,
- treated as though nothing is ever good enough,
- not allowed to make mistakes,
- overly focused on for intelligence and being smart,
- not allowed to pursue areas of your interest and having curiosity stifled,
- forced to follow someone else's path or someone else's interests,
- not being offered remedial or special classes or tutoring when needed,
- not supported for continuing education,
- granted no private thoughts, having to tell everything,
- in a living environment full of secrets and false information,
- advanced too rapidly,
- put in situations with too much pressure to perform intellectually and tested too often,
- not encouraged to question things,
- stifled in areas of creativity,
- not intellectually stimulated and
- in a limited environment with the absence of people around who could provide information and stimulation.

Recovery from intellectual boundary violations enables us to enjoy learning and teaching. We can recover our intellectual curiosity, our spiritual process of learning, noticing and seeking. We can feel good about our process of discovery, how we hold and share information. Our recovery needs to involve:

- seeking and sharing information,
- having a realistic evaluation of our learning processes and style,
- developing ideas and beliefs,
- reading about the things that interest us,
- finding and giving ourselves affirmation for our ability to reason,
- learning to process information and speak to others,
- becoming knowledgeable about the world and what's going on,
- intellectual, vocational and educational challenges,
- speaking out about what we believe,
- giving ourselves permission to ask questions and make mistakes and
- learning it is OK not to know, but *not OK not to ask.*

Many people who have had intellectual boundaries violated, left their families feeling stupid and have found in going back to school in later years that they do well and were not stupid at all. We become brainwashed and were sold a bad bill of goods. Often, our intellectual capacity is much higher than we could ever imagine or our ability to learn is much better than we believe. Sometimes the process by which we learn is different than the process by which we've been taught. Part of recovery is understanding how we learn so we can find appropriate teaching. Einstein said, "Everyone's a genius, some are just less damaged than others." In recovery, we find mentors, teachers and guides—not gurus. Intellectual boundary violations make us vulnerable to cults of various types and live with self-doubt and fear. Recovery gives us the ability to sort out and decide, utilizing what we know and what we're told.

Emotional Boundary Violations

When our emotional boundaries are violated we lose the ability to enhance and share our feelings which affects intimacy. We lose the gifts of our emotional life guidelines.

Emotional violations include:
- abandonment,
- neglect,
- feelings denied and made fun of,
- being told what we can feel and when we can feel,
- being raged at,
- constant criticism,
- finger-pointing,
- name-calling, ridicule,
- sarcasm,
- comparisons,
- blaming,
- living with put downs,
- being belittled and scapegoated,
- unrealistic or lack of expectations,
- excess or no pressure to succeed,
- being judged and never good enough or always better than,
- excessive focus on repetitive, negative comments,
- double binds,
- double messages,
- being terrorized,
- lack of affirmation,
- no structure or limits or overly structured with excess limits,

- over protected, smothered and not being made responsible for behaviors,
- no consequences,
- no protection from the emotional abuse of others,
- poor modeling of relationships and feelings,
- lack of affirmation of feelings,
- people projecting their feelings,
- racism and other prejudices and isms,
- being rejected,
- not being taught to care for self,
- not being taught gentleness or given warmth,
- living with addictions or addicts,
- living with depression or illness and not being able to talk about it,
- living with denial and denied feelings,
- being shamed for the feelings we have or how we expressed them,
- being taught some feelings are OK and others are not,
- not being taught appropriate expression of feelings,
- not being taught there's a time and a place for feelings,
- living with many secrets,
- sticky non-directive parenting,
- excess guilting,
- not being listened to,
- being the favorite kid or the little prince or princess or a parent's best buddy,
- inappropriate roles in families,
- having to be an extension of parents or scripted by the parent,
- being over bonded to a parent,
- living in isolation,
- being placed in inappropriate settings and around inappropriate people,
- excess suspicion,
- getting overinvolved in parents' problems,
- living with people who are phobic, worrisome, obsessive and overindulgent and
- excess emphasis on externals—physical appearance, possessions, performance, and manners.

In recovery for emotional abuse we need to learn we have the choice about how to express our feelings—when, where, with whom and what feelings to express. Some of us need to learn to stuff our feelings, some of us need to learn to express our feelings appropriately and some of us need to learn both at various times. Forget the "let it all hang out." We need to be around people who can affirm our feelings but not always affirm our behavior. Behavior is based on feeling and it is important to affirm the feeling behind the behavior and define it. Sometimes it is important to gently challenge or confront and notice the behavior as inappropriate. We also need to accept that other people *can* tell us how we feel. In addition to recovery from emotional boundary violations we need to:

- learn the language of feelings and become emotionally fluent,
- have a support network of people who will listen to our feelings and share theirs with us,
- learn not to medicate or distract ourselves from our feelings, but to face them and move through them,
- learn to embrace our feelings as Scott Peck pointed out: the only path away from our suffering is to embrace our suffering,
- understand and learn about the grieving process, and
- be able to connect our feelings to the realities of our lives.

Physical Boundary Violations

Physical violence in our culture is commonplace. It stems from family violence, the violation of our bodies, physical space and physical needs. Most of us have experienced some physical violence and it has an impact on our lives. To deal with the impact of the violation we must recognize and deal with the violence itself. Nothing changes until it becomes real. The following is a checklist of physical boundary violations that may help us identify the reality of the violence in our lives. The violence we do to self, others and our planet will only change when we recognize and heal the violence that has been done to us. This recognition will heal and change our collusion, our altered tolerance level for violence and abuse. Physical boundary violations include:

- hitting,
- slapping,
- excess spanking,
- kicking,
- biting,
- pushing,
- shoving,
- pinching,
- choking,
- shaking,

163

- twisting,
- use of objects in hitting: branches, boards, belts, saplings, whips, straps, etc.,
- knocks on the head,
- excess squeezing,
- being physically restrained, tied up and tortured,
- burns with cigarettes, matches, stove and fires,
- threatened with violence and hitting,
- tossed around,
- lack of space,
- lack of privacy,
- no rights to property,
- constant mussing,
- hair tossing and pulling,
- excess tickling,
- deprivation of food, shelter, clothing and warmth,
- being physically tested beyond your abilities,
- being pushed too hard physically with work,
- not being protected from:
  - —sibling abuse (older, younger, or same age)
  - —being beaten in school by bullies or teachers
  - —excessive housework (my kids added this!),
- lack of personal hygiene modeled and taught,
- lack of nutritional support and information,
- touch deprivation,
- under or over feeding,
- excessive scrubbing and abrasion of hands and ears (my dog added this!),
- being exposed to unsanitary living conditions, rats, roaches, dirt, insects, plumbing that doesn't work, odors,
- lack of dental and medical care,
- clothing that is improperly fitted, inappropriate, dirty, worn out,
- lack of information about body
- being teased about body,
- not having one's physical appearance or body affirmed,
- excess emphasis on external appearance, clothing, hygiene, handwashing, nutrition or diet, body functions, body growth or development,
- being shamed or teased about body functions or formation,
- physical punishment by relatives, ministers, strangers,
- being kidnapped,

- constant moving, relocations,
- being in close proximity to nicotine smoke,
- being locked in house, rooms, closets,
- not being protected from someone else's rage, anger, temper, hitting walls, thrashing, destroying property,
- not being protected from one's own rage,
- not being taken care of when sick or ill nor supported when sick,
- not having regular medical and dental checkups,
- people or things that we become attached to being destroyed or removed from our lives,
- not being allowed to have pets, friends, things to be attached to, stay in one place, have a sense of community, opportunities in sports, academics, art,
- overexposed to the elements,
- pushed into violent sports,
- no sense of ownership or learning about property, money, spending and the cost of things,
- physical abuse of parents,
- witnessing violence,
- living through earthquakes, tornadoes, storms, wars, excess crime and
- not being allowed to have feelings, to talk about physical pain or abuse or not being protected.

Recovery from physical boundary violations includes:
- debriefing the violence,
- learning to accept and cherish our bodies,
- caring of our bodies,
- challenging ourselves physically,
- finding touch and nurturing,
- learning about healthy nutrition,
- recreation,
- developing a sensory awareness,
- being able to take pleasure in our bodies,
- learning gentleness,
- proper hygiene,
- giving nurturing to others,
- privacy,
- setting appropriate distance,

- finding an environment that feels safe, is clean—an environment we make a commitment to, take care of, make a connection to and know that it will be there,
- learning to take pride in our physical appearance without overly focusing on it,
- medical and dental care and attention,
- support and help for proper grooming,
- getting feedback, support and help from others for appropriate clothing,
- debriefing the physical violence that we've experienced and connect it to our responses to that violence,
- talking about both the response and the violence,
- learning to use our body in sports, dance, exercise, recreation, fun and play and
- we need to challenge ourselves physically in healthy ways.

Sexual Boundary Violations, Sexual Abuse

Sexual violence is common in our culture. There has been no taboo on incest in our culture, the taboo has been on talking about incest. Forty percent of women and possibly over 20% of men have been sexually abused. If we look at what really constitutes sexual violations the number increases to include almost all of us.

Sexual boundary violations include:
- lack of:
  —information about sex, puberty, our bodies,
  —physical affirmation
  —right to privacy (no door, no lock on bathroom, etc.)
  —values concerning sexuality
- absence of modeling of healthy sexuality,
- being given misinformation about our bodies, puberty or sex,
- too much information too early,
- romanticized relationship with adult or parent,
- shamed for being the wrong sex,
- enmeshed in adult sexual relationship or problems,
- sexualized by inappropriate adult sexual behavior,
- being belittled, over controlled or ignored for sexual feelings or dating relationships,
- exposed to pornography, excess joking, sexual innuendo, sexualized rage, jealousy, fighting,
- living with parents who repress sexuality and physical affection, overdo affection and physical touch, are involved in affairs, sexually addicted or acting out,

166

- being a surrogate spouse to a parent,
- living with an adult who fantasizes or obsesses inappropriately,
- being the victim of covert and seductive glances and behavior,
- exposed to inappropriate nudity,
- living with voyeurism,
- used as a sexual shield or placed in the middle of a parent relationship,
- lack of sexual boundaries in family,
- being set up to act out a parent's fantasy or image (dress seductively, be a little girl for Daddy, or a lady killer for Mom),
- gender identity confusion or denial,
- gender shame,
- woman hate or man hate,
- sexualized rage, anger, cruelty, abuse,
- stripping and sexual punishments,
- forcing or encouraging children to be sexual with other children,
- watching others have sex or be abused,
- pushed into sexual situations too early,
- not taught choices, the right to say No, the right to change your mind at any time, the right to ask for what you need,
- being exposed to weird sex, and
- not being taught safe sex.

The following list are sexual boundary violations for children or non-consenting adults including:

- being touched or massaged in a sexual manner,
- sexualized back rubs or hand holding,
- uncomfortable hugs (too close, too long, hands reach too far or no choice),
- wet or lingering kiss,
- seductive dancing,
- discomfort sitting on a lap,
- being exposed to masturbation,
- genital touching or fondling,
- breasts rubbed or fondled,
- sexual games,
- oral sex, anal sex or intercourse,
- mutual masturbation or being used for masturbation,
- penetration with finger or objects,
- sexual torture,

- rape by stranger, friend, acquaintance, date or spouse (marital rape) or
- emotional rape.

In recovery for sexual boundary violations we need to:
- love ourselves as men and women,
- find same sex nurturing and trust of same sex,
- feel safe and comfortable with the other sex, find healthy other sex friends and nurturing,
- get information about sexual functioning,
- become sexually aware,
- practice safe sex,
- recognize abusive sex, addictive sex and healthy sex,
- deal with being sexually intruded on, being around people who use sexual innuendo or become sexually aggressive and
- recognize other people don't make us sexual, that our sexuality is an aspect of our relationship with ourselves.

Also in recovery we need to give ourselves permission to:
- express our sexuality in healthy ways,
- be spontaneous and careful,
- know that we have the right to change our mind about anything sexually at any time that we are doing or that someone else is doing with us or to us,
- be seductive and enjoy that in appropriate settings with appropriate people,
- debrief the way we've been sexually abused and understand and connect the responses to that abuse back to the violence,
- to enjoy being the sex we are and
- to be able to talk about sex, ask questions and find information about sex.

Religious Boundary Violations

When our religious boundaries are violated we are set up for religiosity, vulnerability to religious offenders or wall ourselves off from the community support of religion. Our spirituality is difficult to enjoy when we've been abused spiritually or religiously.

Religious boundary violations include:
- living in a family that's over-religious,
- excess rituals in religion, disconnected from the community,
- no spirituality,
- empty shell religion,
- no sense of prayer or gratitude,
- excess religious rules, anti-sex, anti-pleasure, posture

168

- a fearful god image,
- no spiritual guidance,
- no sense of right and wrong,
- not having our own or differing beliefs allowed,
- being punished for rebelling against the family religious practices,
- being punished for having the wrong religion or the wrong beliefs,
- not being allowed to choose our friends because of their religious beliefs,
- overzealousness,
- obsessiveness,
- fanaticism,
- being involved in religious hate, religious wars,
- overly mystical,
- being involved with cults,
- anti-religious sentiments,
- satanism,
- living with no beliefs,
- religious cynicism,
- women-hate in religion,
- religion as a form of pro-family activity that is actually anti-women and anti-child,
- image of a punishing God,
- too much focus on a father/God image or having a father who acts as God in the system and our image of God is affected by the behavior of our father,
- a gendered diety—male or female,
- religious wars within family,
- excess religious cliches,
- over emphasis on evil,
- seeing children as evil, possessed and bad,
- religious intolerance,
- puritanism, we are pure, chosen—evil must come from outside forces,
- not seeing the duality of humankind as good with a potential for doing harm,
- religious restrictions regarding gender or race,
- fear-based religion,
- legalistic religious practices and inconsistent enforcement,
- no exposure to religious beliefs,
- narrow and rigid interpretation of religious tenets of the bible,

- religious extortion,
- religious exploitation,
- being taught to believe in a meddlesome God of power and miracles rather than a creator of harmony and balance,
- isolation because of rigid, weird or different religious practices,
- religious leaders acting out,
- denying the reality of the real people issues by religious leaders,
- unapproachable ministers,
- arrogant ministry,
- seduction by religious leaders,
- over emotionalized religion,
- religious terrorism,
- excess religious fantasy,
- focus on the devil and
- prayer only offered as mindless repetition or forced prayer.

In recovery for religious boundary violations we need to:
- experiment with different support systems,
- accept religion as community worship, the support of our spirituality,
- find a community which will support our spirituality, one we can disagree with in some areas and still be accepted by the community.
- find a community that is tolerant, not over ritualized, open, affirming, and generous, a community that also sees social action as spirituality, that see that protecting creation, finding balance in life, the spirituality of our guardianship of the earth, of each other, and ourselves is supported and taught and preached.

Religiosity stems from the absence of spirituality. Religion becomes insatiable when it doesn't rest on a spiritual foundation. In our spiritual religious recovery, we need to recognize and accept religion and spirituality as different entities. Religion is supposed to be a support system for spirituality so where there is no spirituality, religion becomes an empty shell. We need to understand spirituality more fully.

Spirituality embraces:
the meaningfulness of life,
the process of creation itself,
our relationship with this creative process,

our guardianship and protection of creation,
our participation in the process of creation and the creation of self.
Spirituality is a higher order value system.
Spirituality is a lifestyle that gives life.
Spirituality is a sense of noticing, of awe and wonder.
Spirituality is an attitude of gratitude.
Spirituality is prayer, not as an activity, but as a posture, an attitude toward life.
Spirituality is the process of each one of us becoming the person we were meant to be by our creator.

Boundary Violations Recovery

Before we can find recovery from the violations, the violence, the boundary breakdown, we have to make the violence real. We have to talk about it, debrief it—the sights, sounds, smells and details. Nothing changes until it becomes real.

None of us have had a perfect childhood; our parents weren't perfect. The problem isn't that there were boundary violations in our families—many of us were physically abused, emotionally, religiously or sexually abused. The more severe and lasting problem is the denial about the abuse. We weren't allowed to have our feelings about it. We weren't allowed to accept the reality of it and to debrief it. With the denial we act out the violence. We respond to it, and lose the connection between the response and the violence. We repress the feelings regarding the violence and the feelings have us rather than us having them. The shame is internalized and becomes part of our low self-esteem, an identity of self-hate. The responses to violence become a function of our codependency, an overreaction and a sense of powerlessness. We develop a victim role that sometimes turns into offending behavior.

Identifying, talking about, having our feelings about the abuse and making it real allows us to be free of the violence controlling us. We may still have responses to it, but we can connect the responses back to the violence. We can work a program of recovery for the responses and debrief the violence as we need to. Many of us forgot much of the violence which occurred to us. The forgetting is a form of self-deception, a form of dissociation that enables us to survive. What we remember is really the tip of the iceberg of the dysfunction or how much violence there was. *Therapy is not a search for memory* about each incidence of abuse, each bit of violence, each chapter of our childhood. ***Memory is a byproduct of the recovery process.*** Early in our recovery we can work on the tip of the iceberg, and the rest may surface months or years later and some not at all.

As we recover we will remember more and more of the details of the scenes. With it comes the shame, terror, sadness or rage. Having a network of support where we can talk about what we remember, to have outlets for the feelings and to be able to accept and embrace these feelings means that we can continue the path of recovery. To repress or be around people that shame us for what we are going through and doing is to continue the path of our codependency.

If we focus on what we don't remember of our childhood, the brain operates in a way that the focusing on the non-remembering seems to shut down more of what we remember. If we look at what we do remember, talk about it, include the sights, sound, colors and what was around us, the brain works so that it opens up further memory. We have more reality to process and work through, so we're no longer as controlled by it. It is important to allow ourselves to have these memories, but to do it in safe settings. Large workshops are *not* the setting to do regression work and to look at what we do remember, to go back to the hurts of childhood. If anybody asks you to do any regressing back to painful places of childhood, to look at abuse and feel it in a group of more than eight or nine people, refuse to go along. We need to find safe, nurturing, supportive settings and healthy guides to bring us through some of the memories of how we've been hurt. Too many people are doing too many workshops in which people are moved into very raw, scary, frightening, harmful areas of their lives. There isn't the necessary backup support system or the gentle nurturing and care available in a large group. Some of us can go into this and feel good because we've done it, but it's still disrespect to self. Many of us go into it and end up getting too opened, too dissociated, not understanding what's going on with us, and become more self-destructive after the experience.

When we look at how we've been hurt, when we open up the memories of this, we will probably feel more compulsive, the responses to our violence will increase for a period of time before, during and after talking about, looking at it or doing work around it. This chapter is strictly a teaching tool, a checklist. This is not the time to go in and process, look at and feel how we've been hurt. It's a time to check off and see what we need to deal with in safer settings. This is an exercise in insight, not the process of healing.

Denial is the fuel of codependency. The boundaries mentioned above are our personal boundaries, ego boundaries. As these become violated in a particular area we lack a sense of that aspect of self. With intellectual boundary violations we become naive, we feel stupid. Sometimes, to counter this, we build a wall. We build a wall that says we don't care what other people think. We overreact and we now only believe what we think. We'll no longer listen to anybody's advice. We no longer accept any information that comes from outside of us or anything that disagrees with us. This wall is no less dysfunctional than not having any boundary sense. We need to develop a permeability of boundaries, to open and close, the ability to trust our own ideas and still be open and respectful of others' ideas. We need to maintain the right to change our mind and the right to assert what we believe.

Emotional boundary violations cause us to live without emotional boundaries. We become emotional sponges without emotional boundaries. We become emotional sponges absorbing people's feelings that appear on TV, stories that we hear third and fourth hand. We become boundariless about our own feelings, talking about our pain with strangers on the street and in the supermarket. In our recovery attempts, we can build a wall around our feelings. We shut down our feelings, we don't notice other's feelings. This isn't recovery; it is further isolation. We need the permeability of emotional boundaries as well, the ability to sift, to allow feelings in and to allow feelings out, but to learn the choice and the appropriateness of both.

Past physical boundary violations often cause us to become used. Our children run roughshod over us. We can't find privacy, space, keep what's ours. People cut us off, borrow our stuff, never return it or take care of it. In reaction to that, we oftentimes build a wall around us, don't let anybody touch, don't let anybody close, don't let anybody borrow or touch anything we own. We isolate. We need the permeability of physical boundaries as well. The ability to take care of what's ours, to find privacy but still be a part of community, to still be a part of our network and family, to touch, be touched, and share.

Without sexual boundaries we become used and victims. We can't stand up for ourselves, defend against harassment or innuendo or say no to people and mean it. In reaction to that we often shut ourselves down, we cut off anybody's noticing, anybody's sharing of any aspect of their sexuality and we close down our own. This isolation is as dysfunctional as the absence of boundaries. The permeability of our sexual boundaries means that we can share and we can allow ourselves to enjoy, notice and receive other people's sexuality. But we do it with a sense of boundary, appropriateness, choice and freedom.

The same is true of religious boundary violations. Many people who have been religiously abused are real vulnerable to fad religions, pseudo religions. We become a Moonie one week, a Buddhist the next, we become Catholic for a month or we might be tempted to go to South America with Jim Jones and sign up for a Shirley MacLaine workshop the week after. We bounce around from one sect to another, we're vulnerable to cults. After being used for a period of time we finally decide that we've had enough of it and we set this boundary. Except that it's not a boundary; once again it is a wall. We decide that all religion is a fake, that God is dead, so we become agnostics, atheists, heretics. We shut ourselves off from any religious or spiritual community sense. We close ourselves off from our own need to have a sense of spirituality. In developing spiritual and religious boundaries we develop our own beliefs, and we develop a support system. We can share what we have with others, and can accept, receive and hear what other people share with us without always having to agree or to follow. We find a healthy sense of community rather than a cult.

Boundaries are necessary, they are an aspect of identity that enables us to live with others. Absence of boundaries produces codependent enmeshment, the loss of self. The building of boundaries from within enables us to have and risk, to care and detach. Dealing with the violations of boundary helps us rebuild and recover. Wear your boundaries well, use them not to hide but to connect to life and its offerings.

9

A Small But Traumatic Chapter
Post Traumatic Stress Disorder

"Nothing changes until it becomes real."

The previous chapter outlined several types of violence, this chapter will focus on some aspects of post trauma effect. In the sequel to *Broken Toys Broken Dreams*, responses and recovery to trauma and violence will be explored in depth.

A trauma is an event or experience of violence or a disruption of what is normal. It impacts our life in ways that are difficult to handle and this places us in "overwhelm." Abuse is trauma, natural disasters are trauma, war is trauma. The impact of trauma on people's lives is best illustrated by the lives of the Vietnam vets returning from the war in the 1960s and 1970s.

Of the half million plus Americans, mostly adolescent males with an average age of 19 (58,000 never got any older) sent to Vietnam, studies have shown that over half of them have had some adjustment reactions since their return. These reactions include an escalated suicide rate, mental and emotional disturbances, delayed recovery syndromes when injured on jobs or in sports, difficulty maintaining a balanced lifestyle, adjustment disorders, anxiety reactions, memory problems, energy loss, lack of coordination, eye hand motor control difficulties, sleep disorders, sexual problems, startle responses, relationship withdrawal, voices and hopelessness. If much of this sounds like codependency, there's an excellent reason for this. Codependency and post trauma effects are parallel concepts. Depending on one's definition of trauma, I believe codependency could be considered a sibling of post trauma stress disorder. Post trauma stress disorder occurs following a trauma. People usually don't break down before or even during a trauma. The real impact of the trauma occurs after the event. Codependency follows the trauma of a troubled childhood.

Post Traumatic Stress Disorder

Post traumatic stress disorder (PTSD) is the common term for the Vietnam syndrome. When young people went into the war they invariably adopted roles. Some might say they were survival roles, but only some were survival. Others may have been non-survival or self-destructive. They were reactions to or ways of maintaining the system around them. The roles frequently involved a continuing loss of identity, loss of self-direction and loss of emotional connectedness. Many of the roles were like the roles of the alcoholic or violent family—hero, lost children, spiritual leaders, tension relievers, organizers, mediators, protectors, addicts, insightful overseers, victims, offenders that committed atrocities, manipulators, scapegoats and caretakers. Regardless of the roles, most of the vets really just wanted to survive and get out of there. Some of them did, all but the 58,000.

The Vietnam experience wasn't left behind. It was brought home. When the disturbances began to show up among the Vietnam vet population—sometimes immediately and sometimes several years after they were back, mental health practitioners really didn't help them very much. The vets were frequently misdiagnosed; they wouldn't continue therapy or often even begin therapy. Their trust level was low (for good reason). They were often avoided or shamed on their return. Gradually, it was noticed that the Vietnam vets and others who have endured trauma or shock had much in common. Earthquake victims, kidnap victims, refugees, victims of violent crimes and rape victims seem to share common reactive characteristics.

Having worked with several victims of chronic shock and post trauma stress disorder, some of them victims of the Vietnam war, I've noticed that a very high percentage of the more severe sufferers of PTSD came from violent or alcoholic families. The trauma experience was frequently "the straw that broke the camel's back." Often the experience that we attribute the post trauma

176

stress disorder to is really a culmination or a final event in a series of traumas that causes a person to deteriorate or break down. If previous incidents of trauma don't get dealt with, the results get focused on the one event the person can point to as the most recent and least threatening to identify. I've had Vietnam vets that would rather talk about the war than some of their childhood family experiences.

Many people believe that going through horrible situations or trauma is going to toughen them up, especially children. Lenore Terr studied thirty-two children who had been kidnapped and held hostage on a bus in Chauchilla, California for eight days. Five years after their experience she noticed they all had symptoms of post trauma stress disorder. The severity of these symptoms depended on their chronological and developmental ages. It seems that when one is developmentally thwarted, as people in dysfunctional families would normally be, their reaction to trauma may increase. In other words, codependents are more likely to suffer more severe after effects of shock'and trauma, regardless of whether this be a loss, grief issue, injury, war or being the victim of a crime, accident or disaster. Abused children may have a more difficult time than someone who has been raised in a safe and functional environment and has been affirmed and nurtured through the developmental processes of childhood.

The trauma that impacts us does not have to be a particular event. It can be a series of events or a long-term event as in a process. For some of us, crazy-making messages will have a similar impact as an earthquake or kidnapping. These crazy-making messages might be: being told something isn't happening while it's happening, or being told it is, even though it's not; being given reasons for things or approaches to life that don't make sense or deny reality. The trauma can be physical, emotional, intellectual, sexual or spiritual abuse of any type. It can be incidental, ongoing, or short term episodic. It can happen early in childhood or later in our lives. The trauma may be covert or overt, subtle or obvious. It can even relate to the constant fear of living with unpredictability, double binds and double messages or the burden of secrets.

Many children and adults are still reflecting, still reacting to the trauma that has never been sorted out, expressed or debriefed. Many children and adults have ruined lives because of post trauma stress that's never been diagnosed.

177

Why did the Vietnam vets seem to suffer more post trauma stress reaction than survivors of other wars? First, other wars have produced PTSD, and it's gone by different names—battle fatigue or shell shock. A lot of times the diagnosis wasn't made because of the extreme time lapse between the trauma and the event itself. The massive amount of post trauma stress disorder associated with Vietnam partially lies in the nature of the conflict itself. The post trauma reaction increases as the ability to ascribe meaningfulness to the experience decreases. The Nazi concentration camp survivors who somehow attributed meaningfulness to the "experience" seem to have had fewer life problems, fewer post trauma effects. The Vietnam experience, for many, seemed meaningless, futile and hopeless. It was a conflict within a conflict, and there was conflict about the conflict. It was hard to figure out who the enemy was, who were the bad guys and where the next problem or attack would come from. Nothing made sense. There was a lack of direction, goals and support. On return to the States, it seemed even more meaningless. Instead of a hero's welcome, the Vietnam vets were often treated either as criminals or non-existent. The war was an anathema; they were ignored—the "no-talk" rule was in effect. No one wanted to hear. Maybe we believed, with a collective denial, the guilt and shame and the split of the country that the war represented would go away.

The Vietnam war was like a national tolerance break of a codependent culture, a futile involvement without goals, direction or support. This is similar for the victim of child abuse. Where is the meaningfulness of adults bringing a precious, helpless life into the world and then neglecting, abusing, abandoning, battering or incesting that child? What sense does it make? Where is the next attack going to come from? Who's the enemy? Who's the good guy? This is the unpredictability of living with addicts. Mood swings, covert messages, covert violence, overt violence. What could be more meaningless? This is the helplessness of childhood, a true powerlessness to understand or alter the situation. This is the ambivalence our culture has regarding children and child abuse. The denial, the no-talk rules continue into adulthood throughout our culture. The past decade is the first decade in which children of abuse, as with victims of war, have been given a voice. Yet it is a voice that is still heard with muffled ears and ambivalence.

How did the Vietnam vet get help? Not until they started meeting with each other and talking about the sights, sounds, smells and details of the experience did they begin to be relieved of some of the burden and symptoms of the trauma. The grip of the trauma is loosened by debriefing. Gradually, this debriefing enabled many vets to be able to talk about it elsewhere and go public. The very talking about it tends to give it meaning. The meaning might vary for each teller, but the helping of others through each debriefing increases its meaningfulness.

The healing for many began through the debriefing and the debriefing itself enabled many of them to continue working through the effects of the trauma in other helping situations and therapy. It's interesting to me that the Adult Children of Alcoholics (ACA) twelve step program for people raised in alcoholic or dysfunctional homes is the fastest growing self help movement in the United States today. Often accused of staying stuck in the problem, the ACA group's process of debriefing, talking about the details of their childhood, sharing some of the sights, sounds and pain and sharing the feelings enables them to be free of it. When an adult child is debriefed enough they help others do the same. The support, safety and awareness of ACA groups also tends to help the ACA seek and utilize other helping resources and other recovery processes. The impact of the trauma, the consequences of the trauma, the PTSD, is lessened.

Victims Of Violence

There are many victims of trauma in our culture. Children who are:
- incested,
- assaulted,
- sexually abused,
- physically abused,
- battered,
- neglected,
- witnesses of violence around them and
- victims of violent acts.

Also traumatized are adults and children who are:
- dislocated,
- refugees,
- immigrants,
- rape victims,
- victims of war,
- victims of natural disasters,

- living in poverty, sometimes to the point where their very existence is not secure,
- living in high crime areas and threatened, bullied or beaten at school or on the streets,
- hated because of their ethnic background, religion, skin color or their sexual orientation and
- from broken marriages, divorce and separation.

Impacts of Trauma

Some people experience trauma and seem resilient. Its impact is not as great as on others. People who do seem to survive trauma are people who have been able to ascribe some meaningfulness to the experience or have debriefed it along the way, people who have confidants in their lives where they can talk about the details and feelings of the trauma as it happens or shortly after it occurs. When the reality of the trauma is repressed and the meaninglessness is present, the trauma continues to hold the person. Some of the impact or earmarks of PTSD include:

• *A loss of the belief in the meaningfulness of life.* This is also the beginning of our loss of spirituality, for what is spirituality but the meaning of life? Trauma contributes to spiritual bankruptcy that contributes to addiction which continues the process of spiritual bankruptcy. Violence creates a feeling of randomness and coldness about life. What one sees and notices and perceives are framed by the trauma reference. This absence of meaningfulness effects other aspects of life. It diminishes care, hope, energy, parenting, intimacy and relationship with self.

• *A loss of the belief that one can have an impact on one's own destiny.* A sense of helplessness can pervade the trauma victim's life. Power is outside of self. There is no power within. There is no control of our own destiny. We can't determine our direction. It happens to us from the outside. Little difference can be made. We are powerless to ward off future trauma. Self-protectiveness means little. We feel small and insignificant. The process of life itself feels overwhelming. The winds of chance blow us around like leaves in a parking lot. This is the basis for the victim posture of codependency, for the feeling of martyrdom, helplessness and powerlessness that we get stuck in.

• *Magical thinking, the voices inside one's head.* Out of a need for control in the face of a loss of control, we invent mind games and imagined realities. We fantasize a false impact on the cosmic forces and imagine parallel realities. Voices instruct us when our

180

common sense fails. What we can't explain and tolerate shuts down. Voices in our head can instruct us in a pretend pattern or tell us what our psyche wants to hear, to find direction or to stir up crazy feelings in our guts. These are voices that bounce like billiard balls through our mind; it is thinking that reflects the insanity of our life position. Some of these voices are the reenactment of the voices heard in the trauma—a victim of rape or an incest victim that is told it's not happening, the death threats, the denial, the crazy messages. The insanity reflected in the trauma itself becomes part of our thinking.

• *Memory loss.* This loss can flow into memory flooding. We can bounce back and forth between the two positions or maintain one or the other. Our best survival technique is to repress the memory and maintain a shock stance with our trauma. Thus, we no longer have to process it, feel it. Lost memory leaves frightening blanks. With no memory there is no facing the fact, no ability to sort out the why. The impact is lost from our consciousness, but not our bodies, feelings or behaviors. Occasionally, something flashes, trips that door to the trauma and the memory flows. And like a raging, swollen river of anguish we become flooded with too much memory to make sense of the process or to sort it out. A flood that leaves us fragile, weak, shaky, split and broken. The memories feel too big and we become overwhelmed. The feelings can cause us to believe that we are going over the edge, over a waterfall, crashing down into an abyss of nothingness, of disappearing, of going crazy. Sometimes we go back and forth between forgetting and remembering and amnesia and hypermnesia. We explode into the fear and anxiety while remembering.

• *Emotional swings.* The swings go from emotional numbing and emotional blocking to emotional flooding. The shock of the swing itself leads to an emotional shutdown. Sometimes the feelings are too big, too painful, they go beyond our threshold and capacity to organize. The trauma, the abuse, the incest can create this numbing, the shutting down of our feeling responses. This flattening effect can be the interlude before a tidal wave of emotion. Like the memory that can flood us, the feelings become too big and now we swim in a futile effort to keep from drowning. We feel like the wave of feelings is going to sweep us over that edge again and there's no climbing back from it. The emotional numbing, the lack of effect, gives us an automated, robot-like gait with an absence of vulnerability. The flooding stage is like a cannibal's cauldron of boiling bits of self, burning our insides and scalding our outsides. We lose appropriateness, we lose all sense of emotional boundary, anxiety becomes free-floating terror, anger becomes rage, pain feels never ending and drowning. The shame is smothering. The numbness becomes relief. We no longer care. Sometimes the numbness pervades and we become like zombies, a sort of living dead with absence of effect, isolated even from ourselves. The swings between the two can give us a manic, hyper effect, frightening the people around us, not knowing which they're going to see, the robot or the raging torrent.

• *Energy swings.* Another swing is energy loss to hyperactivity. Post trauma energy swings effect the codependent as well as the trauma victim. To avoid, we get into frenetic activity, often non-directed and multi-faceted. Projects to the left of us, meetings ahead of us, committees around us and we take on more. Eventually, the crash comes—the loss of energy, the inability to get off the sofa. The crash may take the form of a tolerance break, a nervous breakdown or an anxiety attack. Sometimes it's called a stress reaction or burn out. These tolerance breaks can look like depression. We can't move or get anything done. We lose our drive. Vietnam vets often wouldn't show up for sessions. They just didn't have the motivation, the energy, they couldn't get there. I have seen the same phenomenon with codependents who were so actively involved in so many things and then suddenly just drop out. It all becomes too difficult.

• *Sleep disorders.* Problems sleeping include the inability to sleep, unusual sleep patterns, nightmares, restless sleep, talking in our sleep and using sleep as avoidance. In our society, when we have difficulty sleeping many people begin medicating to go to sleep and then end up using another pill to stay awake. This vicious cycle leads to greater sleep disturbances and complicates our body's ability to maintain healthy sleep patterns.

• *Sexual disorders.* Sexual problems are common with trauma victims, including sexual inadequacy, sexual fears, dysfunction, denial, repression and shame. Sometimes the rage of the trauma are expressed sexually. This may be frightening or painful for the trauma victim as well as their partners. If the trauma was sexual, the sexual response is further complicated. There are frequently fears of intimacy and many relationship issues.

• *Coordination deficit.* Trauma can affect both small motor skills and one's hand eye motor coordination. It decreases the ability to make connections, have the free flow of coordination, experience energy and life. The spirit is broken and the body reflects it.

• **Startle response.** Due to the inability to experience true relaxation a trauma victim lives with some degree of anxiety which results in being startled. These responses might be awakening in the middle of the night with fear or terror, walking along and having an an anxiety attack, breaking out in a cold sweat, a *déjà vu* hallucination of violence, a wave of fear and emptiness that hits us from the inside. Hypervigilence, the watch dog posture common to codependents travels well with startle response.

The symptoms of Post Traumatic Stress Disorder are very similar to many of the things we describe of codependency. The key issues and the resulting behaviors and symptoms manifested are much the same for all victims.

Combining debriefing and a twelve step spiritual program is very effective in recovering from PTSD. The first time I gave a lecture titled "PTSD and Violence in Alcoholic Families" was in the late 1970s. I have little recall of the lecture or the time afterwards since I "fell" into my own lecture. I dissociated and felt strange until I realized talking about it brought out my responses to my family violence. To continue recovery I needed to share, write and feel my history in a safe setting. If you have experienced trauma, find your safe setting and share it.

Addiction is a PTSD symptom.

10

Oedipus Wrecks And Electra Lights
Boundaries, Bonding And Emotional Incest

> *"Our intimacy blocks are more about the parent we protect than the parent we are angry with."*

> *"Vulnerability is the pathway to intimacy."*

Boundaries define the limits of systems. Our families are systems. The concept of the family as a system is relatively young. Prior to the 1950s there was little or no mention of family systems theory. Virginia Satir, one of several pioneers in family systems was the first to use the concept of the mobile to explain the family. Virginia would hit one part of the mobile. As the part she hit moved, the entire mobile would begin to swing and she would say, "See, tension in one part of the family affects the entire family." This is true of all family systems. Any time one aspect of the system is affected, it in turn affects all the other aspects. They in turn will again affect each other, including the aspect that was originally affected. This is reverberation.

In systems theory, we find that systems have components and principles. The components would seem to be the *members* of the family. This isn't true. In a family, the components are the relationships between the members of the family. A family with five members does not have five components, but twenty-five components. They include Mom's relationship with Dad, Mom's relationship with each of three children, as well as Mom's relationship with herself, and so on down the line. As in most systems, some components are more important than others. An automobile engine with six cylinders has six spark plugs. If two of those plugs are fouled, the engine may still run, but it will miss. In an automobile engine a clogged carburetor prevents fuel from getting to the engine, then the engine stops completely. In families, some components prevent the functioning of the family. Some components may create problems. The key components in the family system are the marriage relationship and the marriage partners' relationship with themselves. When these components go awry the family becomes dysfunctional. These components act as a basis of security, the safety net, if you will, of the family system.

Many family systems therapists work with the dynamics of the family in front of them. They work with the marriage, the children's relationships, the parents' relationships with the children, but they do not work with the family systems from the previous generations. A dysfunctional family may have acting-out children, but the child is acting out of the family dysfunction. The child isn't the reason the family is dysfunctional, the marriage is. To work on the marriage may seem helpful, but the marriage problem is usually based on the marriage partners' inability to have a healthy relationship with themselves.

To work on each marriage partner's relationship with self is the real key in family systems therapy. This faulty relationship with self developed in their family of origin. Until spouses sort out what happened to them in their childhood, they aren't going to be able to have a healthy marriage, healthy children or family. Family systems therapy that doesn't deal with family of origins work in the marriage partners is destined to fail. It sets up the recycling of family problems.

Family Problems

When I first began working in this field, I was working with adolescents. I liked working with adolescents because developmentally I was probably just about entering that stage myself. In working with adolescents I soon learned that a lot of the adolescents were using drugs and had come from chemically dependent families. I got training about chemical addiction, thinking I'd be more effective. Even in dealing with the chemical abuse and understanding the chemical dependency in the family, I felt I was

186

spinning my wheels because the real issue wasn't an adolescent problem. Many parents brought their kids in and wanted us to fix their kids. We couldn't do that because we were dealing with a dysfunctional family. So I read books and received training about family systems and family therapy.

In working with families, I still felt I was spinning my wheels because the families would seem to make change—people sat next to each other and talked and did their homework with each other. The change was usually very short-lived and the basic dynamics of the family didn't seem to change much. The dysfunction of the person acting out didn't really change much either—if they changed usually someone else would start acting out.

I decided that this wasn't really a family problem, not really an adolescent problem. This was a marriage problem, so I learned as much as I could about working with couples. I learned about marriage, the foundation of the family. In working with couples, I thought I would really make progress. These people are really beginning to talk to each other, share their feelings and change the relationship. Eventually I decided I was spinning my wheels again because things weren't really changing or the change didn't last, so I separated the couples and began working with them individually.

In working with individuals, invariably I found the codependency issues, low self-esteem, absence of boundaries, repressed anger, fears, phobias, anxieties, resentments and apathy that had begun in their own childhood. In adulthood they were often reenacting, reacting to or attempting to resolve those unprocessed childhood experiences.

Once people began to work on their family of origin issues, they began to make change in their present family, relationships and lives. The pressure to act out in the family was gone. Sometimes the adolescent still acted out, but the family dealt with it through love and support, without enabling. Help became possible and help could then impact the child as well as the family. I soon realized this was not just true for those families I worked with—it was my story as well. My childhood in an alcoholic family had affected my ability to care for myself or anyone else. I was creating a new dysfunctional family that looked different, but was essentially the same as the one I had left. The recovery needs were mine—my self-esteem and sense of boundaries. I was working with clients but, I needed help myself. I came through the back door to get it. I was working with acting-out adolescents because I was one. I could act like an adult, but inside I felt like a child. I couldn't really be a child because I had never been allowed to be one so I couldn't progress to be an adult. I was stuck somewhere in between—the adult child syndrome. In lectures I would frequently talk about being raised in a violent alcoholic family "on my parents' side." We had rage, fighting, neglect, abandonment, jealousy, drugs—and then my parents would come home and things would get bad. My dad got into a fight once; the problem was it lasted fifty years and it was with the world. My mother used to leave a lot; she always left her body behind so it was very hard to find her. I have an obsessive/compulsive sister whom I would worry about all the time. I have a brother who could walk into any twelve step program in the United States and feel right at home. Anything worth doing is worth doing fanatically. I was the good kid; I was so good at caretaking that I once found a piece of petrified wood and spent the next year trying to make it not be so afraid. My younger brother once stole an 8-foot slate top pool table from an open bowling alley. He got caught about ten miles from the bowling alley with the pool table laid over my dad's car. He explained to the police, of course, that he always takes his pool table for a ride at night.

Not only did I learn to take care of people, to look good and to act mature, I also learned to use humor to cover the pain of what happened in the family. I hope I never stop using humor, but I also need to be able to embrace and look at my pain and the feelings of craziness that came from a family that is violent and low functioning. Dealing with family of origin issues has helped a great deal in my life with stress, taking care of myself, parenting and relationships. The baggage of our childhood doesn't go away, it just become lighter. We crawl into it less often and stay there for shorter periods of time.

Principles of Family Systems

In family systems theory, there are principles. The first principle is the whole is greater than the sum of its parts. Each individual in the family carries around the family tree. The trunk of the family tree grows right out of our backs. We each have the burden of our intergenerational history with us. In therapy, if I see a family and work with five individuals, each one after the other, for a period of five hours, I have a lot of information. If I see that family for one hour, all together, I would start to see more of the impact of the family dynamics on the individuals. Working with individual marriage partners, I often couldn't bring their entire family in, especially the family of origin. On occasion I did bring in parents, siblings, or other relatives. More often I would try to construct a picture of what that family was like for this person, so I could get a sense of the "wholeness." The system's premises, beliefs, rules, roles would eventually come out through the history, and looking at present reenactment, the duplication of aspects of the family we came from in our present lives.

Family Rules

Other principles of family systems are the rules and roles. The roles I will cover in the sequel to this book in a chapter called "If All the World's a Stage I Want Better Lighting." The rules are very important, some are covert and others are overt. Overt rules are the ones that we can decide on. If it's a dysfunctional rule and we know it's a rule, we can decide to change the rule, to begin a new rule for ourselves. Sometimes the rules are hard to change, but at least we can make that choice. The real problem rules are covert and dysfunctional because we are not aware of them. It's hard to break a rule until we know it's a rule. Much of recovery involves looking at the patterns of behavior, making some guesses as to what rules we are living by, what rules we've adopted—about our feelings, relationships, intimacy, touch, sex, leisure, love, drugs, food, god, community, the earth, marriage and kids. In my family, there's a rule about weight. It's OK to be twenty pounds overweight, but it's not OK to be forty pounds overweight or normal weight. When I started running a great deal, and training for and running marathons, I went down to what I would consider normal weight for my height. When my family saw me they thought I looked horrible. They thought I wasn't taking care of myself, not eating right. They kept giving me feedback about what I needed to do; in fact, they kept giving me feedback about trying to feed me. This feedback is designed to maintain the homeostasis in the family. Once I stopped running, I went up to twenty-five or thirty pounds overweight, I started getting feedback that I wasn't taking care of myself again, that I was maybe working too hard, eating too much and traveling too much. The feedback went the other way. In my family it's even OK to be very overweight; you just have to have shame about it. You can't appear in a swimming suit and you have to make excuses for it. Once I went back to the fifteen or twenty pounds overweight it was acceptable and everybody thought I was just fine.

My family has a rule about crying. I believe I was a man of the 1980s, even in the 1950s. I remember that my brother would cry, I could cry and we didn't feel too much shame about crying. We had permission. I thought I was a very vulnerable and sensitive kind of person because I could cry. I don't think the people close to me saw me that way. If something happened to someone I cared about, I could cry with the person. I could even cry **for** them, but it still felt like something was missing. I didn't know what it was until my friend, Will Steger, the arctic explorer, gave me a dog. He gave me a large white Husky puppy. She was the daughter of one of his lead dogs. I know I bonded with this dog because I carried her out of the wilderness, she kept trying to run back. In training for my marathons, Mary, my dog, trained with me. She was the first dog I had ever really owned that was mine. Mary and I spent about four years together and then one day Mary disappeared. My reaction to Mary's disappearance was, "We had a good run. I'm not going to feel badly about this." And that was it. A couple of things subsequently happened. Will gave me another dog, a dog that had retired. It was Mary's older brother, Oscar. Oscar was also a wonderful dog; he had been bumped off of Will's North Pole expedition, probably because of his age and Will had gotten some new Alaskan dogs. Oscar used to watch the TV news reports of the expedition, lick my face, and say, "Thank you, thank you, thank you!" He loved the suburbs. However, when I went out to run, I very seldom invited Oscar. When I came back I said, "Hi, Oscar," and walk in the house. I neglected Oscar, I didn't have a bond with him. In addition to Mary, we had a little "cockapoo" dog. This dog, Jazz, was very 'yippy' and couldn't pull a sled for squat. I really didn't like this dog very much, but the family did. Actually, I think the dog thrived on my dislike of it, because this is the only dog we had who lived fourteen years. After Mary died, Jazz died and it was a very sad event in our family. When I was at the little service we had for Jazz, I was crying my eyes out for this little dog I didn't like. I had never shed a tear for the dog I had loved. I couldn't figure out what was wrong until I realized that it wasn't for the loss of the dog that I was crying. It was for the pain of my family. I finally came to the conclusion that the rule in my family was, "Yes, men can cry, but they can't cry for what happens to them. They can only cry for others." I began to realize that this rule was reenacted in my relationships and was a significant problem. I could be there for others; I could let them cry on my shoulder, but didn't feel safe enough to share my sadness with them. It was difficult for me to be vulnerable. Vulnerability is a key aspect of intimacy. I was unable to do my own grieving. I couldn't grieve my losses, so I couldn't connect with the new. My inability to bond with Oscar was my inability to grieve Mary. Until we grieve our losses, there is no moving on. Grieving fuels the forward movement of our lives.

The overt rule that men can cry is one thing; it was the covert rule that men can't cry for themselves that kept getting me in trouble in my life. We need to know what the rules are. We need to look at, talk about and make decisions about them. Nothing changes until it becomes real. Remember that much of therapy is making the covert explicit, especially the rules we live by. In families, there are many rules, some of the more common ones include:

- 'no talk' rules—don't talk about certain things,
- don't make waves,
- rules about not trusting outsiders,
- don't apologize,
- never lose,
- don't *ever* do better or get better than Dad,
- don't ask questions,
- don't draw attention to yourself,
- never pay retail,
- don't cry, don't get angry,
- never admit to mistakes,
- don't ask for what you want, only what you need,
- never testify against each other and
- always wear clean underwear in case you get run over by a truck!

Sometimes different rules apply to different people in the family. The rules differ depending on roles, age and gender. A healthy lifestyle requires rules. We have to learn to play by the rules, but they need to be healthy rules and guidelines.

Another principle of family systems is dynamic homeostasis, a tendency for things to remain the same over a period of time. If I took Virginia Satir's mobile and hit a part of the mobile, the whole thing would move. But if I walked away and came back a little while later, the mobile would move back to where it started. Families are very much like this. The same conflicts, problems, issues, disagreements and disputes show up over and over again. If the mobile has a dysfunctional balance to it we could provide some tension for change, to get the mobile moving with a new energy, a new dynamic. If we allow ourselves to walk away after providing this tension for change, it goes back to the old dysfunction, the old dynamic homeostasis. To have change in our families, our lives, we have to provide ongoing tension, ongoing positive recovery decisions to maintain that change.

There is no complete recovery in the sense that we are ever *recovered*. It's a message that the alcoholics have been trying to give us for over half a century. An alcoholic who doesn't work an ongoing program, doesn't stay current with their disease, falls back into the throes of the disease—the denial, the delusions, and has a wet or dry drunk. The same is true for codependents, those of us who came from family dysfunction. The homeostasis of our life becomes the codependency, the dysfunction. In recovery we have to learn to take care of ourselves in an ongoing way, work the process of recovery on a daily basis. Recovery is a journey without a destination; the journey itself is the destination. It's a journey that we keep beginning.

One more principle of family systems is *everything gets acted out*. There are no secrets, only denial, in dysfunctional families. The denial may be pretending there is no dysfunction, we can deny the impact of the dysfunction on family members or deny feelings about the dysfunction. The denied dysfunction may be an addiction, abuse, depression or a suicidal ideation. Regardless of what is denied it all gets acted out. People get enmeshed in the denial more than they get enmeshed in the overt behavior or obvious messages. Everybody in the family is really aware of what's going on with each member of the family, often not in a way that we can talk about, but in a way that we can respond to it. We can act it out, we can react to it, so we must know it. To illustrate this principle, if I took Virginia's mobile again, and I hit a part of the mobile, the whole thing moves. If I grab the part I just hit and hold it still, the rest of the mobile keeps on moving. The rest of the moving mobile feels crazy because it doesn't know why it's moving. The acting out response is no longer connected to anything overt. We call the results of this principle enmeshment. We get enmeshed in the denial, in the covert, in the hidden issues of our family systems.

The next principle is that family systems are intergenerational. The issues, the conflicts and the strengths of one generation get passed on to the next. The family serves as an architectural training school for children. They leave school—the family—and tend to build a new system, a new family based on what they learned in their own childhood, in their family of origin. The biblical message that the sins of the parents shall be visited upon the children for three to four generations covers the intergenerational and dysfunctional legacies of families. Many strengths of our present families were learned intergenerationally as well.

Another important systems principle is all systems have boundaries. Without boundaries there is no system. I've discussed ego boundaries, but certain boundaries define the family itself. System boundaries affect people leaving the family and people coming into the family; they affect information leaving the family and information coming into the family.

Boundaries

We need a sense of boundaries. Through boundaries we can define the family. The unity and wholeness of family gives us a sense of identity, belonging, pride and self-awareness. Generally, the more dysfunctional the family, the more rigid the boundaries. Information isn't allowed in or out, people are not allowed in or out. No free flow exists. As I repeat, 180 degrees from sick is still sick, so some families become dysfunctional because there are excessively weak boundaries or no boundaries present.

Healthy boundaries are permeable. Alcoholic families have rigid boundaries about information coming in, especially about the disease or helping resources. Many families in our culture have no idea that there are places you can get help for a problem when a parent drinks too much because the information, even though it's on TV, in the newspapers, on the radio, isn't really allowed to enter the system. In incest families, information about the incest doesn't get out. In fact, the bind of the incest victim is that if they talk about it, they destroy the family; if they don't talk about it, they get hurt even more. An incest family becomes a closed system with very rigid boundaries. Few people and very little information get into the system and nothing or no one is allowed to leave.

How people enter a family is also affected by boundaries. The boundaries don't just affect information; they affect people. In childhood, I would visit one of my friends and if no one was home I would walk in, grab a soda out of the refrigerator, watch TV and when they came home I'd have dinner. I'd pray the rosary after dinner with them and I often did my homework there. I wasn't the only one doing this, it was a very open system. I felt as though I was a part of the family, it was actually my surrogate family. With a different friend, I would knock on his door, the door would open four inches and I'd ask if John could come out and I'd hear one word, "Wait." And I'd wait ten minutes, an hour, a week, whatever it took because I was a patient kid. But I never set a foot in the foyer. I never saw what the inside of that house was like. I never saw any of the other family members, but I did learn in later years it was a very dysfunctional family.

A study was done in Florida of children who were well-adjusted, well-liked and doing well in school. The adolescents whose families were studied (both of them) came from the same kind of families. One of the key factors was that each family was an open system, with lots of flow of people and information, the kind of families where people could and would often walk up to the house, knock on the door and walk in. They still had a sense of pride, a sense of identity about belonging to this family, but this didn't keep others away.

How people leave families is also affected by boundaries. In many families it's hard to leave. I've had clients get jobs in other cities and enjoy their lives, but they didn't quite feel comfortable, so they moved back to their small town in Minnesota, bought a house two blocks from Mom and Dad and went on unemployment. The message may be geographically you can't go too far from the nest. A person may live on a subsistence level farm in a mobile home next to a brother in another mobile home, and the oldest sister has the old farmhouse and the parents are living in a bungalow. The message is clear. You can leave to find someone, but you bring them back. Everybody stays on the homestead. Many of us can leave our families geographically, but not really leave. We still have to follow the family tenets, rules, expectations and rituals. Weekend visits, evenings, Sundays or holidays are controlled by the family. What we do, how we act and where we work is predetermined. To break one of these family rules may be the only way out of the family. We may get kicked out, but the pain of being ostracized is sometimes not worth the price, so we continue to do it in the dysfunctional way we are expected to. Even if Grandpa drinks, shames and frightens the children, we still bring the kids to Grandpa's on Sunday. The guilt is too great if we don't.

The messages regarding coming and going from a family are also heavily influenced by our cultural heritage. Where and how far away family members live varies greatly with every culture. There is no set geographic distance between family members that is deemed correct or healthy. Some families may live in the same apartment complex and still have healthy boundaries, while others may live across the country and function well. Boundaries are not about geographic distance but rather are about how family members relate, regardless of their physical proximity.

Information is filtered through family boundaries. Some of the information in this book or the information we get in therapy and lectures doesn't quite come through, because once we accept the information it will often destroy the image that we have of our families. We filter the information out, space out, dissociate and get confused. Our loyalty to family is a tough one to break, but it isn't real loyalty. It's a protection racket which helps maintain dysfunction. It is the enabling and denial of our codependency.

The sharing of information is affected by boundaries. In an appropriate setting we may talk about our families and share at a very deep, gut-wrenching level about childhood, but every once in awhile we'll hit one thing that will be uncomfortable. We stop there. It might be Mom's nervous breakdown, Dad's dishonesty, embezzlement, sexual problems or affairs. It could be any one of a number of things, but we know when we hit the family boundaries. We know when we're supposed to keep the family secrets. Much of our recovery involves going through the discomfort, the guilt, and sometimes the shame or the fear of survival about breaking the secrets. The secrets keep us sick, and remember, there are no secrets—only denial. Many of us keep the secrets and we keep the hidden shame that is interwoven with the secrets. Many of us maintain our shame, hidden, so that our parents don't have to feel guilt. We have a feeling of betrayal of our parents if we talk about certain things. The price of maintaining denial is usually too high. We must do the sharing, but practice judicious evaluation about when it will be done and with whom. The sharing does not have to be done with parents at all. Our goal is not to change our parents but to change us; not to punish them but to heal ourselves. This work is forgiveness even when it looks like blame. It isn't to fix a relationship but to allow the possibility of intergenerational healing and to reach a spiritual healing of self.

Family Structure Boundaries

Another kind of boundary in family systems are the structural boundaries of the family itself. All systems need structural boundaries or you get mush. Everything runs together. The structural boundaries are the boundaries between people in the family.

When two people get married the rhetoric of flesh unto flesh, become like one person, cling onto thee, is definitely rich in symbolism, but not emphasized much anymore. We presently hear more about separate property contracts, child raising agreements and job delineation. It's usually all posted on the refrigerator door (the family billboard). When two people get married or into a relationship now, they realize they need to maintain their own interests, hobbies, talents, occupation and friends. You cannot totally enmesh yourself into the other person and give up everything of yourself and remain healthy. We need to keep a relationship boundary sense.

When adults get into a relationship and have children, there also needs to be a boundary between the adults and the children. This is a boundary that allows the parent to be available to the child. There is a bond to the child, but the bond is that the parents notice, affirm and take care of the child. The children are not there to give the parents' lives meaning, to take care of the parents' feelings, or to be available to the parents. The natural boundary between parents and children is a bit like a bridge made of bricks and the process of parenting is that the parents guide the child's removal of the bricks from the bridge. The parents don't remove the bridge because the child feels shame, cut off and abandoned. If the parent hangs onto the bridge too tightly, the child gets used and becomes insecure. The boundary is there so that parents can enjoy children and children can feel safe with the parents, so that the parents don't use, abuse or over invest in the child.

Siblings have a boundary sense with each other as well. Siblings do act out. Siblings will even incest each other; but usually where there is sibling incest, there is other sexual acting out already going on—or severe neglect—within the system. Siblings will talk in a different way and about different things with each other than they will with other people. Many families have relationship problems—rage, fights, siblings wanting to hurt each other. These incidents are usually about boundary violations. Boundaries are taught as honesty is taught; when parents have healthy boundaries the children have boundaries. A child will get off a chair after watching TV to get a snack, another one will sit on the chair, and when the first one gets back they want to "kill" each other. Someone will buy a sweater and the sibling will see the sweater and wear it the next day and they want to "kill" each other. These are examples of boundary violations. Boundaries are the key to the smooth flowing of a family system.

Broken Boundaries

The initial breakdown of boundaries in a family is usually in the marriage. The intimacy, or even the enmeshment we may have in a relationship often deteriorates. Gradually we build walls in the marriage. Every time we feel vulnerable or need something, we run into this wall. We can't ask, we don't feel listened to, we don't want to listen to the other person and we don't feel any connectedness or closeness. Of all the painful things that can happen to a person in their life, of all the things that we invest in, hope for, dream about, most important is that one primary relationship with another person, the true friend, the marriage partner or committed relationship that we hope to spend our life with. When we hit the wall, it's one of the most disappointing and devastating things that can happen to anybody. All of a sudden we're isolated in the system. The isolation feels awful, so we try to leave the system to meet our needs. We'll go back to school, have an affair, get a second or third job, play poker every night, go hunting every weekend, join bridge clubs, volunteer ourselves to death, but we still come back to the system and we still feel the isolation and loneliness. So, being the sneaky little buggers that we are, we cross the boundary between us and our children, and we begin to use our children to take care of our needs, isolation and loneliness.

How often, when a mother or father is alone, feeling isolated, lost, needing affection, and there's a child around, does the parent turn to the child? It looks like the parent is giving the child affection, but in reality, the parent is using the child for their own affectional needs. It looks like nurturing, and it is, but the child is doing the nurturing.

Any consistent pattern of this taking from the child, this setting the child up to take care of the parent's feelings and needs creates a bond, an inappropriate bond, a bond where the child believes that the parent is there for the child. This is how the child feels safe and feels guaranteed in their survival. Unfortunately this is mythical, a fantasy bond. The child is there for the parent rather than the parent being there for the child. The child is deluded into thinking the parent is there and taking care of me. On the inside the child always knows, always feels the being used, the being taken from. More and more the child becomes defended, defended from within. As the child gets older and enters relationships, most relationships will continue that element of being used by others or using others. They will have fantasy bonds and mythical relationships. They'll say things such as, "He or she isn't really like that," when he or she actually is like that. They will fantasize that the other person is there for them, even while the other person is using them. On the inside they are so defended they are unavailable for real intimacy and are unavailable for the true sharing of a committed relationship. Their own defendedness keeps them from the kind of love they fantasized. They recreated the mythical bond and they stay defended. This is the reenactment of the childhood experience.

The Little Princess

Often the bonding between the parent and the child, the inappropriate bonding, is other sex bonding—a father who feels not cared for, who can't openly ask for what he needs, feels like he's not getting enough affection and doesn't know how to give it or ask for it—will oftentimes have a little girl, Daddy's little princess that becomes the object of his affections. He can give freely to his little girl where he can't with adults. He may make her his big girl but he is in control. He may come home from work and dance around the living room with baby daughter, showering her with kisses and affection. The more he does it, the more excited she gets when Daddy comes home. He may set her on his lap and bounce her up and down on his leg and this playful, spontaneous, affectionate relationship looks like it's wonderful fathering. It could be good parenting, but it might be that the child is being used. If there is tension and rigid boundaries between Mom and Dad, then the child may be triangulated in the marriage relationship and the child is being set up. This inappropriate bond usually breaks off at some point in the little girl's life. It may break when she begins to notice and ask questions—three, four, five years old. Maybe Dad doesn't want a relationship with someone who notices and asks questions. So Daddy's little princess gets abandons and become lost. The princess knows there is something wrong with someone now, and the person she assumes there is something wrong with is her, which is why Daddy abandoned her. She also knows there is something wrong with noticing and asking questions, which may enable her to get into relationships with addicts, with people who are dishonest, because she learns not to notice and not to ask the questions that are needed to stay current with what's going on. The princess may not get abandoned until she begins puberty.

Dad's system may be a woman-hate system. He is threatened by women, but it's OK to have a relationship with a little girl who's not

198

threatening, but once that little girl starts to become a woman, Dad distances, withdraws and he becomes more angry and punishing. Abandonment takes place in this process with still the same result. Daddy's little girl knows there's something wrong with her and also that there's something wrong with being a woman. She too, may now participate in woman-hate or feel shame about becoming a woman.

Sometimes the abandonment doesn't take place until she starts dating. In a workshop on relationships, I had two women in one small group write the same sentence. The sentence was, "I started dating other men when I was fifteen years old." My question to them was, "How do you start dating *other* men?" In each case the relationship with father had been a courtship, a romanticized dating relationship. One was around horses, horse shows and breakfast in the morning. The other dad took his daughter on business trips, to movies and they shared many interests together. In both cases this looked like wonderful fathering, but as soon as the daughters started dating, one father became physically abusive and the other withdrew and became passive. The broken relationship with Dad again produced the result of "There's something wrong with me and there's something wrong with my need or my attraction or my sexuality or my being a woman."

Frequently, Daddy's little princess moves to become a lost child, feeling like an orphan, abandoned, often a victim of neglect, sometimes a victim of innuendo, emotional abuse, sexual abuse, physical abuse, violence or passive aggressiveness. Still the image of Daddy and being Daddy's princess persists. Daddy usually remains on a pedestal but the child has been used and abandoned. As I reflect on the number of clients I have had, the number of women I have met who have felt used and abandoned in their relationships with men, it seems so often to begin with this relationship with Dad. The protective using father must be dealt with to find intimacy.

Daddy's princess may leave the family and begin a dating relationship, a courtship. Of course courtship is difficult because it's hard to find someone who makes you feel like a princess. It is hard to find someone who can live up to the fantasy of what Dad was like. It is also difficult because of the prior abandonment; it produces a fear of being spontaneous, open, vulnerable and hurt again. Frequently, there is a reenactment of the abandonment. The person keeps finding relationships with people that will give them a whirlwind princess romance and then be completely unavailable for a real relationship, for intimacy and commitment. It looks as though it is always about the other person rather than about our selections. What doesn't show up is the defendedness within self that keeps us from having intimacy, that having been used and abandoned produces a withdrawal of the deepest aspect of ourselves, our real vulnerability which is necessary for intimacy.

Sometimes the courtship will progress into marriage. A few years into the marriage Daddy's former princess now feels like she's becoming a raging lunatic. Maybe she has attempted to write a book called My Mother, Myself because this is how Mom appeared to her and she figures it must be genetic. She's becoming exactly like her mother.

Dad may be seen as an easy-going, nice, gentle, quiet person. What's missed is that Dad's quietness and gentleness was really withdrawal and passive aggressiveness. Dad was really controlling the situation and Mom was going crazy because of the withdrawal, of not having needs met, because of being triangulated in a relationship with her daughter. Mom was dealing with her own rage, her anger and the anger that wasn't being dealt with in the marriage and by her husband. This can be reversed—Dad may be rageful and Mom passive aggressive, but the effect is similar. Daddy's former princess now is angry, lost and alone, sees no correlation in her marriage and her mother's marriage because she is still convinced that her mother is responsible for the dysfunctional marriage—if Mom had not nagged so much or been so passive, Dad wouldn't have withdrawn, drank, worked so much or become rageful. She doesn't see that she just repeated the relationship. She does not see because Dad is still on a pedestal. She still has the child image of a father who loved her and was there for her. But was he really? Was he there when she needed him or was she there when he needed her?

Oftentimes, Daddy's princess has never been allowed to grow up at all. In discovering that if I become a woman Dad will abandon me, sometimes staying immature, developing a little girl affection, a little girl voice, a little girl naïvete and never gaining independence will ensure that Daddy will remain. Perhaps it may be manifested as a refusal to eat, become anorexic so that we don't develop and become women. Many women with anorexia, who I have worked with, have been in the Daddy's little princess role. This little girl role carries over into relationships with others and because of the little girl role, one may not be taken seriously. Self-image deteriorates even further. The strength is never found to make the choices of adulthood.

And Now The Little Prince

After Dad has abandoned the princess, he may find another little princess to bond with, a younger sibling. It could be a little prince, Daddy's best buddy. It could be one of his sons who is there to meet his needs, to be an extension of him, to give his life meaning, to provide affection and to be a pal. The same process is true with inappropriate bonding whether it is same sex or other sex bonding — the parent isn't really there for the child; the child has to be there for the parent. The child has the same distrust, the same feelings that there's something wrong with me if abandonment takes place, the same sense of being used and the same placement of the parent on a pedestal. The reenactment of the unrealistic, mythical relationship takes place in adulthood. A son or daughter of the same sex parent with inappropriate bonding will have a hard time bonding appropriately with men or women. The real issue when a parent uses a child for the parent's need is the child's developmental process is thwarted. The child's relationship with self is broken. Again, this is the core of codependency.

Mom, in the meantime, has probably found her little prince, her special child, the one who takes care of her affectional needs, the one that gives her life meaning. The surrogate spouse for mom learns early in life to entertain Mom, notice Mom's feelings, take care of Mom, talk to Mom about her day, distract her from her pain, give her advice about her relationships, marriage, life, depression, let her cry on his shoulder and be the best boy possible so Mom will feel better. Mama's little boy learns to be a parent, a spouse, a therapist all rolled into one. Mama's little boy is used, but when the time comes to leave, it is Mama's little boy that does the abandoning of Mom rather than being abandoned by Mom. Usually, when the bonded partner to Dad is a little girl, she gets used and abandoned. The bonded partner to Mom, if it's a boy, does get used but feels like he's doing the abandoning. I reflect on how many men I've worked with who have felt used by women and also felt that they have abandoned them. This is often another reenactment of the relationship with the parent.

The Ultimate Boundaries Broken —
Emotional and Sexual Incest

These relationships are also sexual relationships. They exist to take care of the parent's sexual affectional needs. They may not get acted out physically, but it is an incest dynamic nonetheless and is usually acted out emotionally. It is *emotional incest*. The most powerful seduction process on earth is the parent's seduction of their own child. Sometimes there is a sexual stimulation within the seduction process that the child is left to deal with. If it is Mom's surrogate spouse, the surrogate spouse has all the duties that a husband has but often little of the sexual privileges, often little of the sexual expression is present. A covert sexual dynamic is usually present. The male child being sexualized by this emotional incest may be expected to affirm Mom's sexuality, how Mom looks in a bathing suit, Mom's relationships with men, to listen to Mom talk about men, talk about sex or to flirt with Mom. It may go to the extreme of taking care of Mom's covert or overt sexual needs. To the child it is a no-win situation. If the child feels sexual toward Mom, there is a great deal of shame regarding the feelings. If they decide they're going to deal with it by asking Mom for sex, that is a definite no-win situation, since if Mom says "Yes," they are in deep trouble and if Mom says "No," they are in deep trouble. These confusing sexual issues, these confusing sexual feelings at times get repressed and other times get acted out.

Sometimes a child in reaction to this will shut down their sexuality, not feel sexual, avoiding it. They may have a difficult time finding sexual feelings in their relationships with others. Sometimes a child will shut down and find the idea of having sex with Mom (or Dad) disgusting as a way of avoiding having to feel the sexuality. Maybe sex with women (or men) becomes disgusting. The emotional incest affects appropriate gender preference as much as any other kind of sexual abuse. Gender preference confusion is one of the results of being sexually abused, either overtly or covertly. Maybe the disgust with a parent means that one cannot have a sexual relationship with someone they are close to, intimate with and bonded to. Then, casual sex, non-bonded sex, impersonal sex, bought sex can be the only way to find the high, the expression of all the sexual stimulus and the seductive relationship with the mother.

Sexual addiction as a result of emotional incest is common — sexualizing feelings, objects and activities to the point of destructiveness and obsession in one's life. Maybe getting into a relationship, getting married, and then making extreme sexual demands that everything in the relationship is sexualized, so the relationship doesn't have a chance to be intimate because of the overwhelming need for the sexual expression since sexuality was never allowed but always stimulated in the emotional incest with the parent.

Sex can also get mixed up with anger since the relationship with the parent is a using relationship. We all get angry when we are used. Then sex can become a punishing experience, an angry experience and a way to get even, a way to use back and to continue being used. Shutting down, getting used, becoming obsessed, acting out, being confused, having difficulty in sorting out gender preference, repressed shame can all be results of emotional incest. Especially a fear of intimacy because of a fear of being smothered or used.

In our relationships we look for the parenting, the bonding, a reenactment of the surrogate spouse role. We set other people up to be that parent and covertly begin to act out our anger toward them about being used. The surrogate spouse son leaves home, abandoning Mom, and begins a relationship. Maybe the courtship is wonderful because the surrogate spouse son has learned to talk to women, understand women, notice feelings and take care of needs. After courtship, there may be a commitment to the relationship, possibly marriage. Suddenly the marriage doesn't seem to be going well. The anger that comes from being used in the relationship with Mom begins to seep out in the new relationship. The anger at Mom that was never dealt with because we were taking care of Mom, protecting her, begins to spill out, oftentimes passively, with put downs, withdrawal, innuendo and criticism. Sometimes it's active, with threats, physical abuse and violence. The anger comes out and the marriage is destroyed. Usually, a divorce is the next step. I believe the mistake at this point is that most people divorce the wrong person.

Breaking Unhealthy Bonds

The real divorce needs to be made with the parent because the emotional bond is still present. The anger that is getting poured into the marriage is really the emotional bond with the parent. The sexual issues, the fears of intimacy, are all a part of that emotional bond. A marriage isn't really a legal contract; it's an emotional connectedness, an emotional bonding. Sometimes the marriage with the parent must be broken, the anger directed at the parent, the feelings about the parental relationship, about being used made real. Very few people get a divorce before they get angry. Usually, we get the wrong divorce and get angry at the wrong people.

This divorce process doesn't even have to be in the presence of the parent. The parent doesn't have to know anything about it. It is possible for us to confront parents and deal with these issues, but we can do the same work symbolically or internally. The divorce process is a process of our freeing ourselves, our becoming aware of how we've been used, having our feelings and being able to move toward a commitment, vulnerability and intimacy. We must also do our grieving.

The divorce is difficult because we so often have the parent on a pedestal. Why do we keep the parent on the pedestal? Why don't we accept that we were used? Why is it so difficult for us to chip away at the pedestal in our therapy, in our recovery? Because if we take that person off the pedestal, what do we have to face? We have to face that many of us didn't have anybody there for us in our childhood, that the people we thought were there for us, we had to be there for. That is the bottom line, was it that they were there when we needed them? Or that we were there when they needed us? Sometimes we might think that Grandma or Grandpa or an uncle or a cousin was there for us, but even then, oftentimes we were sent to live with Grandma for the summer, not because it was a good place for us. We were there to be gotten rid of or we were there to take care of Grandma. Although it might have been the best time of our lives, the best part of our youth, if we were there to take care of someone else, what we reenact in our life is being happiest when we are taking care of other people. You can only be happy for a short time when you're giving and not receiving. Eventually we run out of fuel, we burn out and we fall apart.

Usually we are the most protective of the parent with whom we become the most bonded. The parent we are the least angry at or have the hardest time being angry at is possibly the one who used us the most. When we get into therapy the therapist might help us deal with our family of origins and have us talk about our parents. We want to get angry at the parent we saw as the offensive parent, the unavailable, the angry or the alcoholic parent, our pain and our rage seems as though it is about the abusive parent. Our intimacy blocks are about the non-offending parent. The real bonding, the one we protect, is usually the one we see as the non-offending parent. Sometimes the covert anger of the insidiousness of the relationship keeps us from having intimacy and controls us more than the relationship with the parent that we seem so angry at. When the therapist mentions this non-offending parent, we get defensive, we get protective and shut down. Sometimes the hardest thing to do in recovery is to have our anger at the parent we protected, at the parent who used us. This anger may be more difficult than finally receiving the nurturing, especially same sex nurturing, the nurturing that we missed from both parents, or either parent. To have the anger and receive the nurturing are both difficult and both important, especially for those of us who came from families where the bonding was inappropriate.

People who keep the parents who used them on pedestals, usually end up being in relationships which are extremely codependent and get used and abused repetitively while making excuses for the user or abuser. They may project all of their anger at the parent that they protect into their relationships with their spouses. Many of us participate in a national parent protection racket. We follow the commandment, "Protect thy father and thy mother." Although, more of us rewrite the commandment as, "Protect thy father *or* mother." We see one as the bad guy and the other as the good guy, and very seldom is it completely true.

In doing our family of origins work we have to deal with our relationships with both parents. We have to deal with the anger, the hurts, the neglect, the not being protected and the being used on both sides.

Meanwhile, back at the ranch, the mother who has lost her surrogate spouse, whose favorite son has left, might have another child that she can bond with, male or female. Sometimes, one child gets bonded to both parents, and this is called double bonding. Many people have a life of confusion, they feel pulled in several directions and are unable to sort their lives out. This very confusion may be the result of being double bonded. One can be Dad's best buddy and Mom's surrogate spouse, but the *confusion* (the very word itself means "with the fusion" of two realities) can literally pull us apart. Frequently "only" children experience this.

There may be someone in the family that doesn't get bonded at all, the true lost child, maybe the one who feels like an orphan, brought in off the street, plopped in the corner of the living room and forgotten about. This orphan, this lost child, sees what is happening with the siblings and thinks what others are getting looks very good. The lost child feels jealous and isolated. There is a tremendous contrast between their neglect and the others' being used, but they don't recognize their siblings are being used. To them it looks like love. The one positive part about being the orphan, the lost child, is that you don't have to get a divorce to get married. The down side is being able to get into a relationship with another person is a little bit like, "I wouldn't belong to a club that would have me." Our feeling bad about ourselves, our feelings of inadequacy, our lack of socialization causes us to feel left out, to stay lost, to get into relationships where we are ignored.

The other role in the family that doesn't look like a bonded role is the scapegoat, the victim. Even in the most violent families, the violence gets encapsulated more or differently on one child than the others. Even in the least violent families, there is usually one child that is seen as different, that is blamed somewhat more, that the family is a little bit harder on. This scapegoat, this victim role is also a role of bonding. As a victim, they become bonded to the perpetrator, the aggressor. This is true of battered women, as well. It's one of the primary reasons that battered women don't leave battering relationships. Even with all the economic dependency issues or the children involvement, the real reason for not leaving, even for decades, is that the process of battering is an enslavement process. As one is battered, one becomes less and less able to make choices. One loses a sense of their own power, their own process, their own ability to be out of the relationship. A person who's being battered usually stays beyond the first few incidences of battering because of an intergenerational familiarity with battering. They've been around it, they've had it threatened, they've experienced it. People who have never been battered before in their life, if they get hit, slapped, beaten in adulthood by someone in a relationship, would more likely say, "What's this? I'm out of here. You're sick. Go get help." But if we have some familiarity with it from our background, we may stay beyond the first incident. After that, the battering becomes an eroding of our boundaries, our self-esteem, power and choices.

The same is true for children. Children actually get bonded to the people who batter them. A child who is being abused by the mother may go to sleep saying, "I hate Mother," but the child may well spend the rest of their life trying to win, buy, beg, borrow, or steal the mother's love, attention, approval, and affection. A child is very likely to reenact that in the relationships they get into—trying to buy affection, trying to prove themselves, trying to take care of people—but still ending up getting neglected, getting abused, getting battered or giving it.

This inappropriate bonding, favorite kid stuff, seduction of children, using of children, emotional incest, abusing and neglecting of children, affects everybody in the family and everybody's chances for intimacy. Most families have this happening, primarily as a result of the dysfunctional marriage. Rather than dealing with the marriage, resolving the adult relationship problems, it's too easy to turn to the kids, to begin to use the kids to meet needs.

Appropriate Bonding

What children really need in a family is not to be loved to death, because, in fact, that is what it often does. What they need is to see parents modeling healthy adult relationship. Kids will do well in a family where they are even benignly neglected, at least allowed to pursue their own interests, their own way, their own friends. When the parents don't focus so much on the child, but show a loving, caring relationship with each other, this provides the children with a safety net, enabling them to go and explore and discover themselves and the world. It gives them the incentive to leave and find that kind of relationship for themselves. It also gives them the ability to do it, for they know what they are looking for. They have seen it. They feel the sense of the marriage within themselves, the security, nurturing, care and intimacy.

To have intimacy modeled for us in our parents' relationship is more important than having parents who are intimate with us. To maintain healthy structural boundaries in the parents, to let children be children, and to have adults bonded with adults in the family will reflect in non-enmeshed boundaries. Healthy intimacy is a key in the recovery and prevention of codependency. Even in families with no marriage, a healthy adult relationship must be modeled—not necessarily a committed sexual relationship, but healthy adult intimacy. Single parents often use their children; the children become the salve for the hurt and loneliness. The children replace the missing parent. Whether in committed same sex or other sex relationships, single or married, rather than using our children for our love and intimacy, we must model love and intimacy with other adults for our children.

11

Know Thyself
Identity And Recovery

> *"Prayer and humor are not activities they are postures toward life."*

> *"Prayer is child awareness with adult gratitude, child honesty with adult forgiveness, child acceptance with adult action."*

Codependency recovery was summed up over 2,000 years ago by a Greek philosopher who said, "Know thyself." This is the basis of the spiritual process of dependency recovery. Specific recovery processes for codependency include accepting the label. What does it mean to us to be codependent? How do we feel about having the label of codependency? Can we accept the label as something that we have, as something about us, without it *being* all of us, without it being *who* we are? The label, imperfect as it may be, does directly address our dependency problems. We have to look at who we depend on, if the dependency needs are appropriate, if the people we depend on are dependable and whether we can depend on ourselves. To be able to label what we have is a relief. For a long time in recovery we've known something was wrong and we've known that the programs didn't seem to work. There was no treatment which addressed what was going on. Oftentimes, we were diagnosed improperly, went into inappropriate programs and were dealing with the wrong issues. Finally, we have a label and a process for recovery.

Recovery is a process, it is not an event. It is an ongoing process.

Recovery is a daily program that does not have a fixed ending or a closing date.

Recovery is intergenerational, our recovery affects the lives of those around us and those who follow us, not by giving them recovery, but by offering the opportunity to choose, which is the gift of freedom.

Telling Our Story

After accepting the label, it is important that we share our stories, and listen to other people's codependency stories. Some of the stories may be shared with pain, some with humor. In the sharing of the stories there is a lessened sense of shame, and greater awareness and insight into our dependency. These are stories of how we have been used and used others. Stories of over responsiblity, enabling, how we have been hurt and how we keep looking for our children's shoes even though they're in college or how the mailman stops at our house and pours his heart out about the affairs his wife is having. Some of the stories are about how hard it is to tell our stories. The stories reflect how we keep finding ourselves lonely and used.

Journal

Another form of telling our story is to journal. The journal keeping is a process of telling our story as it occurs. The journal is our record of us, our life, thoughts, activities. We write things that happened and are happening to us, around us, what we're told and how we perceive things. To journal in our recovery keeps the focus of our attention inward, towards us. It helps us build identity. Journal writing gives us insights into our motivations. It is telling a story of the patterns in our life, whether functional or dysfunctional. Keeping a journal is a recording of our recovery, a chronicle of growth. As codependents we often see life as a problem to be solved. We get so mired down in the pain and the problems that even well into our recovery we think we haven't recovered very much. Taking a look at a journal of six weeks or six months ago, we can see our progress, how far we've really come. We may backslide some and yet our journal is usually a record of a progression toward self-care and identity. We think we might be sick now, but when we look at how sick we were a year ago, we can give ourselves a pat on the back. (Be careful not to stretch one arm longer than the other—be sure and switch arms!)

Sharing parts of our journals in our groups can be helpful. It is important to save a part of our journal just for ourselves. Oftentimes, when we're writing for ourselves we write more freely, and we won't edit. When we write for others, we change things, perform for the audience. We try to write what might please people, or what might impress people. Journal writing on a regular basis works well, especially if we do not get overly structured or too hard on ourselves about what or how we write. Our journal can include drawings, questions, feelings, doodling, fantasies, ideas and lists. It is not homework, it is creativity. The creation of us.

Journal writing forces us to face ourselves, to look at our selections, clarify feelings, thoughts and ideas. It forces us to examine our choices and create options and is the beginning of building an intimate relationship with us, a conversation that leads to increased awareness. Our journal becomes a reflection of our thought talk.

Another written exercise that works well in the process of recovery is an autobiography, a story of our life, a story of us. An autobiography which includes early childhood memories, pre-school issues, what we know about our infancy, what was going on in the world and in our families that might have impacted us, what our early days at school were like, our first friends. We can include patterns, problems, things we liked, people that were important, abusive, friendly or supportive. Teachers, romantic relationships, early sexual experiences, recreational activities, sports, academics, family time, vacations and losses are all part of our history. The autobiography is another example of our telling our story, of knowing ourselves. In it we can also include our hopes and our dreams, our successes and failures. We can see the patterns in our life. We can see our early adulthood, trace our codependency, we can see more of who we really are to help us get back on the track of becoming ourselves. As codependents, it's important not to let others write our autobiographies; neither should we write someone else's.

Family History

We continue to develop identity by doing a family history, going back beyond our autobiography. Asking yourself and other family members the following questions may help you uncover your family history:

- What were our grandparents like?
- What were the myths in the family?

- What were the premises about life that the family carried through?
- Where did they come from?
- What did they believe?
- What happened to them?
- Were there suicides?
- Were there abortions?
- Were their other children?
- Were there blended marriages, divorces?
- Were there tyrannical rulers, alcoholics, gamblers, sex addicts, criminals, politicians?
- Was the family political, adventurous or self-destructive?
- What were the secrets?

In conjunction with the questions it is helpful to draw a genogram, a family tree. Doing a genogram gives us a sense of family patterns which can reflect the continuation of some of the issues that we face now. To build our family history we can do research, similar to the research that a person might do for a thesis. In the autobiography we can look at old pictures of ourselves, we can talk to old friends, we can just start writing and remember. In the family history we can find relatives, people with information, siblings, parents and grandparents if they're still alive. We may find letters. It is important get information and break denial but not get obsessed or hung up on too many details. We can look through the mythology. A family myth may be that Grandpa was a ladies' man, when in fact Grandpa was a sex addict. Grandma was authoritarian instead of accepting Grandma was physically violent and abusive. Mom had her moods occasionally rather than Mom was a manic depressive, alcoholic or "rageaholic." Looking through the mythology back to the reality is important because the realities that get denied keep resurfacing.

Feelings in Recovery

In recovery we learn to share our feelings and do our grieving. As we debrief and talk about some of the things in our life and in our past, it is important to embrace the feelings about these things. I don't think we truly embrace until we share with others, until we acknowledge that the feelings are OK, until we attach them to what they're really about.

In embracing our feelings and bodies, we also embrace our memory. Our feelings are the access to our memories; feelings can be memories. Children don't learn cognitively as much as they learn emotionally. We can give our feelings sound and words and live through them. Sometimes we know what has happened to us, what the realities of our lives were, why we were afraid or responded the way we did because of our body memories. Our memories are stored in our bodies—our minds may forget; our bodies will not. The embracing of the physical responses, the using of our bodies, will increase memory. Sometimes the feelings will access memory. Even if we never find the videotape in our head of what specifically happened, we can know with the memory of our bodies and feelings.

Information, Lists and Role Models For Recovery

In treatment and recovery, information is vital. We find books, tapes, videos, workshops, lectures, information from friends at meetings, speakers and seminars. With awareness we already enter recovery. Information helps us break the denial, make choices and it helps us to feel less crazy—though not always right away.

I also recommend list work for clients as part of the building of identity, of getting to know oneself, and developing boundaries. Lists of illnesses, likes, dislikes, wants, needs, past events that we've enjoyed, our favorite activities, our favorite people, movies or whatever. The lists need to include values, priorities, shameful things that have happened to us and things that make us angry. Lists can be about clarifying, developing beliefs, writing about what we believe about women and men, love, God, people, relationships. These lists can be incorporated in our journal or they can be done separately. The list work forces us to have likes, it forces us to remember losses or illness. Lists help us see the patterns and clarify who we are. Lists enable us to be serious, playful, they help us prioritize and discover. Our lists are like surprise packages; our lists are our identity.

In recovery we learn that we have choices, that we really are not stuck, that we can make decisions and we have the right to make mistakes in the decisions. We have the right to make the wrong choice and at any given time we can change our mind and make another choice, move in another direction. We have choices about relationships, religion, sex, how to take care of ourselves, anything we decide which requires or represents options and choices. We learn the right to not be or look perfect, not to have to know everything or even always do the right thing. We need to learn that we are lovable, and being lovable is not based upon perfection. It's just based on who we are and accepting ourselves as we are.

Leaving a relationship does not cure codependency. Sometimes we need separation time so we can deal with our codependency. If we're being abused we need to leave. We need detachment rather than separation. Detachment means we can be in a relationship with another person and still maintain the one with self.

Role models are important in our recovery. We need to find people who we respect, who teach us how to model boundaries, have intimacy and share feelings. Do *not* have gurus, do not put anybody on the pedestal, spend time knowing the people whom we respect and who will also respect us.

Inner Direction and Detachment

In recovery, we need to become more inner-directed and see our limitations. We have to look at the involuntary aspects of the codependency, the compulsive and addictive aspects. Recognize there is little choice in codependency. So much of our behavior in relationships seems as though it's chosen, but it really isn't. Addicts don't choose. Codependents are addicts. We have to become aware of our pain. We need to make the connection between the pain and isolation, hurts and anger with our codependent behaviors and relationships. Learning detachment allows us to develop enough ego strength and not get enmeshed, to keep the detachment while learning healthy adult dependency. We must depend on several people in our lives and let what they give us be enough. We need to find the parenting we lacked, but not so that people have to be our parents.

Become a Social Animal!

Learn small talk, we need to be able to socialize. I've always believed that before we have intimacy, it's important to have friends. Before we have friends, it's helpful to have acquaintances. Before we can have acquaintances, it's important to learn to talk to people. We need to be able to talk to people about the kinds of things they chat about and discuss. It doesn't always have to be heavy and deep. Many of us were raised in families where we never got a chance to talk to anybody about anything. We didn't see normal chatting or small talk modeled. We never talked about the big things either. In fact, no one talked about anything very real. We get into therapy and learn how to talk about the big things, but we leave therapy, still unable to have relationships because we can't socialize and are unable to talk about the small, everyday stuff. We can blow people away talking about alcoholic parents, incest issues, suicide in our families, when they are just interested in a pleasant evening of dinner and a walk around the lake.

In learning to socialize and do small talk, it is important to learn about the things that people talk about. Read *People* magazine so we can talk to people, the *National Enquirer* if we want to talk to lots of people! There are many topics for beginning, light conversations—take up a hobby, read a book, go to a play, try a new recipe, play a new game, visit an art gallery, talk a wilderness hike, volunteer at a local library—you will have new stimulations, thoughts, and things to chat about. You don't need to be an expert, you can ask questions and simply talk about your new interests and share some thoughts. Show interest in the other person by asking about their hobbies and activities and balance it with sharing your own.

Take Up Challenges

We avoid many of life's possibilities because we become so problem oriented, depressed and lose energy. In recovery we have to bring back physical and intellectual challenge into our lives. Play games that stimulate—chess as an example. Enjoy sports—climbing, hiking, camping, skiing, working out, biking, aerobics. Challenge our minds, read, learn, take classes, develop new skills. Challenge what we learn, don't believe all you read, including this. The challenges help us handle the problems of life. Outward Bound courses, physically exhausting and challenging adventures, are a way to get the rest of our lives into perspective.

The challenges must include body work that helps build a relationship with our bodies. Make a decision to like your body, to learn to take care of it, to affirm and nurture, to keep our bodies fit. Learn to strengthen and build our endurance. A resource I highly recommend for learning a balance and loving acceptance of our body is *attrACTIVE WOMAN A Physical Approach To Emotional and Spiritual Well-being.* Although written for women, I personally found this special book very supportive in my journey to reclaim and accept my body, a step in my recovery which I recently rediscovered. The authors, Marvel Harrison and Catharine Stewart-Roache have outlined a practical, insightful and gentle way to self-care and developing a healthy relationship with our body.

Prayer and Humor

Other aspects of recovery are to learn prayer and humor and playfulness. Prayer isn't something that we do. It's a posture toward life. It's the attitude of gratitude; it is the noticing, the awareness, a sense of awe of creation. It's how we protect and how we participate in and care about creation and the world around us, the people around us and ourselves.

Humor is the aspect of our humanity which is human, a sense of noticing, a playful posture; it is a view of life, an attitude. It's not laughing, it's not joking, it's a way of seeing our reality. Prayer and humor are interwoven. Nothing is sacred and everything is sacred.

Affirmations

We need to get and give affirmations. From our self-affirmations we can learn to affirm others more easily. Isaiah, chapter 55, verse 11: "So shall my word be that go forth out of my mouth and shall not return unto me void, but it shall accomplish that which I propose and prosper in the thing for which I said it."

Affirmations should be said, read, or heard on a daily basis. I think it is helpful to do it privately. Sit and relax, hands on lap, going into a relaxed state for a few minutes, then say whatever affirmation we need to say four or five times. Some people write their affirmations on their bathroom mirrors or carry little affirmation notes with them. Affirmations should be kept simple:

I like myself.
I have warm regard for people.
I value myself.
I am alive and positive in my thoughts.
I enjoy my career.
I am patient with my children.
I don't need a cigarette.
My thoughts are OK.
My feelings are OK.
My body is strong.
I have a right to enjoy my sexuality.
I have choices.
I am a sexual being.
I enjoy taking care of myself.
I am patient.
I am active.
I like noticing the little things around me.

Creation is a wonder.

There is a warm, caring god.

I can say, "No."

Oops, I almost forgot this next one—I have a good memory!

Affirmations must be taken from the context of our lives. You can't just pick an affirmation out of a book; you can get ideas which might fit but they must come from within. Affirmations should not be out of the possibility or reality of our lives so much that they are ludicrous. They need to be connected to where we want to go and to real possibilities of getting there. Affirmations are a powerful tool in recovery from codependency. They can counter so much of the negative thought talk.

Receiving affirmations from others is also very important. Learning to give them to the people around us is part of recovery. The affirmations we give to people need to follow similar guidelines as the ones we give to ourselves. Make them simple, realistic and genuine. Affirmations to others are not compliments about how someone is dressed or how they look but the noticing of who someone is. See the book **Hummingbird Words**—*affirmations for your spirit to soar and notes to nurture by,* which is another BRAT Publication co-authored by Marvel Harrison and myself. It is part two of the **Raindrops Trilogy**—*Creating Balance.* Also in the trilogy are **Butterfly Kisses**—*little intimacies, that can't be bought, sometimes noticed, sometimes not* and **Roots and Wings**—*words for growing a family.* The **Raindrops Trilogy** are hardbound, artistically illustrated, children's style books for everyone who hasn't given up completely and even they might secretly enjoy them!

The "Oh, no!"

Part of recovery is learning to say "No" and "Oh." Saying "No" helps us define our limits; it's part of boundary creation. Saying "Oh" helps us learn detachment. Rather than having a campaign for our children of "Just Say No to Drugs," which in reality is a double message since we're telling them to say no to drugs while, as adults, we are saying yes to drugs, my suggestion is to start a whole new campaign for codependents, called, "Just Say Oh." If one of our children wants to have a graduation party from high school, they might decide they want a keg and we've told them they can't have it; if they come up before the party and say, "But Dad, I just have to have a keg," I think rather than arguing I could just say, "Oh?" "But Dad, no one will come if I don't have a keg." "Oh?" "But Dad, you said you'd think about it, you might change your mind." "Oh." I think as long as I just say "Oh," I'm getting the message across, that nothing is changing, but I'm not getting into power struggles. I'd already said my "No," so at this point, any further information is just "Oh." Explanations are important, but once we've given them, we often get embroiled in power struggles with our children. Parents need to learn the importance of the "Oh Zone as well as the No Zone." It's hard to get in trouble. It's hard to get enmeshed when we just say "Oh." I'm suggesting "Just Say Oh" T-shirts for all the codependents in the world. Being reasonable, gentle, kind and flexible with children is important but many of us go beyond reasonable and get used and angry.

Saying, "No," has been one of the most difficult parts of my own recovery. I found that there were requests for my time, returning phone calls or speaking engagements that I am not able to do, because of scheduling, family commitment and the need to take care of myself. One of the most difficult things for a recovering codependent is learning to say, "No."

We also need to go slow. A lot of us want it right now. We want recovery immediately. We want the changes in our lives, healthier relationships, a fix, to like ourselves—instantly. We want firm, slim, beautiful, attractive bodies, successful careers—all of it, right now.

As we go slow, we need to be aware of flare ups and increases of pain and compulsive behaviors as we process the losses, family of origin issues and pain of relationships. There will be a great deal of fear as changes in our relationships occur. Partners feel threatened as we change. Our children react, sometimes act out violently. Increasing compulsion, increase in relationship problems, or problems with our children can be part of the recovery process. It doesn't mean that recovery isn't working; it can mean that it is working.

Networking. No one recovers alone. We network with friends, people in recovery, other dependents, with twelve step groups. We find confidants, people with whom we can share, solve problems, people who will listen to us and affirm our feelings. Before recovery our networking was often with people who either reenacted the family dysfunction—ignored, neglected or hurt us—or we networked with our families, where we couldn't find the space to grow and experience healthy relationship. In recovery, we move toward healthier relationships and healthier networking.

Control and Letting Go

As we give up certain behaviors and people, it may threaten what identity we do have. Beginning recovery is like a dive off a cliff. We may have faith that the water is deep enough and we can swim well enough, but we still have fears that we will hit a rock or not come back up. We might be giving up what we believe is the only *place* we have in our relationships, the only way we have of being worthwhile, of being noticed or needed. We need to accept the loss of control in our lives, the control we thought we had. Willpower alone isn't enough to change our lives and other people. In some ways, our codependency was a dysfunction of our willpower. We thought we could will things to happen and they would.

See what stage of dependency we are in. Stages vary from looking good, developing tolerance breaks, doing more and more controlling, defending ourselves with anger, getting helpless and out of control, projecting, rage, moving into offender issues, eventually becoming physically ill and phobic. The enabling that we've done, eliminating the consequences of other people's behavior, was disrespectful. We need to learn to talk about love, what love is to us, what it really means to love someone else, the difference between love and enabling or possession. We need to learn the issues about tough love, firmness and gentleness in love, how love really comes from love of self. It's an outpouring of relationship with self. Love isn't something that we fall into. Love is something that we do. It's a willing and doing the good of another. It's the sharing of ourselves with others and mostly it's a feeling to be embraced.

Understand our defenses, not to get rid of them, but to be able to use them to prevent having to walk around like an open wound. We do need to know when we're using a defense, why we're using it and what defense we're using.

Look at the rules we live by, rules we learned in our family systems, rules that we make up to support our dependent behaviors. Talk about self-denial, victimization, martyrdom and neglect of our needs.

Look at the things we have done to try to get people to love us or to accept us, or how we tried to hide the fact that we felt unlovable. We need to look at anxiety in our life, our phobias, how we deal with fear. Look at repressed shame and how it has controlled our lives, at the ways that we deal with our anger, rage, passive aggressiveness. Do we "somatize" feelings into illness. Learn healthy fighting and healthy anger. Recovery involves debriefing the abuse, abandonment, neglect and enmeshment. Learn the responses to those issues and link the two together, link the response back to the violence.

Learn assertiveness and how it's different than aggressiveness. Understand decision-making processes, understand our rights as human beings, learn to do things for ourselves and learn to not do things for others what we won't do for ourselves. All of life is not black and white, there is much gray. There are always options and choices, we need to notice and find them. Learn to differentiate between caring and codependency.

Have a crisis list, things that we can do when we're in trouble. Call a friend, take time out, take a bath, do our daily reading, exercise, share feelings, find someone to chat with, go to a meeting, take a walk, meditate, pray, write in our journal, write a letter to someone we care about, read an old letter, plan a vacation, set up a therapy session, join a group, find a hobby, renew an old interest, listen to music, create a frozen health food treat, go play outside, jump on a trampoline, find a body of water and sit by it, build a snowman, tell someone we care about them, ask someone if they care about us—preferably someone who does. Learn about time, its value to us, its value to others, how to have time balance for ourselves and others, for play and work. Balancing time often prevents crises.

More Focuses For Recovery

Look at talking too much, watch who we talk to, watch who we get advice from and who we give advice to. Sometimes we're not selective in what we share with people. Observe our self in our groups, Do I do too much encouraging of other people to feel, am I defensive, do I get enmeshed and end up feeling for other people, do I abort feelings and "intellectualize" them—the feelings of others or ourselves. We also can get too controlling in our groups; we want to share all of our recovery insights, all of what we've read or heard; we focus it on others and we don't allow silences. Sometimes we try to force the group to keep working.

Learn parenting skills. Read a book on basic child development. Move through the forgiveness process. Affirm and notice the people we care about. See *our self-destructive behaviors as being about what happened to us rather than who we are.* Accept our need for therapy and do the therapy with therapists rather than with friends or in twelve step programs. Be able to choose therapists, change therapists, question the direction of our therapy and question our therapists. Work a twelve step program for our spirituality and allow the awe-like wonderment for the world to come back into our lives. Notice the small things and deal with the details, notice the details of our lives.

Give up our illusions about life, have realistic expectations. Learn to suffer and feel bad. Learn to accept fluctuations between joy and pain, self-esteem and shame. It is important for us to see hopelessness as a symptom rather than a reality. Acknowledge our talents, skills and strengths, including the talents, skills and strengths that we learned or see in our families.

It helps to know what trips up our low self-esteem, the buttons that can be pushed that get us into our shame or rage. Learn that talking is like checkers—we take turns. Learn the difference between privacy and secrets, that we must have privacy but secrets mess us up. Secrets involve boundary violation.

Embrace the joy of recovery, the discovery of self-identity—making a friend, the building of self-friendship. Let yourself feel the good stuff too!

Look at the options for treatment and recovery—twelve step programs, therapy, workshops and primary residential treatment. Sometimes a residential treatment is not necessary to break down our delusion and denial or to deal with our addictiveness, but rather a place to find safety, a place to find a chance to accept the reality and talk about and deal with the hurts that have happened to us. It can be a chance to find separateness, break our denial and give us the strength to make the decisions we need to make about our lives and relationships; an opportunity to do the grieving so that we're not stuck to the old losses; a chance to heal and feel, to know us and find a new family; a chance to deal with incest, physical abuse, neglect, or break the enmeshment and the dysfunctional patterns of our family lives.

Being Realistic

We also need to become realistic—about 20% of everything we try or do isn't going to work, about 20% of everything we own isn't going to work. Follow the rules, learn to accept authority in our lives, but do not be abused by it. Accept that people are the way they are, and not make excuses for others, but be gentle and understanding. New rules can be it is OK to ask for what we need; it is OK to say, "I don't care." It is OK to say, "I don't know," and it's OK to love ourselves. Remember, there is always time to go to the

221

bathroom. When I first started counseling I would set up appointments at 9:00 AM, 10:00 AM, and 11:00 AM. Then, about noon, I'd have lunch. My 50-minute hours were not fifty minute hours; they were seventy-five minute hours. I had a hard time closing things down, ending the session. People seemed to need more. My 9:00 session would go until 10:15. At that point, though, my 10:00 session had been waiting 15 minutes. I would usher them in. The 10:15 session was then going until 11:30, and so the next session had been waiting a half hour. I had to go to the bathroom, but I would feel so guilty that I would take them immediately and wait. By the next session, which was 12:45, I not only hadn't had time to go to the bathroom, but I had missed lunch. Who wants to see a therapist that needs to pee and is starving? That is codependency.

We have to face that we got damaged, accepting that the damage is there; it's going to be there, and it's a handicap. We live with a handicap as codependents. What matters is what we do with what we have, not what we have. We don't have to let the handicap of our codependency keep us from getting what we want and deserve out of life. Know that within us we have what it takes to do the healing, to have intimacy, to love ourselves.

Know also that protecting our family is a symptom of the family dysfunction. A healthy family doesn't need protecting or defending. People can look at the problems in a healthy family without getting defensive, especially about parents.

We can discontinue the perpetuation of our childhood experiences. We can deal with the abuse from childhood and experience the pain, but we don't have to continue it. We have to grow away from our own cynicism and hopelessness. Notice and affirm the needs we meet in the relationships we have. Decide if the price we pay is too high. Affirm what we want in the relationship and be realistic about what we're getting. Before we can detach from a need we have to accept that it is a need, affirm the need, and then we're free to move on. We cannot control anybody else. We cannot control the relationship. We have to face our powerlessness in our relationships. Sometimes it's important to see the helplessness before we can accept the powerlessness. We also need to learn and accept that life is not a popularity contest. Not everybody is going to like us, like what we do, like where we're going.

Our preoccupation with relationships and some of our destructive obsessions will continue and sometimes increase as we get healthier. This separation anxiety, the moving away from, creates an increase of preoccupation and obsession.

In recovery we can expect to feel some physical discomfort, withdrawal. Sometimes it's just beginning to notice who we are and know it's our body that feels kind of weird. We can expect some agitation and irritability. Our temper may get shorter in recovery for a period of time. We also feel diminished. We have to face the fact that we were half empty, and we need to feel the impact. When we face what we are giving up and how we tried to fill ourselves, we feel even more empty. There is a sense of loss as we move away from codependency and we have to grieve the loss of it, grieve what we wanted it to be, grieve the needs in us that it met. Grieving is a part of the feeling and if we cannot feel, we cannot grieve. And if we can't feel, we can't heal. All relationships that we move away from, regardless of how unhealthy they are, require the grieving process.

We need to know that the anger and rage are there, about being used, about what happened to us, and what we have to do. Any addictive relationship that is given up usually involves anger and rage at having to move away from it.

We also have to accept the confusion — where do I go from here? *We don't have to know where we are going from here.* Look at the shame and embarrassment of having been human doings instead of human beings. Human doings can't introspect or look at themselves. We can now look at the fear that we won't be in control anymore.

We can understand our dissociation and treat our dissociative responses as friends because they have been our survival. Often the dissociation sets us up to get into addictive, codependent relationships so we can stay grounded with someone else's reality, because we really can't connect to our own. Much of recovery is learning separation, surrender, and acceptance. Our addictions can become our friends. We can embrace the demons.

can become our friends. We can embrace the demons.

Recovery involves the healing of our spirituality as well as the healing of our sexuality. Our spiritual recovery programs are available. Our sexuality recovery programs are scarce. It's more difficult to find support, to debrief, and to identify the problems around our sexual issues.

Managing Stress In Recovery

When I repress my emotions, my body keeps score. What the mind dwells on, the body reveals. If we repress our emotions, our bodies somatize. This is what we call stress. Stress management is continued healthy adjustment of the internal relationships to external relationships. The external always impacts the internal, and vice versa. We need to learn to match our bodies' reactions, the cause of stress and our feelings. Management is different than control. There are some things we can't control, but we can still manage to be appropriate. Stress is positive; there is no energy without stress. All change involves stress. All recovery is change. There is always the need for management of lifestyle. Stress is positive, but when it gets out of whack, it becomes "dis-stress." We need distress management. As we move along, we tell our bodies to handle this, and this, and a little bit more, and eventually, our bodies say, "I'm fed up, I'm on overload, I'm going to break down, I'm going to fall apart." We develop hives, a headache, a backache. This is what stress is. Physical activity, laughter, spirituality, rest and play help us deal with stress. Learn stress management, look at what causes our stress in our lives, learn relaxation techniques, prayer and meditation.

The more covert the abuse in our lives, the longer it's going to take to work them out in recovery. It's also important to know that we can swing into offender behavior even though our primary role as a victim is being dealt with. Stress comes from the victimization and the offending. Stress can be positive. It includes feeling. How to cope and learn to deal with stress is learned in our families. Some of us become stress-addicted. We take on too much responsibility, try to do too much through willpower. Stress become the dis-stress of our lives, depending on what we do with it—whether we somatize it or act out inappropriately. As long as we have balance in our lives, our stress becomes a healthy motivator and a source of energy. When we lack balance, stress becomes distress. Taking care of the small irritations—the tail light that's out, the lawn mower that needs fixing, balancing the checkbook—can greatly reduce stress. Sometimes the small things produce more stress in our lives than the big things.

If we make a list of primary stressors in life and put them in priority—the biggest down to the smallest we may find the best way to deal with lessening the stress can be to take the smallest items first, working our way up the list rather than down. Sometimes we get overwhelmed by the *big* stresses in our lives. They sometimes feel impossible to deal with and at this point of overwhelm the Serenity Prayer can offer a moment of peacefulness:

Serenity Prayer
God grant me the serenity to
Accept the things I cannot change,
The courage to change the things I can and
The wisdom to know the difference.

Recognizing Roles In Recovery

Many of our life roles do not have much to do with us. There are roles we get set up to play out and we continue playing them out in adulthood. We didn't choose the role. Children don't make these choices. Don't give up, give away, or get rid of feelings. Some catharsis—the physical discharge in a highly emotional state—is OK, but catharsis can be addictive. We have to practice vulnerability to be able to find intimacy. We really do remember and we really do know, but sometimes we just don't recognize how we remember or what we know. In recovery, to focus on what we don't remember shuts down what we do remember. It's also important to accept that a lot of us remember emotionally or physically what we can't envision in our minds. Children learn emotionally more than they learn intellectually. Our bodies can be the access to our memories. Our feelings can be the memories themselves. Regression is OK, but too much regression is like too much catharsis. Role playing is a very powerful tool in recovery, but we should never role play any abuse issue. Memory comes as a by-product of recovery, but there is always enough memory present to do the work we need to do. We can feel it, image it, surmise, reconstruct and work on what we know and what we feel. Our autobiographies, genograms, family histories, journal keeping, photos, family interviews, revisiting the geography of our childhood, sometimes hypnosis and regression and role play all help us with remembering. The real key is in trusting our feelings, trusting our bodies, and giving our feelings and our bodies sound, noise, movement, and allowing them to become the memories and to access some of the mental images in safe places.

Spirituality and Forgiveness

The key in forgiveness is self-forgiveness. Forgiveness is a part of the spiritual healing, but there is more to spirituality than forgiveness. I was also raised Catholic on my parents' side. Guilt and all you could eat. We had religion, but we really didn't have a sense of spirituality, a noticing, an attitude and posture of prayer and gratitude. We went to church, but the church was just a ritual. It was form without substance. I left my family and worked in the Bahamas for two years for the Catholic Church as a lay missionary. I laid on the beaches a lot! In the Bahamas, I felt very religious. I was serving mass on a regular basis, going to mass even more frequently. However, when I left the Bahamas I lost, not just that sense of connectedness to the church, but any sense of spirituality that I thought I had. It wasn't until several years later when I got into therapy and a twelve step program that a sense of spirituality began to creep back into my life. I still had a problem. Every time I started to think about being in the hands of a nurturing creator, a God who cared and guided, who was involved in my life, I lost it. I had a hard time believing in a God who cared at all. I definitely believed in God—Catholics generally do—I believed in a creator, but I didn't believe in a God who was intrinsically involved in the creative process. I had friends that were going through conversion, being born again. I once snidely told them that "once was enough for me!" I was actually jealous of some of what they had. Some of them seemed to belong to the church of "perpetual proselytizing" and I wasn't too jealous of them because I thought they had a tenuous grip on what they thought they had. Others, however, really went through a transformation, found peace and meaningfulness in life that I didn't have. They felt safe in the hands of their creator, a personal God. In doing some work in therapy, I found myself doing some anger work about my father, his unavailability, his seemingly uncaring attitude. I knew much of that was about the disease of alcoholism; I knew about the absence of fathering in his life but I was angry. In saying the anger, I kept saying he just didn't care. Later on, in remembering that, an insight hit me. That's what I kept saying about God, that I didn't believe in a God who cared. What I did was a transference of the feelings and concept of God, "Our Father," from God to those feelings about my dad. In our culture, we do this anyway, with the image of god as a patriarch, our prayers to God, the Father. It's as though the father is the authority in the family, and God is the ultimate authority figure. Some of us "adult children" have authority problems that effect our relationship with God because we see God as an authority. In dealing with my father and his lack of caring, I thought this might facilitate my healing with God as well. Even now, though, when I try to define God, I get in trouble. I think some of the definition of authority and my father get back into it. I believe in God, and I stopped trying to define

God—God doesn't need a definition. What I started doing was defining my spirituality instead.

In defining spirituality, I realized that it certainly has a lot of meanings to me.

Spirituality is a *higher* order value system. What I value is a reflection of my spirituality, having values is spirituality. Cherishing, protecting and guarding those values is knowing them.

Spirituality also includes a sense of *meaningfulness* of life. Part of the past trauma in our lives is a removal of that meaningfulness. That is why abuse and violence is always spiritual abuse. In recovery, we find life has meaning, that there is love, caring, direction, movement, hopes and dreams.

Spirituality is also *lifestyle*. It's what gives life, leading a life that enhances and supports life. Some of us lead a "deathstyle"— absence of spirituality, addictive behaviors, self-destructiveness, suicidal fantasies, not taking care of ourselves. I think spirituality includes how we treat *our bodies,* our nutrition, recreation, laughter, love, play and work, it is a lifestyle.

Spirituality is *noticing,* a sense of wonder, a sense of awe toward creation. The biblical message, "To become like children," is very essential in learning spirituality. We have to do the childlike noticing, wonderment and awe of the unfolding of creation. Noticing is intrinsic to spirituality. This is why we keep going back to our childness and doing child work. Back to the spontaneity, magical noticing and wonder of the splendor of creation. Spirituality is when we *integrate* that wonder, childness and noticing into the adult ability to experience, have wisdom and be the guardians of this creation.

Spirituality is a mission and sense of our *guardianship* of creation. Without the sense of our adulthood, our strengths and abilities, the child is lost, and creation is in trouble.

Spirituality is our *participation* in the creative process. That can be through family, the building, cherishing, respecting and guarding of life itself, for each other, plants, animals, the earth. It's participating in creation by allowing the creative forces within us to build, to create art, dreams, visions, sculptures, music and writing. All of what we create is participatory in the creation of the universe.

Our emotional healing process, our *recovery* is a spiritual journey that invites us to protect life, enjoy life, to integrate our childness and adulthood and to find both spontaneity and responsibility. Spirituality includes a sense of *prayer,* the joyfulness

227

of child noticing entering adult guardianship—an adult gratitude. Our spirituality is an attitude of gratitude for the gifts we've been given.

The essence of spirituality is the *process of each of us becoming the person we were meant* to be by our creator. My spirituality is my becoming me. That is why I believe that all abuse is spiritual abuse; all abuse keeps us from becoming who we were meant to be.

Twelve Step Programs

During my therapy I realized some of my spiritual growth, but I was unable to really feel it and work on it until I got involved in twelve step programs. Alanon saved my life. I have heard clients say it for twenty years, and now I know it is also true for me. My first introduction to twelve step work was at an Alanon meeting. The meeting almost drove me *nuts* because I was told to detach. At that point, some of the people who were talking about detachment seemed to indicate that it meant not having my feelings. I know now that isn't true. What I found in terms of the support and caring, the community and the spirituality was the key in my continuing recovery process.

The twelve step program is a key in spiritual recovery. It is a grief process for the loss of the relationship with our addictions— or addictive relationships. It helps us deal with denial, helps us open up and see the impact of who we are on ourselves, others and families. It helps us with honesty, patience, anger and receiving support. There are many messages about not carrying resentments in the Big Book, and sometimes this is interpreted to mean we shouldn't be angry. Not carrying resentments means that we have to deal with our anger, be up front with it. Otherwise, the resentments fester and kill our spirituality. The twelve step program helps us with sadness and depression. Through the steps we work out much of what the sadness and depression are about. The program moves us toward serenity and acceptances.

The twelve step program was originally for alcoholics, but the rest of us are catching on. The twelve step program is a potential recovery program for everybody. It isn't just for alcoholics, about children or spouses of alcoholics or smokers or overeaters. It's for people. It's the spiritual answer to our human race's spiritual bankruptcy. The twelve step program provides a system for the recovery of our belief system, values, honesty, rituals, meaning and purpose.

The Twelve Steps

1. We admitted we were powerless over _____ —that our lives had become unmanageable.
2. Came to believe that a Power greater than ourselves could restore us to sanity.
3. Made a decision to turn our will and our lives over to the care of God as we understood Him.
4. Made a searching and fearless moral inventory of ourselves.
5. Admitted to God, to ourselves, and to another human being the exact nature of our wrongs.
6. Were entirely ready to have God remove all these defects of character.
7. Humbly asked him to remove our shortcomings.
8. Made a list of all persons we had harmed, and became willing to make amends to them all.
9. Made direct amends to such people whenever possible, except when to do so would injure them or others.
10. Continued to take personal inventory and, when we were wrong, promptly admitted it.
11. Sought through prayer and meditation to improve our conscious contact with God as we understood Him, praying only for knowledge of His will for us and for the power to carry that out.
12. Having had a spiritual awakening as a result of these steps, we tried to carry this message to others, and to practice these principles in all our affairs.

Recovery Beyond Ourselves

In the recovery from codependency and the development of our own identity, our own ability to have intimacy, our own respect for life, a flowing out of this is a respect for creation. This is a way of seeing behavior in terms of its long term impact, as consequences, a way of knowing that we can make a difference, we can stand up in the strength of our outrage, with the wisdom of our fear, with the healing of our sadness and pain, with a sense of guardianship from our shame, and the voice of conscience from our guilt. We can heal ourselves, our families, our relationships. We can heal our communities, and maybe most importantly, we can heal our planet.

Part of this recovery involves embracing the reality of our feelings, to face our fears, embrace them, our fear of extinction, our fear of pain, and use it as a source of wisdom. Pause to reflect, the ability to be careful—full of care—to look at the consequences of the decisions we make. We face our pain, we embrace our pain, our grieving of losses, which enables us to make new attachments which prevent us from inflicting needless loss of habitat, life, knowledge and humanity. Facing and being able to realize the pain of loss is an incentive to be rid of the tools that can create loss in numbers difficult to imagine. Facing and embracing the anger, to give us the strength to protect, to fight for life, to maintain dignity, to become outraged at our spiral toward destruction, at the abuse and neglect of vulnerable life.

Recovery Priorities

In the process of recovery there are several areas of living that require our attention. Each area is important and some need to be addressed earlier than others. Following is a list of twelve key life themes building one upon the other. None are isolated from the others. No theme has a particular destination, time line or completion. Each priority is a foundation step for the next focus of work. Begin with number one and continue to work on the first while gradually adding two through twelve. In recovery we work concurrently on themes as we add new dimension.

1. **Identity**—self-awareness, knowledge of one's history, roles, beliefs, needs, character flat spots, pitfalls, likes, dislikes and boundaries. It is the decision to accept oneself, ability to give oneself affirmation, internally validate, to seek an awareness of past boundary violations and ways in which we've been used, neglected, and to look at aspects of our family that were secret, and how we were enmeshed.

2. **Emotional fluency**—the ability to embrace and share our feelings. To identify the feeling and use it as a guide. To find the gift of each feeling. To have our feelings so they don't have us. To discover intimacy through emotional vulnerability.

3. **Friends and family**—social life, emotional support system, people to play with, physical contact, discussion, sharing of losses, hopes, feelings, thoughts and events. It is being cared about, affirmed, gently confronted when off-base, finding our parenting needs, mentors, teachers, guides and role models. It means enjoying a family, whether biological, through marriage or a family of creation—people we choose—to bond with who don't overwhelm us. Be attracted to others similar to us or because of their differences, be able to sustain a sense of cherishing people and differences.

230

4. **Physical balance**—activity, movement, challenge, physical play, dance, massage, fitness, strength, endurance and flexibility. It is choosing to care for our body, here, today—showing self-respect through hygiene, getting rest, doing up our seat belt, learning to compete, to do the best we can physically and to be grateful for our bodies and gentle with ourselves.

5. **Spiritual focus**—Henry Nouen said "The first stage in establing spirituality is to establish a relationship with self." The first three priorities of recovery are about knowing and embracing self and are filled with spiritual essence. If we focus on spirituality *directly* too early in recovery, before relationship with self, others and our bodies, our spirituality often becomes "religiosity," obsessional and empty. Spirituality is the meaningfulness of life, development of a value system, ability to give and receive love. It is developing a sense of guardianship of creation, the ability to notice, the wonder, the awe of little things around us, seeking a sense of gratitude, taking an active participation in creation and allowing the process of ourselves to become the person we are meant to be by our creator. Spirituality is childness entering adulthood and is called growing up—becoming an adult without losing our childness. A spiritual focus includes learning prayer, not as an activity, something done or said but as a posture toward life. Prayer is childness woven into adulthood. It is:
Child noticing with adult gratitude.
Child honesty with adult forgiveness.
Child acceptance with adult action.
Child newness with adult experience.
Child naïvete with adult wisdom.
Child vulnerability with adult strength.

6. **Sexuality**—gender pride, loving ourselves as men, as women, having same sex and other sex trust, nurturing, noticing, advice, care and contact. It is the awareness of sexual boundaries of self and others, choices we have regarding our sexuality and needs and knowing a sense of satisfactory loving in a physical relationship according to our desires and sexual preference. Gaining sexual information, sexual and physical affirmation, recognizing that other people don't make us sexual and acceptance that our sexuality is not about our genitals or having sex are all part of sexual recovery. Building relationship with selves as women and men.

7. **Play and recreation**—experience the world in a childlike and playful manner. Re-creation through recreating, the spirit in our spiritual journey, the humor in our humanity.
8. **Nutrition and food balance**—moderate use of food, accepting that diets do not work, getting off the dieting roller coaster stopping harmful weight loss routines and not being rigid with food. It means being gentle and nurturing with food, learning to experience pleasure and fun with food, being able to be spontaneous and social with food, knowing what foods affect us and how. It is giving ourselves permission to eat in a gentle and loving way and if we are compulsive, developing a proper support system and program.
9. **Intellectual balance and creativity**—challenging ourselves intellectually, playing intellectual games with self and others, continue to learn, read, attend workshops. Find places to teach what we know, to continue the discovery of the world around us, knowing where to find information, having the ability to ask questions and make mistakes, develop belief systems, the ability to see the relatedness of what we learn, and utilize our learning to change our lives, our behaviors, and the world around us.
10. **Career**—being able to be productive, choosing what we do, having a career in an area we can respect, enjoying commensurate rewards offered according to our efforts and career position. It is getting appropriate feedback from people around us, being able to respect authority and having the support to protect ourselves from abusive authority. It also means being able to make a positive social contribution, building through our career, finding the ability to feel productive in our leisure time, having opportunities of leadership, advancement, being able to practice our skills, to do the kinds of things that we are good at doing and being able to find some diversity in what we do to the extent of our desire for diversity.
11. **Community**—involvement, participating in community projects and improvement, voting, political involvement. It is working for school issues, helping with campaigns, planting parks, meetings, bonding local and community involvement to city, county, state and national involvement. Besides being aware and involved in local and world issues, community recovery means recognizing our individual role and impact on our environment through our consumptive patterns and

participating in recycling, working for clean air and water, limiting our personal consumption and waste. It is finding our niche in the protection of our planet.

12. **Passion**—finding something we can believe in and work for, that we can be passionate about—a cause, a need, something that will make a difference without becoming obsessed with it, without it controlling our lives (passion is sometimes misunderstood as intensity for the sake of intensity). Passion is the breath of life energy. It is important to not just believe in something, but to back up that belief with activity, personal choices, energy and passion. To bring passion into our lives, our relationship and our guardianship is one part of our spiritual journey. It continues by maintaining the guardianship and respect for life, having beliefs and following those with actions in our life choices. Passion is the emotional fuel supply for our values, decisions, relationships, parenting— our journey through life.

For more information on each priority see *Finding Balance: 12 Priorities for Interdependence and Joyful Living*—Health Communications by Kellogg and Harrison.

Life Lines

Through the twelve priorities, our major life lines are *humor* and *balance*. They add direction, stability and keep us from sinking—out of balance, out of humor, out of sight!

Humor develops as a posture toward life. Humor shortcuts shame, heals the body, lifts the spirit, facilitates change and grief, diffuses hopelessness and secrecy. Humor and human are synonymous. Laugh lines are life lines.

Balance is the design for the priorities together. As shared by Marvel Harrison in the following passage from her book *Gentle Eating:*

The *key* to making the body•mind•spirit connection, above all else is:

Balance

Balance in life. Balance of committments. Balance in decisions. Balance of choices. Balance of foods. Balance in caring for others and taking care of ourselves. Balance with play and work. Balance of intensity and relaxation. Some of the time you may feel out of balance, off balance. It feels unsteady, unsure, unsafe, off base or not grounded. Other times you may feel in balance, on target, centered, steady and sure. Living is a process of balancing life choices.

Balance is the dance of life. When we feel *in* balance, steady and sure we can take a few dips, twirls and extra steps without falling. When we feel a little *off* balance, out of step or not in tune, a swirl, an extra move or step may be too much, may result in a fall. We might need to keep a steady beat and follow a simple rhythm for a short while, get the basic steps down, gain some confidence before moving on. We may have to repeat the steps time and time again. We might need to go over the moves on our own, take some lessons and dance with others; you have to do it *for* yourself, not *by* yourself! The exciting part is we are not practicing or preparing for a big event, major production or grand finale. Each step and every move along the way counts. This is it. This is *not* a dress rehearsal. This is the *dance of life!* Throughout recovery we weave the uniqueness of us in the fabric of recovery. We use threads of humor to create a design of balance. The artist's creation is the quilt of recovery.

Ultimately in our recovery, we have to accept that life is a free fall and we can fall through time, screaming in terror, filled with anxiety about the landing. Or we can scream joyfully, with the breathless exhilaration of the journey we have been fortunate enough to have been given. We can even have faith that the landing of the journey will be gentle, in the arms of the life source. Whatever we believe, *enjoy the ride!*

In Closing

"Recovery is not to change who we are, but to become who we are and not to become who we are but to be who we are. The loving of who we are allows the being of who we are.

Recovery is the Spiritual journey of self discovery.

Recovery is a journey without a destination. The journey itself is the destination.

Recovery is the journey we keep beginning.

Recovery is the joy of falling in love, finding a soul mate and having a friend that will never leave us.

It is the never ending story of us."

Terry Kellogg

The Kellogg Epilogue

*"Rather than being made in the image
and likeness of God we have made God
in our image and likeness."*

*"Our dominion over the earth is the gift
of guardianship."*

On this planet Earth, life is common, abundant, but in the immensity of the universe and the limits of our awareness of creation, we are told that life may well be a rare occurrence. The likelihood of other planets orbiting in the billions of galaxies is high. There is a good likelihood that some have conditions present to nurture life, and a real possibility that life has developed on a number of these planets in orbit around their nuclear furnaces. It is even possible that on a few of these other planets, life has achieved an awareness, a consciousness of consciousness, the ability to wonder and dream, the ability and the desire to search for more of its own, to pray, to notice, to be filled with gratitude for and awareness of, this gift of life itself.

We may not be alone in the universe, but we are rare. Life is not cheap; it is precious. The human mind, the human soul, the life spark of our being, are unique. With its possibilities, curiosities, noticing, wondering, and craving, human life is one of the most precious and rare items in the entire universe. To stifle it, confuse it, threaten it, deprive it—of nutrition, information, freedom, a chance to achieve its potential—may be the most heinous, insidious crime in our universe.

Each child is the culmination of the potential of this universe. To provide the child with safety, gentleness and awareness of that uniqueness and preciousness, to provide all of the encouragement

235

and information they can handle, is the prime responsibility of adulthood. This guardianship of children, of our own potential, includes the nurturing of our own childness, our newness in our expanding universe.

Following is a poem I would like to share. It is reprinted with permission of the author, my sixteen-year-old son:

David's Thoughts

Experience our children need to gain
The gentle feel of summer rain
Not acid rain destroying grain

Things our children need to know
How to eat and how to grow
Not that Iraq is a threatening foe

Lessons our children need to learn
How the sun helps grow a fern
Not sun's light will instantly burn

What our children need for warming
Go inside when clouds are storming
Not dreading clouds of global warming

What our children need to do
Read and play and go to schools
Not build shelters from nuclear tools

What our children need decide
Be a doctor or writer of Sci Fi
Not take this drug and maybe die

What our children need to say
"Mom and Dad what a wonderful day"
Not "Mom I'll live with Dad today"

What our children need to hear
"We love you so much you are so dear"
Not, "You are so dumb, why are you here"

What our parents need to know
A world like this will never grow

What I see is pretty crummy
Change may happen with lots of money

Most of you have some time left
Do what you can, no time to rest

Give us a chance we know you care
Time to live and breathe fresh air

David Kellogg, 1990

Children learn cruelty, self-destructiveness, apathy, anger, fears, shame, anxieties that not only prevent the continuation of learning and seeking, the enjoying of the adventure of life, but it begins a legacy of cruelty, greed, narcissism, judgments, parochial defensiveness, covert manipulation, violence, abuse, neglect, and carelessness. This spreads like a fire, burning and destroying the potential and the gratitude, the chance for more awareness, to achieve new heights of conscious being.

The real parent of this precious, aware, unique form of life is the beautiful blue planet we inhabit. We spring from the waters and are nurtured in the soil of the earth itself. All of life on earth are our cousins and siblings. The earth is a parent without consciousness, without a conscience. We are the eyes, ears, voice, awareness, sentience, and conscience of our planet—our parent, the Earth. Our primary responsibility and goal should be as guardians, not only of our children who we participate in the creation of, but of our parent, the earth itself, the vehicle of our creation. The first priority in our own awareness must be to protect the basis for and of our existence, to look at the consequences of our behavior, to be gentle and supportive of all life itself, and to insure the survival and balance of our planet. Earth is the source of the continuing nurturance of life. It is the life giving vehicle of the creator and our continuing quest must be to ensure its protection. Accepting the challenge of guiding and loving children, the lives that we produce, involves a teaching and modeling of love and respect for life itself and for the place of lifespring, Earth.

We live in a garden. We did not fall from the garden. With our growing awareness, we became more than "of the garden." We became the keepers of the garden, the guardians of all that grows there. Our survival now depends upon taking the message of this guardianship seriously.

Recently, with our growing awareness of the need for personal healing because of past hurts, addictions, relationship problems or poor self-esteem, there is awareness of the processes of recovery. From this awareness, a recognition of the impact and concepts of recovery is also developing. Most of codependency has been described in the context of its symptoms—relationship with alcoholics, painful patterns of living, dependency problems and other definitions I've discussed in this book. I hope I've gone beyond the symptoms and immediate consequences and opened up some of the core issues of family and culture that create codependency. I hope I have helped expose the continuing impact of codependency in our lives and on our planet.

The concept must move beyond the enabling spouse of an alcoholic and must be seen as a basis for intimacy problems, our addictive and self-destructive behaviors, including the crimes against each other and our planet. Our consumption is an issue of planetary existence, survival and health. Addiction becomes a destructive force because it involves an absence of self-respect, a lack of respect for life, manipulation and denial of consequences. It involves the absence of boundaries that enables and creates violence, that includes and creates collusion and the enabling of inappropriate activities, the violations of environment and of people. We experience a growing sense of helplessness and unwillingness to make the changes we need to make. In healing our families we may be taking the most important step in the healing of our planet. We have become the collusive enablers and participants in the destruction of our planet, in the ignoring of vulnerable life on our planet and in the neglect of self. This is recovery from the self hate and fear that prevents us from accepting the interdependency of all of life, and of life with the planet that gave life. Recovery is the healing of relationship, first with self, then others and then our environment. The problem goes beyond the lack of identity. It goes beyond addiction. It goes beyond family systems. It goes beyond lost intimacy. Child Abuse threatens the survival of all of us. It is the basis of the victim/ offender relationship, the need for control and power to destroy and hurt. It creates the inability to stand up for what we believe and feel. In the face of crazy, destructive courses, it is the feeling of helplessness to impact change and bring about peace.

Affected are our lives, organizations, government and culture. Despair is born in dysfunction, in not recognizing the preciousness of children and not teaching gentleness and respect for life, of not modeling healthy boundaries and in giving up the ability to impact toward sanity, peace, care and spirituality.

Despair occurs in dysfunctional families, families with addiction, neglect, abandonment, abuse, victimization, dishonesty, unpredictability and denial and it affects all levels of our society. Children who are abused, hurt, neglected tend to continue this pattern, not just toward themselves, their relationships, and their children, but toward their physical environment as well. Children who have been hurt will hurt their surroundings. Pollution comes naturally to someone who has been boundary-violated, because pollution is essentially a violation of our physical boundaries, the boundaries of our life source, the boundaries of our planet. The ozone layer disappearing, the greenhouse effect, oil spills, acid rain, air pollution, our garbage crisis, nuclear waste, exhaust poisons, the disappearing wilderness, the destruction of our planet's lungs, the burning of the rain forests, the killing of the dolphins and whales, the cutting of the redwoods, threats to rare plant and animal life come from people who have not been taught to respect life, cherish vulnerability, or take the time to look at consequences. This is the result of careless families, of child abuse, neglect and denial, of not teaching limits, impulse control, of the need for immediate gratification and insatiability of addictive systems. A dysfunctional family creates this lack of respect for life and creates in its members, in children, the codependency, that continues the dysfunction through our adult lives. Codependency is a by-product of how we treat our children. How we deal with children is a result of cultural misogyny, the fear and hatred of vulnerability. In our culture, vulnerable peoples do not fare well—infants, children, adolescents, disabled, mentally ill, immigrants, minorities, poor, Native Americans, homeless, women—any group with vulnerability, with differences. The worship of power is the flip side of misogyny. Cultural and family despair is the result. The antidote is hope, the true recovery gift.

Following is another poem my son David wrote that I would like to share.

More of David's Thoughts

I am peaceful simply knowing
I am part of all that's growing
Flower trees all life flowing

I am happy with the thought
when I die I will not stop
I'll still exist in nature's lot

I am spirited clearly seeing
All creation includes my being
An organic part of cosmic seeding

Enlightened now I understand
The earth, ocean, sky and land
Linked to me hand in hand

With this brotherhood comes a treaty
Cease forest slaughter stop being greedy

End pollution of our lakes
Acid rain our fish can't take

Stop burning the fuels, read the warning
Drought, no crops, global warming

Cease the products that deplete ozone
Our future's unhappy under a dome

Nature and I go hand in hand
I am sick if so is my land

David Kellogg, 1990

Recovery or discovery is the development of identity, the ability to have intimacy and a respect for life, an acceptance and cherishing of vulnerability and fragility, the ability to find strength through vulnerability. Flowing out of this is a respect for creation, a way of seeing behavior in terms of its long term impact. We learn we can make a difference. We can stand up in the strength of our outrage. We can move ahead with the wisdom of our fear. We can nurture life with the healing of our sadness and pain. We can protect life with a sense of guardianship from our shame and the voice of conscience from our guilt. We can heal ourselves, our families, relationships and communities. Most importantly, we can heal the planet we live on.

Broken Toys, Broken Dreams has focused on addiction and codependency issues with references to family and recovery. The sequel, *Broken Silence* will focus more on Adult Children issues, adults who grew up in dysfunctional families. In it we will continue to explore the impact of violence in our lives and culture, the violation of self, feelings, rights, needs, wants, our bodies, our sexuality, our spirituality, and how we have responded to the violence which happens to us and around us. I will go further into the family system with chapters on family roles, family secrets, family violence and the responses to violence. I will also discuss the process of recovery as outlined—the insight processes with a focus on realizing, linking and debriefing; the emotional processes, grieving, feeling and healing; the social processes, networking, socializing, parenting; the spiritual processes, forgiving, twelve step work, establishing meaningfulness and values; the self processes of developing identity and integrity—integrity being the integration of sometimes seemingly separate aspects of self, integration of childness and adulthood, sexuality and spirituality, fear and courage, strength and vulnerability, prayer and humor. If you would like information on the sequel to *Broken Toys, Broken Dreams,* please call.

The Mulberry Center at Welborn Hospital in Evansville, Indiana, is one of the places that is discovering a new, gentle means of giving people safety and support, to heal child trauma and build healthy identity while also dealing with their addictiveness. Through the efforts of several people in this field, treatment is changing and responding to the reality of our broken lives and broken dreams. I have found that I now make more referrals to treatment for the safety and gentleness of the setting than the confronting and breaking of denial of a disease. Many of us can benefit from something less than a three to six week residential experience. Outpatient groups, often meeting once a week, can be an important part of this growth experience. Individual therapy, family counseling, couples counseling, but sometimes we need a safer setting, a more intense process. We need more support and community in an ongoing way. Nine years ago I began a program called the Compulsivity Clinics, which are now called Kellogg's Lifeworks Clinics, to deal with Adult Children issues, compulsive behaviors and codependency in an intense, safe, 4 $1/2$ day process. This clinic involves information, small group experiential and personal process work. We keep the group size at six to eight people because I believe catharsis and emotional work should not be done with large audiences and groups. When we're doing this kind of work, we should be the only one doing it, with other people around us for support. Kellogg's Lifeworks are held in different locations throughout the U.S. and Canada. Call 1-800-359-2728 for information.

In the Kellogg's Lifeworks process I have learned about courage from the hundreds of individuals who have faced and embraced their demons, the courage of feeling and moving through hurts and trauma and the courage to change. There are many other short term programs available. I recommend checking around before deciding. Generally, they function as a renewal, a reinforcement and an integration. They are a great beginning for recovery and they can help us get unstuck at points along the way as we grow in our recovery. Other processes which facilitate our growth are conferences, books, tapes and meetings. The *core of recovery* lies within our sense of community with others in recovery. The strongest family of recovering people I know are in twelve step programs.

Recovery Options

• *Life Balance*™ is two week clinic based on didactic and interactive process groups to assist people in finding resolution to disordered eating and body image problems. The Life Balance™ program is treatment designed and directed by Marvel Harrison, Ph.D. and Terry Kellogg, M.A., and the Mulberry Center Staff.

The Clinic is for those with one or more of the following:

• lack of success with weight loss programs.
• a diagnosis of an eating disorder.
• a history of struggling with body acceptance.
• emotional and overeating problems.
• a history of compulsive exercising.
• restrictive eating habits.
• health problems due to body weight.

The process integrates group therapy with focused action therapy, imagery, self reflection, journaling, physical activity, psych education and movement therapy in a safe environment. The personal sharing and connecting with others will help participants find a sense of balance and empowerment in their daily lives.

• *Life Connections* is an eight day process group specializing in Women's issues. Women struggling with life changes, depression, body image problems or losses will find support and mobilizing tools for growth and renewal. Call 1-800-359-2728 for program dates, times, and details.

242

• **_Kellogg Harrison Intensive Treatment Program_** is a safe and gentle therapy process designed to help each participant embrace their childhood, thereby deepening and broadening their recovery. This fourteen day program is based on didactic and interactive process groups to assist people in finding resolution. The intensive program integrates psychodrama, imagery, self reflection, journaling, physical activity, psycho-education and movement therapy in a safe environment of sharing and connecting with others to help participants find a sense of balance and empowerment in their lives.

This treatment is for those who are:

• struggling with issues of compulsive, addictive or self-defeating coping patterns.
• struggling with co-dependency and related intimacy issues.
• adult children of alcoholic or other dysfunctional families.
• survivors of emotional, physical, sexual, or spiritual abuse or neglect.

Call 1-800-359-2728 for program dates, times, and details.

BRAT PUBLISHING ORDER BLANK

Mailing List & Order Blank--Please send books/tapes selected to:
(please print)
Name_____
Street_____
City_____State/Province_____Zip_____
Phone # Day_____Evening_____

# of Copies

BOOKS

_____ Broken Toys Broken Dreams: Terry Kellogg $10.95

_____ Family Matters *The Principles & Roles of Family:* Terry Kellogg $11.95

_____ AttrACTIVE WOMAN *A Physical Fitness Approach To Emotional & Spiritual Well-Being:* Harrison & Stewart-Roache $8.95

_____ Finding Balance: *12 Priorities For Interdependence And Joyful Living* Kellogg & Harrison Family & Relationship Series $10.95

_____ Pathways to Intimacy *Communicating With Care & Resolving Differences* Kellogg Harrison Family & Relationship Series $7.95

_____ The Sacred Trust *The Parenting & Guardianship of Children and Creating Healthy Families* Kellogg Harrison Family & Relationship Series $7.95

_____ Butterfly Kisses *Little Intimacies For Sharing!* Harrison/Kellogg/Michaels $12.95

_____ Hummingbird Words *Self Affirmations Notes To Nurture By* Harrison/Kellogg/Michaels $12.95

_____ Roots & Wings *Words On Growing A Family* Harrison/Kellogg/Michaels $12.95

_____ Reflections *Guideposts and Images For The Journey* Harrison/Kellogg/Michaels $10.00

AUDIO/VIDEO TAPES
(Partial Listing--Call for full brochure of
educational audios/videos on families and relationships)

_____ Gentle Eating-3 Audio Set: Marvel Harrison $24.00

_____ Gentle Eating Experience-Audio w/Manual Set: Marvel Harrison $19.95

_____ Creating Balance Audio: Butterfly/Hummingbird/Roots Books on tape with music $9.95

_____ Trauma Tapes-2 Audio Set: Terry Kellogg $15.95

_____ Trauma Tapes-2 Video Set: Terry Kellogg $99.95

_____ Sexuality & Spirituality-2 Video Set: Terry Kellogg $99.95

_____ Family Roles Video: Terry Kellogg $48.95

Also Available from BRAT Publishing: marvel notes™ Elegant & delightful greeting cards

Add $4.00 S/H per order please. $_____ TOTAL ENCLOSED. Make check/MO payable to
BRAT Publishing. or MC/VISA #_____exp_____
Signature_____

BRAT PUBLISHING, 369 Montezuma St., Suite 203, Santa Fe, NM 87501
505-662-9200 or 800-359-2728; Fax 505-662-4044; Email «marvel@trail.com«